2008 Supplement

Constitutional Law

ASPEN PUBLISHERS

2008 Supplement

Constitutional Law

Fifth Edition

Geoffrey R. Stone
Harry Kalven, Jr., Distinguished Service Professor of Law
University of Chicago Law School

Louis Michael Seidman
Carmack Waterhouse Professor of Constitutional Law
Georgetown University Law Center

Cass R. Sunstein
Felix Frankfurter Professor of Law
Harvard Law School

Mark V. Tushnet
William Nelson Cromwell Professor of Law
Harvard Law School

Pamela S. Karlan
Kenneth & Harle Montgomery Professor of Public Interest Law
Stanford Law School

Wolters Kluwer
Law & Business

AUSTIN   BOSTON   CHICAGO   NEW YORK   THE NETHERLANDS

Aspen Publishers
Attn: Permissions Department
76 Ninth Avenue, 7th Floor
New York, NY 10011-5201

To contact Customer Care, e-mail customer.care@aspenpublishers.com, call 1-800-234-1660, fax 1-800-901-9075, or mail correspondence to:

Aspen Publishers
Attn: Order Department
PO Box 990
Frederick, MD 21705

Printed in the United States of America.

1 2 3 4 5 6 7 8 9 0

ISBN 978-0-7355-7233-1

Library of Congress Cataloging-in-Publication Data

Constitutional law / Geoffrey R. Stone ... [et al.]. — 5th ed.
    p. cm.
  Includes index.
  ISBN 0-7355-5014-8 (case bound)
       978-0-7355-7233-1 (supplement)
  1. Constitutional law — United States. I. Stone, Geoffrey R.

KF4549.C647 2205
342.73 — dc22   2005000567

About Wolters Kluwer Law & Business

Wolters Kluwer Law & Business is a leading provider of research information and workflow solutions in key specialty areas. The strengths of the individual brands of Aspen Publishers, CCH, Kluwer Law International and Loislaw are aligned within Wolters Kluwer Law & Business to provide comprehensive, in-depth solutions and expert-authored content for the legal, professional and education markets.

CCH was founded in 1913 and has served more than four generations of business professionals and their clients. The CCH products in the Wolters Kluwer Law & Business group are highly regarded electronic and print resources for legal, securities, antitrust and trade regulation, government contracting, banking, pension, payroll, employment and labor, and healthcare reimbursement and compliance professionals.

Aspen Publishers is a leading information provider for attorneys, business professionals and law students. Written by preeminent authorities, Aspen products offer analytical and practical information in a range of specialty practice areas from securities law and intellectual property to mergers and acquisitions and pension/benefits. Aspen's trusted legal education resources provide professors and students with high-quality, up-to-date and effective resources for successful instruction and study in all areas of the law.

Kluwer Law International supplies the global business community with comprehensive English-language international legal information. Legal practitioners, corporate counsel and business executives around the world rely on the Kluwer Law International journals, loose-leafs, books and electronic products for authoritative information in many areas of international legal practice.

Loislaw is a premier provider of digitized legal content to small law firm practitioners of various specializations. Loislaw provides attorneys with the ability to quickly and efficiently find the necessary legal information they need, when and where they need it, by facilitating access to primary law as well as state-specific law, records, forms and treatises.

Wolters Kluwer Law & Business, a unit of Wolters Kluwer, is headquartered in New York and Riverwoods, Illinois. Wolters Kluwer is a leading multinational publisher and information services company.

Contents

CHAPTER 3.   THE SCOPE OF CONGRESS'S POWERS: TAXING AND SPENDING, WAR POWERS, INDIVIDUAL RIGHTS, AND STATE AUTONOMY

CHAPTER 4.   THE DISTRIBUTION OF NATIONAL POWERS

CHAPTER 5.   EQUALITY AND THE CONSTITUTION

Table of Cases

Table of Authorities

Constitutional Law

BIOGRAPHICAL NOTES ON SELECTED U.S. SUPREME COURT JUSTICES

Page lxi.   Before the biography of Hugo Black, add the following:

SAMUEL A. ALITO, JR. (1950-): The son of two school teachers (his father went on to become New Jersey's first Director of the Office of Legislative Services), Justice Alito graduated from Princeton and then from Yale Law School where he served as an editor of the Yale Law Journal. He served as an assistant to the United States Solicitor General and Deputy Assistant to the Attorney General before becoming the United States Attorney for the District of New Jersey. He developed the reputation of a tough but fair prosecutor and was known especially for his efforts directed against drug trafficking and organized crime. Before his Supreme Court appointment, he served for sixteen years as a judge on the United States Court of Appeals for the Third Circuit.

Page lxxiv.   After the biography of William Rehnquist, add the following:

JOHN G. ROBERTS, JR. (1955-): Originally nominated by President George W. Bush to replace Justice O'Connor, John Roberts was renominated for the position of Chief Justice of the United States following the death of Chief Justice Rehnquist. Upon his confirmation, he became the third youngest Chief Justice in American history and the first justice to replace the justice for whom he had clerked. After graduating magna cum laude from Harvard Law School, Roberts served as a special assistant to the Attorney General, Associate Counsel to the President, and the Principal Deputy Solicitor General. He is one

1

of the most experienced and successful Supreme Court advocates ever to have been appointed to the Court. While in government service, he argued thirty-nine cases before the Supreme Court, winning twenty-five of them. Upon leaving government, he became head of the appellate practice of a major Washington law firm, in which capacity he argued fourteen additional cases before the Court. In 2003, he became a judge on the United States Court of Appeals for the District of Columbia Circuit.

1

THE ROLE OF THE SUPREME COURT IN THE CONSTITUTIONAL ORDER

A. Introduction: Creating a Constitution that Binds the Future

Page 8.   Before Section B, add the following:

DISTRICT OF COLUMBIA v. HELLER

554 U.S. ____ (2008)

JUSTICE SCALIA delivered the opinion of the Court.

We consider whether a District of Columbia prohibition on the possession of usable handguns in the home violates the Second Amendment to the Constitution....

II

A

The Second Amendment provides: "A well regulated Militia, being necessary to the security of a free State, the right of the people to keep and bear Arms, shall not be infringed." In interpreting this text, we are guided by the principle that "[t]he Constitution was written to be understood by the voters; its words and phrases were used in their normal and ordinary as distinguished from technical meaning."....

The two sides in this case have set out very different interpretations of the Amendment. Petitioners and today's dissenting Justices believe that it protects only the right to possess and carry a firearm in connection with militia service. Respondent argues that it protects an individual right to possess a firearm unconnected with service in a militia, and to use that arm for traditionally lawful purposes, such as self-defense within the home.

The Second Amendment is naturally divided into two parts: its prefatory clause and its operative clause. The former does not limit the latter grammatically, but rather announces a purpose....

Logic demands that there be a link between the stated purpose and the command. The Second Amendment would be nonsensical if it read, "A well regulated Militia, being necessary to the security of a free State, the right of the people to petition for redress of grievances shall not be infringed."....But...a prefatory clause does not limit or expand the scope of the operative clause.... Therefore, while we will begin our textual analysis with the operative clause, we will return to the prefatory clause to ensure that our reading of the operative clause is consistent with the announced purpose.

1. Operative Clause.

a. "Right of the People."   The first salient feature of the operative clause is that it codifies a "right of the people." The unamended Constitution and the Bill of Rights use the phrase "right of the people" two other times, in the First Amendment's Assembly-and-Petition Clause and in the Fourth Amendment's Search-and-Seizure Clause. The Ninth Amendment uses very similar terminology.... All three of these instances unambiguously refer to individual rights, not "collective" rights, or rights that may be exercised only through participation in some corporate body....

What is more, in all six other provisions of the Constitution that mention "the people," the term unambiguously refers to all members of the political community, not an unspecified subset.....

This contrasts markedly with the phrase "the militia" in the prefatory clause. As we will describe below, the "militia" in colonial America consisted of a subset of "the people" — those who were male, able bodied, and within a certain age range. Reading the Second Amendment as protecting only the right to "keep and bear Arms" in an organized militia therefore fits poorly with the operative clause's description of the holder of that right as "the people."

We start therefore with a strong presumption that the Second Amendment right is exercised individually and belongs to all Americans.

b. "Keep and bear Arms."   We move now from the holder of the right — "the people" — to the substance of the right: "to keep and bear Arms." Before addressing the verbs "keep" and "bear," we interpret their object: "Arms." The 18th-century meaning is no different from the meaning today. The 1773 edition of Samuel Johnson's dictionary defined "arms" as "weapons of offence, or armour of defence." Timothy Cunningham's important 1771 legal dictionary defined "arms" as "any thing that a man wears for his defence, or takes into his hands, or useth in wrath to cast at or strike another."

The term was applied, then as now, to weapons that were not specifically designed for military use and were not employed in a military capacity. For instance, Cunningham's legal dictionary gave as an example of usage: "Servants and labourers shall use bows and arrows on Sundays, &c. and not bear other arms." ... Although one founding-era thesaurus limited "arms" (as opposed to "weapons") to "instruments of offence *generally* made use of in war," even that source stated that all firearms constituted "arms."

Some have made the argument, bordering on the frivolous, that only those arms in existence in the 18th century are protected by the Second Amendment. We do not interpret constitutional rights that way. Just as the First Amendment protects modern forms of communications, and the Fourth Amendment applies to modern forms of search, the Second Amendment extends, prima facie, to all instruments that constitute bearable arms, even those that were not in existence at the time of the founding.

We turn to the phrases "keep arms" and "bear arms." Johnson defined "keep" as, most relevantly, "[t]o retain; not to lose," and "[t]o have in custody." Webster defined it as "[t]o hold; to retain in one's power or possession." No party has apprised us of an idiomatic meaning of "keep Arms." Thus, the most natural reading of "keep Arms" in the Second Amendment is to "have weapons."

The phrase "keep arms" was not prevalent in the written documents of the founding period that we have found, but there are a few examples, all of which favor viewing the right to "keep Arms" as an individual right unconnected with militia service. William Blackstone, for example, wrote that Catholics convicted of not attending service in the Church of England suffered certain penalties, one of which was that they were not permitted to "keep arms in their houses." .... "Keep arms" was simply a common way of referring to possessing arms, for militiamen *and everyone else.*

At the time of the founding, as now, to "bear" meant to "carry." When used with "arms," however, the term has a meaning that refers to carrying for a particular purpose — confrontation. ... Although the phrase implies that the carrying of the weapon is for the purpose of "offensive or defensive action," it in no way connotes participation in a structured military organization.

From our review of founding-era sources, we conclude that this natural meaning was also the meaning that "bear arms" had in the 18th century. In numerous instances, "bear arms" was unambiguously used to refer to the carrying of weapons outside of an organized militia. The most prominent examples are those most relevant to the Second Amendment: Nine state constitutional provisions written in the 18th century or the first two decades of the

5

19th, which enshrined a right of citizens to "bear arms in defense of themselves and the state" or "bear arms in defense of himself and the state." It is clear from those formulations that "bear arms" did not refer only to carrying a weapon in an organized military unit. Justice James Wilson interpreted the Pennsylvania Constitution's arms-bearing right, for example, as a recognition of the natural right of defense "of one's person or house" — what he called the law of "self preservation." That was also the interpretation of those state constitutional provisions adopted by pre-Civil War state courts....

The phrase "bear Arms" also had at the time of the founding an idiomatic meaning that was significantly different from its natural meaning: "to serve as a soldier, do military service, fight" or "to wage war." But it *unequivocally* bore that idiomatic meaning only when followed by the preposition "against," which was in turn followed by the target of the hostilities. (That is how, for example, our Declaration of Independence ¶28, used the phrase: "He has constrained our fellow Citizens taken Captive on the high Seas to bear Arms against their Country....")...

In any event, the meaning of "bear arms" that petitioners and Justice Stevens propose is *not even* the (sometimes) idiomatic meaning. Rather, they manufacture a hybrid definition, whereby "bear arms" connotes the actual carrying of arms (and therefore is not really an idiom) but only in the service of an organized militia. No dictionary has ever adopted that definition, and we have been apprised of no source that indicates that it carried that meaning at the time of the founding. But it is easy to see why petitioners and the dissent are driven to the hybrid definition. Giving "bear Arms" its idiomatic meaning would cause the protected right to consist of the right to be a soldier or to wage war — an absurdity that no commentator has ever endorsed. Worse still, the phrase "keep and bear Arms" would be incoherent. The word "Arms" would have two different meanings at once: "weapons" (as the object of "keep") and (as the object of "bear") one-half of an idiom. It would be rather like saying "He filled and kicked the bucket" to mean "He filled the bucket and died." Grotesque....

Justice Stevens places great weight on James Madison's inclusion of a conscientious-objector clause in his original draft of the Second Amendment: "but no person religiously scrupulous of bearing arms, shall be compelled to render military service in person." He argues that this clause establishes that the drafters of the Second Amendment intended "bear Arms" to refer only to military service. It is always perilous to derive the meaning of an adopted provision from another provision deleted in the drafting process. In any case, what Justice Stevens would conclude from the deleted provision does not follow. It was not meant to exempt from military service those who objected to going to war but had no scruples about personal gunfights. Quakers opposed the use of arms not just for militia service, but for any violent purpose whatsoever—so much so that Quaker frontiersmen were forbidden to use arms to defend their families, even though "[i]n such circumstances the temptation to seize a hunting rifle or knife in self-defense... must sometimes have been almost overwhelming."... Thus, the most natural interpretation of Madison's deleted text is that those opposed to carrying weapons for potential violent confrontation would not be "compelled to render military service," in which such carrying would be required.

Finally, Justice Stevens suggests that "keep and bear Arms" was some sort of term of art, presumably akin to "hue and cry" or "cease and desist."....Justice Stevens believes that the unitary meaning of "keep and bear Arms" is established by the Second Amendment's calling it a "right" (singular) rather than "rights" (plural). There is nothing to this. State constitutions of the founding period routinely grouped multiple (related) guarantees under a singular "right," and the First Amendment protects the "right [singular] of the people peaceably to assemble, and to petition the Government for a redress of grievances."....

c. Meaning of the Operative Clause.   Putting all of these textual elements together, we find that they guarantee the individual right to possess and carry weapons in case of confrontation. This meaning is strongly confirmed by the historical background of the Second Amendment. We look to this because it has always been widely understood that the Second Amendment, like the First and Fourth Amendments, codified a *pre-existing* right. The very text of the Second Amendment implicitly recognizes the pre-existence of the right and declares only that it "shall not be infringed." As we said in *United States v. Cruikshank*, 92 U.S. 542, 553 (1876), "[t]his is not a right granted by the Constitution. Neither is it in any manner dependent upon that instrument for its existence. The Second amendment declares that it shall not be infringed...."

Between the Restoration and the Glorious Revolution, the Stuart Kings Charles II and James II succeeded in using select militias loyal to them to suppress political dissidents, in part by disarming their opponents.... These experiences caused Englishmen to be extremely wary of concentrated military forces run by the state and to be jealous of their arms. They accordingly obtained an assurance from William and Mary, in the Declaration of Right (which was codified as the English Bill of Rights), that Protestants would never be disarmed: "That the subjects which are Protestants may have arms for their defense suitable to their conditions and as allowed by law." This right has long been understood to be the predecessor to our Second Amendment. It was clearly an individual right, having nothing whatever to do with service in a militia. To be sure, it was an individual right not available to the whole population, given that it was restricted to Protestants, and like all written English rights it was held only against the Crown, not Parliament. But it was secured to them as individuals, according to "libertarian political principles," not as members of a fighting force.

By the time of the founding, the right to have arms had become fundamental for English subjects. Blackstone, whose works, we have said, "constituted the preeminent authority on English law for the founding generation," cited the arms provision of the Bill of Rights as one of the fundamental rights of Englishmen.... It was, he said, "the natural right of resistance and self-preservation," and "the right of having and using arms for self-preservation and defence." Thus, the right secured in 1689 as a result of the Stuarts' abuses was by the time of the founding understood to be an individual right protecting against both public and private violence.

And, of course, what the Stuarts had tried to do to their political enemies, George III had tried to do to the colonists. In the tumultuous decades of the 1760's and 1770's, the Crown began to disarm the inhabitants of the most rebellious areas.... [The colonists] understood the right to enable individuals to defend themselves. As the most important early American edition of Blackstone's Commentaries (by the law professor and former Antifederalist St. George Tucker) made clear in the notes to the description of the arms right, Americans understood the "right of self-preservation" as permitting a citizen to "repe[l] force by force" when "the intervention of society in his behalf, may be too late to prevent an injury."

There seems to us no doubt, on the basis of both text and history, that the Second Amendment conferred an individual right to keep and bear arms. Of course the right was not unlimited, just as the First Amendment's right of free speech was not. Thus, we do not read the Second Amendment to protect the right of citizens to carry arms for *any sort* of confrontation, just as we do not read the First Amendment to protect the right of citizens to speak for *any purpose*. Before turning to limitations upon the individual right, however, we must determine whether the prefatory clause of the Second Amendment comports with our interpretation of the operative clause.

2. Prefatory Clause.

The prefatory clause reads: "A well regulated Militia, being necessary to the security of a free State...."

a. "Well-Regulated Militia."   In *United States v. Miller*, 307 U.S. 174, 179 (1939), we explained that "the Militia comprised all males physically capable of acting in concert for the common defense." That definition comports with founding-era sources.

Petitioners take a seemingly narrower view of the militia, stating that "[m]ilitias are the state- and congressionally-regulated military forces described in the Militia Clauses (art. I, § 8, cls. 15-16)."…. [W]e believe that petitioners identify the wrong thing, namely, the organized militia. Unlike armies and navies, which Congress is given the power to create ("to raise... Armies"; "to provide... a Navy," Art. I, § 8, cls. 12-13), the militia is assumed by

Article I already to be *in existence....* [and to consist of] all able-bodied men.... Although the militia consists of all able-bodied men, the federally organized militia may consist of a subset of them.

Finally, the adjective "well-regulated" implies nothing more than the imposition of proper discipline and training.

b. "Security of a Free State."....

There are many reasons why the militia was thought to be "necessary to the security of a free state." First, of course, it is useful in repelling invasions and suppressing insurrections. Second, it renders large standing armies unnecessary.... Third, when the able-bodied men of a nation are trained in arms and organized, they are better able to resist tyranny.

3.   Relationship between Prefatory Clause and Operative Clause

We reach the question, then: Does the preface fit with an operative clause that creates an individual right to keep and bear arms? It fits perfectly, once one knows the history that the founding generation knew and that we have described above. That history showed that the way tyrants had eliminated a militia consisting of all the able-bodied men was not by banning the militia but simply by taking away the people's arms, enabling a select militia or standing army to suppress political opponents. This is what had occurred in England that prompted codification of the right to have arms in the English Bill of Rights.

[D]uring the 1788 ratification debates, the fear that the federal government would disarm the people in order to impose rule through a standing army or select militia was pervasive in Antifederalist rhetoric....

It is therefore entirely sensible that the Second Amendment's prefatory clause announces the purpose for which the right was codified: to prevent elimination of the militia. The prefatory clause does not suggest that preserving the militia was the only reason Americans valued the ancient right; most undoubtedly thought it even more important for self-defense and hunting. But the threat that the new Federal Government would destroy the citizens' militia by taking away their arms was the reason that right — unlike some other English rights — was codified in a written Constitution....

B

Our interpretation is confirmed by analogous arms-bearing rights in state constitutions that preceded and immediately followed adoption of the Second Amendment....

Between 1789 and 1820, nine States adopted Second Amendment analogues. Four of them... referred to the right of the people to "bear arms in defence of themselves and the State." Another three States... used the even more individualistic phrasing that each citizen has the "right to bear arms in defence of himself and the State." Finally, two States... used... "common defence" language....

9

D

We now address how the Second Amendment was interpreted from immediately after its ratification through the end of the 19th century. Before proceeding, however, we take issue with Justice Stevens' equating of these sources with postenactment legislative history, a comparison that betrays a fundamental misunderstanding of a court's interpretive task.... [That phrase] most certainly does not refer to the examination of a variety of legal and other sources to determine *the public understanding* of a legal text in the period after its enactment or ratification. That sort of inquiry is a critical tool of constitutional interpretation. As we will show, virtually all interpreters of the Second Amendment in the century after its enactment interpreted the amendment as we do.

1. Post-ratification Commentary

Three important founding-era legal scholars interpreted the Second Amendment in published writings. All three understood it to protect an individual right unconnected with militia service....

2. Pre-Civil War Case Law

The 19th-century cases that interpreted the Second Amendment universally support an individual right unconnected to militia service....

Many early 19th-century state cases indicated that the Second Amendment right to bear arms was an individual right unconnected to militia service, though subject to certain restrictions. A Virginia case in 1824 holding that the Constitution did not extend to free blacks explained that "numerous restrictions imposed on [blacks] in our Statute Book, many of which are inconsistent with the letter and spirit of the Constitution, both of this State and of the United States as respects the free whites, demonstrate, that, here, those instruments have not been considered to extend equally to both classes of our population. We will only instance the restriction upon the migration of free blacks into this State, and upon their right to bear arms." *Aldridge v. Commonwealth*, 4 Va. 447 (Gen. Ct.).... An 1829 decision by the Supreme Court of Michigan said: "The constitution of the United States also grants to the citizen the right to keep and bear arms. But the grant of this privilege cannot be construed into the right in him who keeps a gun to destroy his neighbor. No rights are intended to be granted by the constitution for an unlawful or unjustifiable purpose."

In *Nunn v. State*, 1 Ga. 243, 251 (1846), the Georgia Supreme Court construed the Second Amendment as protecting the "*natural* right of self-defence" and therefore struck down a ban on carrying pistols openly....

Likewise, in *State v. Chandler*, 5 La. Ann. 489, 490 (1850), the Louisiana Supreme Court held that citizens had a right to carry arms openly: "This is the right guaranteed by the Constitution of the United States, and which is calculated to incite men to a manly and noble defence of themselves, if necessary, and of their country, without any tendency to secret advantages and unmanly assassinations."....

3. Post-Civil War Legislation

In the aftermath of the Civil War, there was an outpouring of discussion of the Second Amendment in Congress and in public discourse, as people debated whether and how to secure constitutional rights for newly free slaves. Since those discussions took place 75 years after the ratification of the Second Amendment, they do not provide as much insight into its original meaning as earlier sources. Yet those born and educated in the early 19th century faced a widespread effort to limit arms ownership by a large number of citizens; their understanding of the origins and continuing significance of the Amendment is instructive.

Blacks were routinely disarmed by Southern States after the Civil War. Those who opposed these injustices frequently stated that they infringed blacks' constitutional right to keep and bear arms. Needless to say, the claim was not that blacks were being prohibited from carrying arms in an organized state militia.... A joint congressional Report decried:

> "in some parts of [South Carolina], armed parties are, without proper authority, engaged in seizing all fire-arms found in the hands of the freemen. Such conduct is in clear and direct violation of their personal rights as guaranteed by the Constitution of the United States, which declares that 'the right of the people to keep and bear arms shall not be infringed.' The freedmen of South Carolina have shown by their peaceful and orderly conduct that they can safely be trusted with fire-arms, and they need them to kill game for subsistence, and to protect their crops from destruction by birds and animals."....

Congress enacted the Freedmen's Bureau Act on July 16, 1866. Section 14 stated:

> "[T]he right ... to have full and equal benefit of all laws and proceedings concerning personal liberty, personal security, and the acquisition, enjoyment, and disposition of estate, real and personal, including the constitutional right to bear arms, shall be secured to and enjoyed by all the citizens ... without respect to race or color, or previous condition of slavery...."

The understanding that the Second Amendment gave freed blacks the right to keep and bear arms was reflected in congressional discussion of the bill...

Similar discussion attended the passage of the Civil Rights Act of 1871 and the Fourteenth Amendment....

4. Post-Civil War Commentators.

Every late-19th-century legal scholar that we have read interpreted the Second Amendment to secure an individual right unconnected with militia service. The most famous was the judge and professor Thomas Cooley, who wrote a massively popular 1868 Treatise on Constitutional Limitations. Concerning the Second Amendment it said:

> "Among the other defences to personal liberty should be mentioned the right of the people to keep and bear arms.... The alternative to a standing army is 'a well-regulated militia,' but this cannot exist unless the people are trained to bearing arms. How far it is in the power of the legislature to regulate this right, we shall not undertake to say, as happily there has been very little occasion to discuss that subject by the courts." ...

E

We now ask whether any of our precedents forecloses the conclusions we have reached about the meaning of the Second Amendment.

United States v. Cruikshank, in the course of vacating the convictions of members of a white mob for depriving blacks of their right to keep and bear arms, held that the Second Amendment does not by its own force apply to anyone other than the Federal Government.... The limited discussion of the Second Amendment in *Cruikshank* supports, if anything, the individual-rights interpretation. There was no claim in *Cruikshank* that the victims had been deprived of their right to carry arms in a militia; indeed, the Governor had disbanded the local militia unit the year before the mob's attack....

Presser v. Illinois, 116 U.S. 252 (1886), held that the right to keep and bear arms was not violated by a law that forbade "bodies of men to associate together as military organizations, or to drill or parade with arms in cities and towns unless authorized by law." This does not refute the individual-rights interpretation of the Amendment; no one supporting that interpretation has contended that States may not ban such groups....

Justice Stevens places overwhelming reliance upon this Court's decision in *United States v. Miller*, 307 U.S. 174 (1939). "[H]undreds of judges," we are told, "have relied on the view of the amendment we endorsed there," and "[e]ven if the textual and historical arguments on both side of the issue were evenly balanced, respect for the well-settled views of all of our predecessors on this Court, and for the rule of law itself... would prevent most jurists from endorsing such a dramatic upheaval in the law." And what is, according to Justice Stevens, the holding of *Miller* that demands such obeisance? That the Second Amendment "protects the right to keep and bear arms for certain military purposes, but that it does not curtail the legislature's power to regulate the nonmilitary use and ownership of weapons."

Nothing so clearly demonstrates the weakness of Justice Stevens' case. *Miller* did not hold that and cannot possibly be read to have held that. The judgment in the case upheld against a Second Amendment challenge two men's federal convictions for transporting an unregistered short-barreled shotgun in interstate commerce, in violation of the National Firearms Act. It is entirely clear that the Court's basis for saying that the Second Amendment did not apply was *not* that the defendants were "bear[ing] arms" not "for... military purposes" but for "nonmilitary use." Rather, it was that the *type of weapon at issue* was not eligible for Second Amendment protection:...

This holding is not only consistent with, but positively suggests, that the Second Amendment confers an individual right to keep and bear arms (though only arms that "have some reasonable relationship to the preservation or efficiency of a well regulated militia"). Had the Court believed that the Second Amendment protects only those serving in the militia, it would have been odd to examine the character of the weapon rather than simply note that the two crooks were not militiamen....

It is particularly wrongheaded to read *Miller* for more than what it said, because the case did not even purport to be a thorough examination of the Second Amendment. Justice Stevens claims that the opinion reached its conclusion "[a]fter reviewing many of the same sources that are discussed at greater length by the Court today." Not many, which was not entirely the Court's fault. The respondent made no appearance in the case, neither filing a brief nor appearing at oral argument; the Court heard from no one but the Government (reason enough, one would think, not to make that case the beginning and the end of this Court's consideration of the Second Amendment).... This is the mighty rock upon which the dissent rests its case.[24]

We may as well consider at this point (for we will have to consider eventually) *what* types of weapons *Miller* permits. Read in isolation, *Miller*'s phrase "part of ordinary military equipment" could mean that only those weapons useful in warfare are protected. That would be a startling reading of the opinion, since it would mean that the National Firearms Act's restrictions on machineguns (not challenged in *Miller*) might be unconstitutional, machineguns being useful in warfare in 1939. We think that *Miller*'s "ordinary military equipment" language must be read in tandem with what comes after: "[O]rdinarily when

---

24. As for the "hundreds of judges" who have relied on the view of the Second Amendment Justice Stevens claims we endorsed in *Miller*: If so, they overread *Miller*. And their erroneous reliance upon an uncontested and virtually unreasoned case cannot nullify the reliance of millions of Americans (as our historical analysis has shown) upon the true meaning of the right to keep and bear arms. In any event, it should not be thought that the cases decided by these judges would necessarily have come out differently under a proper interpretation of the right.

called for [militia] service [able-bodied] men were expected to appear bearing arms supplied by themselves and of the kind in common use at the time." The traditional militia was formed from a pool of men bringing arms "in common use at the time" for lawful purposes like self-defense. "In the colonial and revolutionary war era, [small-arms] weapons used by militiamen and weapons used in defense of person and home were one and the same.".... We therefore read *Miller* to say only that the Second Amendment does not protect those weapons not typically possessed by law-abiding citizens for lawful purposes, such as short-barreled shotguns. That accords with the historical understanding of the scope of the right, see Part III, *infra*....

We conclude that nothing in our precedents forecloses our adoption of the original understanding of the Second Amendment. It should be unsurprising that such a significant matter has been for so long judicially unresolved. For most of our history, the Bill of Rights was not thought applicable to the States, and the Federal Government did not significantly regulate the possession of firearms by law-abiding citizens. Other provisions of the Bill of Rights have similarly remained unilluminated for lengthy periods. This Court first held a law to violate the *First Amendment's* guarantee of freedom of speech in 1931, almost 150 years after the Amendment was ratified, see *Near v. Minnesota ex rel. Olson*, 283 U.S. 697 (1931), and it was not until after World War II that we held a law invalid under the Establishment Clause, see *Illinois ex rel. McCollum v. Bd. of Educ.*, 333 U.S. 203 (1948)....

III

Like most rights, the right secured by the Second Amendment is not unlimited. From Blackstone through the 19th-century cases, commentators and courts routinely explained that the right was not a right to keep and carry any weapon whatsoever in any manner whatsoever and for whatever purpose. For example, the majority of the 19th-century courts to consider the question held that prohibitions on carrying concealed weapons were lawful under the Second Amendment or state analogues. Although we do not undertake an exhaustive historical analysis today of the full scope of the Second Amendment, nothing in our opinion should be taken to cast doubt on longstanding prohibitions on the possession of firearms by felons and the mentally ill, or laws forbidding the carrying of firearms in sensitive places such as schools and government buildings, or laws imposing conditions and qualifications on the commercial sale of arms.[26]

---

26. We identify these presumptively lawful regulatory measures only as examples; our list does not purport to be exhaustive.

We also recognize another important limitation on the right to keep and carry arms. *Miller* said, as we have explained, that the sorts of weapons protected were those "in common use at the time." We think that limitation is fairly supported by the historical tradition of prohibiting the carrying of "dangerous and unusual weapons."

It may be objected that if weapons that are most useful in military service — M-16 rifles and the like — may be banned, then the Second Amendment right is completely detached from the prefatory clause. But as we have said, the conception of the militia at the time of the Second Amendment's ratification was the body of all citizens capable of military service, who would bring the sorts of lawful weapons that they possessed at home to militia duty. It may well be true today that a militia, to be as effective as militias in the 18th century, would require sophisticated arms that are highly unusual in society at large. Indeed, it may be true that no amount of small arms could be useful against modern-day bombers and tanks. But the fact that modern developments have limited the degree of fit between the prefatory clause and the protected right cannot change our interpretation of the right.

IV

We turn finally to the law at issue here. As we have said, the law totally bans handgun possession in the home. It also requires that any lawful firearm in the home be disassembled or bound by a trigger lock at all times, rendering it inoperable.

As the quotations earlier in this opinion demonstrate, the inherent right of self-defense has been central to the Second Amendment right. The handgun ban amounts to a prohibition of an entire class of "arms" that is overwhelmingly chosen by American society for that lawful purpose. The prohibition extends, moreover, to the home, where the need for defense of self, family, and property is most acute. Under any of the standards of scrutiny that we have applied to enumerated constitutional rights,[27] banning from the home "the most preferred

---

27. Justice Breyer correctly notes that this law, like almost all laws, would pass rational-basis scrutiny. But rational-basis scrutiny is a mode of analysis we have used when evaluating laws under constitutional commands that are themselves prohibitions on irrational laws. In those cases, "rational basis" is not just the standard of scrutiny, but the very substance of the constitutional guarantee. Obviously, the same test could not be used to evaluate the extent to which a legislature may regulate a specific, enumerated right, be it the freedom of speech, the guarantee against double jeopardy, the right to counsel, or the right to keep and bear arms. See *United States v. Carolene Products Co.*, 304 U.S. 144, 152, n. 4 (1938) ("There may be narrower scope for operation of the presumption of constitutionality [*i.e.*, narrower than that provided by rational-basis review] when legislation appears

firearm in the nation to 'keep' and use for protection of one's home and family," would fail constitutional muster....

It is no answer to say... that it is permissible to ban the possession of handguns so long as the possession of other firearms (*i.e.*, long guns) is allowed. It is enough to note, as we have observed, that the American people have considered the handgun to be the quintessential self-defense weapon. There are many reasons that a citizen may prefer a handgun for home defense: It is easier to store in a location that is readily accessible in an emergency; it cannot easily be redirected or wrestled away by an attacker; it is easier to use for those without the upper-body strength to lift and aim a long gun; it can be pointed at a burglar with one hand while the other hand dials the police. Whatever the reason, handguns are the most popular weapon chosen by Americans for self-defense in the home, and a complete prohibition of their use is invalid....

Justice Breyer has devoted most of his separate dissent to the handgun ban. He says that, even assuming the Second Amendment is a personal guarantee of the right to bear arms, the District's prohibition is valid. He first tries to establish this by founding-era historical precedent, pointing to various restrictive laws in the colonial period.... A 1783 Massachusetts law forbade the residents of Boston to "take into" or "receive into" "any Dwelling House, Stable, Barn, Out-house, Ware-house, Store, Shop or other Building" loaded firearms, and permitted the seizure of any loaded firearms that "shall be found" there. That statute's text and its prologue, which makes clear that the purpose of the prohibition was to eliminate the danger to firefighters posed by the "depositing of loaded Arms" in buildings, give reason to doubt that colonial Boston authorities would have enforced that general prohibition against someone who temporarily loaded a firearm to confront an intruder (despite the law's application in that case). In any case, we would not stake our interpretation of the Second Amendment upon a single law, in effect in a single city, that contradicts the overwhelming weight of other evidence regarding the right to keep and bear arms for defense of the home. The other laws Justice Breyer cites are gunpowder-storage laws that he concedes did not clearly prohibit loaded weapons, but required only that excess gunpowder be kept in a special container or on the top floor of the home. Nothing about those fire-safety laws undermines our analysis; they do not remotely burden the right of self-defense as much as an absolute ban on handguns. Nor, correspondingly, does our analysis suggest the invalidity of laws regulating the storage of firearms to prevent accidents....

---

on its face to be within a specific prohibition of the Constitution, such as those of the first ten amendments...")。 If all that was required to overcome the right to keep and bear arms was a rational basis, the Second Amendment would be redundant with the separate constitutional prohibitions on irrational laws, and would have no effect.

16

Justice Breyer moves on to make a broad jurisprudential point: He criticizes us for declining to establish a level of scrutiny for evaluating Second Amendment restrictions. He proposes, explicitly at least, none of the traditionally expressed levels (strict scrutiny, intermediate scrutiny, rational basis), but rather a judge-empowering "interest-balancing inquiry" that "asks whether the statute burdens a protected interest in a way or to an extent that is out of proportion to the statute's salutary effects upon other important governmental interests." After an exhaustive discussion of the arguments for and against gun control, Justice Breyer arrives at his interest-balanced answer: because handgun violence is a problem, because the law is limited to an urban area, and because there were somewhat similar restrictions in the founding period (a false proposition that we have already discussed), the interest-balancing inquiry results in the constitutionality of the handgun ban. QED.

We know of no other enumerated constitutional right whose core protection has been subjected to a freestanding "interest-balancing" approach. The very enumeration of the right takes out of the hands of government — even the Third Branch of Government — the power to decide on a case-by-case basis whether the right is *really worth* insisting upon. A constitutional guarantee subject to future judges' assessments of its usefulness is no constitutional guarantee at all. Constitutional rights are enshrined with the scope they were understood to have when the people adopted them, whether or not future legislatures or (yes) even future judges think that scope too broad. We would not apply an "interest-balancing" approach to the prohibition of a peaceful neo-Nazi march through Skokie. See *National Socialist Party of America v. Skokie*, 432 U.S. 43 (1977) (per curiam). The First Amendment contains the freedom-of-speech guarantee that the people ratified, which included exceptions for obscenity, libel, and disclosure of state secrets, but not for the expression of extremely unpopular and wrong-headed views. The Second Amendment is no different. Like the First, it is the very *product* of an interest-balancing by the people — which Justice Breyer would now conduct for them anew. And whatever else it leaves to future evaluation, it surely elevates above all other interests the right of law-abiding, responsible citizens to use arms in defense of hearth and home.

Justice Breyer chides us for leaving so many applications of the right to keep and bear arms in doubt, and for not providing extensive historical justification for those regulations of the right that we describe as permissible. But since this case represents this Court's first in-depth examination of the Second Amendment, one should not expect it to clarify the entire field, any more than *Reynolds v. United States*, 98 U.S. 145 (1879), our first in-depth Free Exercise Clause case, left that area in a state of utter certainty. And there will be time enough to expound upon the historical justifications for the exceptions we have mentioned if and when those exceptions come before us. . . .

* * *

17

We are aware of the problem of handgun violence in this country, and we take seriously the concerns raised by the many *amici* who believe that prohibition of handgun ownership is a solution. The Constitution leaves the District of Columbia a variety of tools for combating that problem, including some measures regulating handguns. But the enshrinement of constitutional rights necessarily takes certain policy choices off the table. These include the absolute prohibition of handguns held and used for self-defense in the home. Undoubtedly some think that the Second Amendment is outmoded in a society where our standing army is the pride of our Nation, where well-trained police forces provide personal security, and where gun violence is a serious problem. That is perhaps debatable, but what is not debatable is that it is not the role of this Court to pronounce the Second Amendment extinct. . . .

JUSTICE STEVENS, with whom JUSTICE SOUTER, JUSTICE GINSBURG, and JUSTICE BREYER join, dissenting.

The question presented by this case is not whether the Second Amendment protects a "collective right" or an "individual right." Surely it protects a right that can be enforced by individuals. But a conclusion that the Second Amendment protects an individual right does not tell us anything about the scope of that right.

Guns are used to hunt, for self-defense, to commit crimes, for sporting activities, and to perform military duties. The Second Amendment plainly does not protect the right to use a gun to rob a bank; it is equally clear that it *does* encompass the right to use weapons for certain military purposes. Whether it also protects the right to possess and use guns for nonmilitary purposes like hunting and personal self-defense is the question presented by this case. The text of the Amendment, its history, and our decision in *United States v. Miller*, 307 U.S. 174 (1939), provide a clear answer to that question.

The Second Amendment was adopted to protect the right of the people of each of the several States to maintain a well-regulated militia. It was a response to concerns raised during the ratification of the Constitution that the power of Congress to disarm the state militias and create a national standing army posed an intolerable threat to the sovereignty of the several States. Neither the text of the Amendment nor the arguments advanced by its proponents evidenced the slightest interest in limiting any legislature's authority to regulate private civilian uses of firearms. Specifically, there is no indication that the Framers of the Amendment intended to enshrine the common-law right of self-defense in the Constitution.

In 1934, Congress enacted the National Firearms Act, the first major federal firearms law. Upholding a conviction under that Act, this Court held that, "[i]n the absence of any evidence tending to show that possession or use of a 'shotgun having a barrel of less than eighteen inches in length' at this time has some reasonable relationship to the preservation or efficiency of a well regulated militia, we cannot say that the Second Amendment guarantees the right to keep and bear such an instrument." The view of the Amendment we took in *Miller*— that it protects the right to keep and bear arms for certain military purposes, but that it does not curtail the Legislature's power to regulate the nonmilitary use and ownership of weapons— is both the most natural reading of the Amendment's text and the interpretation most faithful to the history of its adoption.

Since our decision in *Miller,* hundreds of judges have relied on the view of the Amendment we endorsed there; we ourselves affirmed it in 1980. See *Lewis v. United States*, 445 U.S. 55 (1980).[3] No new evidence has surfaced since 1980 supporting the view that the Amendment was intended to curtail the power of Congress to regulate civilian use or misuse of weapons. Indeed, a review of the drafting history of the Amendment demonstrates that its Framers *rejected* proposals that would have broadened its coverage to include such uses.

The opinion the Court announces today fails to identify any new evidence supporting the view that the Amendment was intended to limit the power of Congress to regulate civilian uses of weapons. Unable to point to any such evidence, the Court stakes its holding on a strained and unpersuasive reading of the Amendment's text; significantly different provisions in the 1689 English Bill of Rights, and in various 19th-century State Constitutions; postenactment commentary that was available to the Court when it decided *Miller;* and, ultimately, a feeble attempt to distinguish *Miller* that places more emphasis on the Court's decisional process than on the reasoning in the opinion itself.

Even if the textual and historical arguments on both sides of the issue were evenly balanced, respect for the well-settled views of all of our predecessors on this Court, and for the rule of law itself, would prevent most jurists from endorsing such a dramatic upheaval in the law. As Justice Cardozo observed years ago, the "labor of judges would be increased almost to the breaking point if every past decision could be reopened in every case, and one could not lay one's own course of bricks on the secure foundation of the courses laid by others who had gone before him." The Nature of the Judicial Process 149 (1921)....

I

[T]hree portions of [the Second Amendment's] text merit special focus: the introductory language defining the Amendment's purpose, the class of persons encompassed within its reach, and the unitary nature of the right that it protects.

---

3. Our discussion in *Lewis* was brief but significant. Upholding a conviction for receipt of a firearm by a felon, we wrote: "These legislative restrictions on the use of firearms are neither based upon constitutionally suspect criteria, nor do they entrench upon any constitutionally protected liberties. See *United States v. Miller* ...."

"A well regulated Militia, being necessary to the security of a free State"

The preamble to the Second Amendment makes three important points. It identifies the preservation of the militia as the Amendment's purpose; it explains that the militia is necessary to the security of a free State; and it recognizes that the militia must be "well regulated."....

[T]he Second Amendment's omission of any statement of purpose related to the right to use firearms for hunting or personal self-defense, is especially striking in light of the fact that the Declarations of Rights of Pennsylvania and Vermont did expressly protect such civilian uses at the time.... The contrast between those two declarations and the Second Amendment reinforces the clear statement of purpose announced in the Amendment's preamble. It confirms that the Framers' single-minded focus in crafting the constitutional guarantee "to keep and bear arms" was on military uses of firearms, which they viewed in the context of service in state militias....

The Court today tries to denigrate the importance of this clause of the Amendment by beginning its analysis with the Amendment's operative provision and returning to the preamble merely "to ensure that our reading of the operative clause is consistent with the announced purpose." That is not how this Court ordinarily reads such texts, and it is not how the preamble would have been viewed at the time the Amendment was adopted...

"The right of the people"

The centerpiece of the Court's textual argument is its insistence that the words "the people" as used in the Second Amendment must have the same meaning, and protect the same class of individuals, as when they are used in the First and Fourth Amendments.... But the Court *itself* reads the Second Amendment to protect a "subset" significantly narrower than the class of persons protected by the First and Fourth Amendments; when it finally drills down on the substantive meaning of the Second Amendment, the Court limits the protected class to "law-abiding, responsible citizens." But the class of persons protected by the First and Fourth Amendments is *not* so limited; for even felons (and presumably irresponsible citizens as well) may invoke the protections of those constitutional provisions. The Court offers no way to harmonize its conflicting pronouncements.

The Court also overlooks the significance of the way the Framers used the phrase "the people" in these constitutional provisions. In the First Amendment,... it is only the right peaceably to assemble, and to petition the Government for a redress of grievances, that is described as a right of "the people." These rights contemplate collective action. While the right peaceably to assemble protects the individual rights of those persons participating in the assembly, its concern is with action engaged in by members of a group, rather than any single individual.

Likewise, although the act of petitioning the Government is a right that can be exercised by individuals, it is primarily collective in nature. . . .

Similarly, the words "the people" in the Second Amendment refer back to the object announced in the Amendment's preamble. They remind us that it is the collective action of individuals having a duty to serve in the militia that the text directly protects and, perhaps more importantly, that the ultimate purpose of the Amendment was to protect the States' share of the divided sovereignty created by the Constitution.

[I]t is true that the Fourth Amendment describes a right that need not be exercised in any collective sense. But that observation does not settle the meaning of the phrase "the people" when used in the Second Amendment. For, as we have seen, the phrase means something quite different in the Petition and Assembly Clauses of the First Amendment. . . .

"To keep and bear Arms"

Although the Court's discussion of these words treats them as two "phrases" — as if they read "to keep" and "to bear" — they describe a unitary right: to possess arms if needed for military purposes and to use them in conjunction with military activities. . . .

The term "bear arms" is a familiar idiom; when used unadorned by any additional words, its meaning is "to serve as a soldier, do military service, fight." One 18th-century dictionary defined "arms" as "weapons of offence, or armour of defence," and another contemporaneous source explained that "[b]y *arms*, we understand those instruments of offence generally made use of in war; such as firearms, swords, & c. By *weapons,* we more particularly mean instruments of other kinds (exclusive of fire-arms), made use of as offensive, on special occasions." Had the Framers wished to expand the meaning of the phrase "bear arms" to encompass civilian possession and use, they could have done so by the addition of phrases such as "for the defense of themselves," as was done in the Pennsylvania and Vermont Declarations of Rights. The *unmodified* use of "bear arms," by contrast, refers most naturally to a military purpose, as evidenced by its use in literally dozens of contemporary texts. . . .

The Amendment's use of the term "keep" in no way contradicts the military meaning conveyed by the phrase "bear arms" and the Amendment's preamble. To the contrary, a number of state militia laws in effect at the time of the Second Amendment's drafting used the term "keep" to describe the requirement that militia members store their arms at their homes, ready to be used for service when necessary. . . .

This reading is confirmed by the fact that the clause protects only one right, rather than two. . . . [T]he single right that it does describe is both a duty and a right to have arms available and ready for military service, and to use them for military purposes when necessary.[13] Different language surely would have been used to protect nonmilitary use and possession of weapons from regulation if such an intent had played any role in the drafting of the Amendment....

II

The proper allocation of military power in the new Nation was an issue of central concern for the Framers. The compromises they ultimately reached, reflected in Article I's Militia Clauses and the Second Amendment, represent quintessential examples of the Framers' "splitting the atom of sovereignty."

Two themes relevant to our current interpretive task ran through the debates on the original Constitution. "On the one hand, there was a widespread fear that a national standing Army posed an intolerable threat to individual liberty and to the sovereignty of the separate States.".... On the other hand, the Framers recognized the dangers inherent in relying on inadequately trained militia members "as the primary means of providing for the common defense"; during the Revolutionary War, "[t]his force, though armed, was largely untrained, and its deficiencies were the subject of bitter complaint." In order to respond to those twin concerns, a compromise was reached: Congress would be authorized to raise and support a national Army and Navy, and also to organize, arm, discipline, and provide for the calling forth of "the Militia." U.S. Const., Art. I, § 8, cls. 12-16. The President, at the same time, was empowered as the "Commander in Chief of the Army and Navy of the United States, and of the Militia of the several States, when called into the actual Service of the United States." Art. II, § 2. But, with respect to the militia, a significant reservation was made to the States: Although Congress would have the power to call forth, organize, arm, and discipline the militia, as well as to govern "such Part of them as may be employed in the Service of the United States," the States respectively would retain the right to appoint the officers and to train the militia in accordance with the discipline prescribed by Congress. Art. I, § 8, cl. 16.

But the original Constitution's retention of the militia and its creation of divided authority over that body did not prove sufficient to allay fears about the dangers posed by a standing army. For it was perceived by some that Article I contained a significant gap: While it empowered Congress to organize, arm, and discipline the militia, it did not prevent Congress from providing for the militia's *dis*armament....

---

13. The Court notes that the *First Amendment* protects two separate rights with the phrase "the 'right [singular] of the people peaceably to assemble, and to petition the Government for a redress of grievances.'" But this only proves the point: In contrast to the language quoted by the Court, the Second Amendment does not protect a "right to keep *and to* bear arms," but rather a "right to keep and bear arms." The state constitutions cited by the Court are distinguishable on the same ground.

[This risk] was one of the primary objections to the original Constitution voiced by its opponents. The Anti-Federalists were ultimately unsuccessful in persuading state ratification conventions to condition their approval of the Constitution upon the eventual inclusion of any particular amendment. But a number of States did propose to the first Federal Congress amendments reflecting a desire to ensure that the institution of the militia would remain protected under the new Government.... [While some proposals] were exclusively concerned with standing armies and conscientious objectors, [others] would have protected a more broadly worded right, less clearly tied to service in a state militia. Faced with all of these options, it is telling that James Madison chose to craft the Second Amendment as he did....

Madison's decision to model the Second Amendment on the distinctly military... proposal is therefore revealing, since it is clear that he considered and rejected formulations that would have unambiguously protected civilian uses of firearms. When Madison prepared his first draft, and when that draft was debated and modified, it is reasonable to assume that all participants in the drafting process were fully aware of the other formulations that would have protected civilian use and possession of weapons and that their choice to craft the Amendment as they did represented a rejection of those alternative formulations.

Madison's initial inclusion of an exemption for conscientious objectors sheds revelatory light on the purpose of the Amendment. It confirms an intent to describe a duty as well as a right, and it unequivocally identifies the military character of both....

III

Although it gives short shrift to the drafting history of the Second Amendment, the Court dwells at length on four other sources: the 17th-century English Bill of Rights; Blackstone's Commentaries on the Laws of England; postenactment commentary on the Second Amendment; and post-Civil War legislative history. All of these sources shed only indirect light on the question before us, and in any event offer little support for the Court's conclusion.

The English Bill of Rights

The Court's reliance on Article VII of the 1689 English Bill of Rights—which, like most of the evidence offered by the Court today, was considered in *Miller*—is misguided both because Article VII was enacted in response to different concerns from those that motivated the Framers of the Second Amendment, and because the guarantees of the two provisions were by no means coextensive. Moreover, the English text contained no preamble or other provision identifying a narrow, militia-related purpose.

23

The English Bill of Rights responded to abuses by the Stuart monarchs; among the grievances set forth in the Bill of Rights was that the King had violated the law "[b]y causing several good Subjects being Protestants to be disarmed at the same time when Papists were both armed and Employed contrary to Law." Article VII of the Bill of Rights was a response to that selective disarmament; it guaranteed that "the Subjects which are Protestants may have Armes for their defence, Suitable to their condition and as allowed by Law." This grant did not establish a general right of all persons, or even of all Protestants, to possess weapons. Rather, the right was qualified in two distinct ways: First, it was restricted to those of adequate social and economic status ("suitable to their Condition"); second, it was only available subject to regulation by Parliament ("as allowed by Law").

The Court may well be correct that the English Bill of Rights protected the right of *some* English subjects to use *some* arms for personal self-defense free from restrictions by the Crown (but not Parliament). But that right — adopted in a different historical and political context and framed in markedly different language — tells us little about the meaning of the Second Amendment.

Blackstone's Commentaries

The Court's reliance on Blackstone's Commentaries on the Laws of England is unpersuasive for the same reason as its reliance on the English Bill of Rights. Blackstone's invocation of "'the natural right of resistance and self-preservation,'" and "'the right of having and using arms for self-preservation and defence'" referred specifically to Article VII in the English Bill of Rights. The excerpt from Blackstone offered by the Court, therefore, is, like Article VII itself, of limited use in interpreting the very differently worded, and differently historically situated, Second Amendment.

What *is* important about Blackstone is the instruction he provided on reading the sort of text before us today. Blackstone described an interpretive approach that gave far more weight to preambles than the Court allows.... "[T]he proeme, or preamble, is often called in to help the construction of an act of parliament."

Postenactment Commentary

The Court also excerpts, without any real analysis, commentary by a number of additional scholars, some near in time to the framing and others post-dating it by close to a century. Those scholars are for the most part of limited relevance in construing the guarantee of the Second Amendment: Their views are not altogether clear, they tended to collapse the Second Amendment with Article VII of the English Bill of Rights, and they appear to have been unfamiliar with the drafting history of the Second Amendment....

Post-Civil War Legislative History

The Court suggests that by the post-Civil War period, the Second Amendment was understood to secure a right to firearm use and ownership for purely private purposes like personal self-defense. While it is true that some of the legislative history on which the Court relies supports that contention, such sources are entitled to limited, if any, weight. All of the statements the Court cites were made long after the framing of the Amendment and cannot possibly supply any insight into the intent of the Framers; and all were made during pitched political debates, so that they are better characterized as advocacy than good-faith attempts at constitutional interpretation.

What is more, much of the evidence the Court offers is decidedly less clear than its discussion allows. The Court notes that "[b]lacks were routinely disarmed by Southern States after the Civil War. Those who opposed these injustices frequently stated that they infringed blacks' constitutional right to keep and bear arms." The Court hastily concludes that "[n]eedless to say, the claim was not that blacks were being prohibited from carrying arms in an organized state militia." But some of the claims of the sort the Court cites may have been just that. In some Southern States, Reconstruction-era Republican governments created state militias in which both blacks and whites were permitted to serve. Because "[t]he decision to allow blacks to serve alongside whites meant that most southerners refused to join the new militia," the bodies were dubbed "Negro militia[s]." . . . .

IV

. . . . [The Second] Amendment played little role in any legislative debate about the civilian use of firearms for most of the 19th century, and it made few appearances in the decisions of this Court. Two 19th-century cases, however, bear mentioning.

In *United States v. Cruikshank*, 92 U.S. 542 (1876), the Court sustained a challenge to respondents' convictions under the Enforcement Act of 1870 for conspiring to deprive any individual of "'any right or privilege granted or secured to him by the constitution or laws of the United States.'" The Court wrote, as to counts 2 and 10 of respondents' indictment:

> "The right there specified is that of 'bearing arms for a lawful purpose.'
> This is not a right granted by the Constitution. Neither is it in any manner
> dependent on that instrument for its existence. The Second amendment
> declares that it shall not be infringed; but this, as has been seen, means
> no more than that it shall not be infringed by Congress. This is one of the
> amendments that has no other effect than to restrict the powers of the
> national government."

25

The majority's assertion that the Court in *Cruikshank* "described the right protected by the Second Amendment as 'bearing arms for a lawful purpose,'" is not accurate. The *Cruikshank* Court explained that the defective *indictment* contained such language, but the Court did not itself describe the right, or endorse the indictment's description of the right....

Only one other 19th-century case in this Court, *Presser v. Illinois*, 116 U.S. 252 (1886), engaged in any significant discussion of the Second Amendment. The petitioner in *Presser* was convicted of violating a state statute that prohibited organizations other than the Illinois National Guard from associating together as military companies or parading with arms. Presser challenged his conviction, asserting, as relevant, that the statute violated both the Second and the Fourteenth Amendments....

[In upholding the conviction,] *Presser,* therefore, both affirmed *Cruikshank*'s holding that the Second Amendment posed no obstacle to regulation by state governments, and suggested that in any event nothing in the Constitution protected the use of arms outside the context of a militia "authorized by law" and organized by the State or Federal Government....

[T]he dominant understanding of the Second Amendment's inapplicability to private gun ownership continued well into the 20th century. The first two federal laws directly restricting civilian use and possession of firearms — the 1927 Act prohibiting mail delivery of "pistols, revolvers, and other firearms capable of being concealed on the person," and the 1934 Act prohibiting the possession of sawed-off shotguns and machine guns — were enacted over minor Second Amendment objections dismissed by the vast majority of the legislators who participated in the debates. Members of Congress clashed over the wisdom and efficacy of such laws as crime-control measures. But since the statutes did not infringe upon the military use or possession of weapons, for most legislators they did not even raise the specter of possible conflict with the Second Amendment.

Thus, for most of our history, the invalidity of Second-Amendment-based objections to firearms regulations has been well settled and uncontroversial.[38]

---

38. The majority appears to suggest that even if the meaning of the Second Amendment has been considered settled by courts and legislatures for over two centuries, that settled meaning is overcome by the "reliance of millions of Americans" "upon the true meaning of the right to keep and bear arms." Presumably by this the Court means that many Americans own guns for self-defense, recreation, and other lawful purposes, and object to government interference with their gun ownership. I do not dispute the correctness of this observation. But it is hard to see how Americans have "relied," in the usual sense of the word, on the existence of a constitutional right that, until 2001, had been rejected by every federal court to take up the question. Rather, gun owners have "relied" on the laws passed by democratically elected legislatures, which have generally adopted only limited gun-control measures.

Indeed, the Second Amendment was not even mentioned in either full House of Congress during the legislative proceedings that led to the passage of the 1934 Act. Yet enforcement of that law produced the judicial decision that confirmed the status of the Amendment as limited in reach to military usage. After reviewing many of the same sources that are discussed at greater length by the Court today, the *Miller* Court unanimously concluded that the Second Amendment did not apply to the possession of a firearm that did not have "some reasonable relationship to the preservation or efficiency of a well regulated militia."

The key to that decision did not, as the Court belatedly suggests, turn on the difference between muskets and sawed-off shotguns; it turned, rather, on the basic difference between the military and nonmilitary use and possession of guns. Indeed, if the Second Amendment were not limited in its coverage to military uses of weapons, why should the Court in *Miller* have suggested that some weapons but not others were eligible for Second Amendment protection? If use for self-defense were the relevant standard, why did the Court not inquire into the suitability of a particular weapon for self-defense purposes?

Perhaps in recognition of the weakness of its attempt to distinguish *Miller*, the Court argues in the alternative that *Miller* should be discounted because of its decisional history. It is true that the appellee in *Miller* did not file a brief or make an appearance, although the court below had held that the relevant provision of the National Firearms Act violated the Second Amendment (albeit without any reasoned opinion). But, as our decision in *Marbury v. Madison*, 5 U.S. 137, in which only one side appeared and presented arguments, demonstrates, the absence of adversarial presentation alone is not a basis for refusing to accord *stare decisis* effect to a decision of this Court.…

The majority cannot seriously believe that the *Miller* Court did not consider any relevant evidence; the majority simply does not approve of the conclusion the *Miller* Court reached on that evidence. Standing alone, that is insufficient reason to disregard a unanimous opinion of this Court, upon which substantial reliance has been placed by legislators and citizens for nearly 70 years.

Indeed, reliance interests surely cut the other way: Even apart from the reliance of judges and legislators who properly believed, until today, that the Second Amendment did not reach possession of firearms for purely private activities, "millions of Americans," have relied on the power of government to protect their safety and well-being, and that of their families. With respect to the case before us, the legislature of the District of Columbia has relied on its ability to act to "reduce the potentiality for gun-related crimes and gun-related deaths from occurring within the District of Columbia," H. Con. Res. 694, 94th Cong., 2d Sess., 25 (1976); so, too have the residents of the District.

V

The Court concludes its opinion by declaring that it is not the proper role of this Court to change the meaning of rights "enshrine[d]" in the Constitution. But the right the Court announces was not "enshrined" in the Second Amendment by the Framers; it is the product of today's law-changing decision. The majority's exegesis has utterly failed to establish that as a matter of text or history, "the right of law-abiding, responsible citizens to use arms in defense of hearth and home" is "elevate[d] above all other interests" by the Second Amendment.

Until today, it has been understood that legislatures may regulate the civilian use and misuse of firearms so long as they do not interfere with the preservation of a well-regulated militia. The Court's announcement of a new constitutional right to own and use firearms for private purposes upsets that settled understanding, but leaves for future cases the formidable task of defining the scope of permissible regulations. Today judicial craftsmen have confidently asserted that a policy choice that denies a "law-abiding, responsible citize[n]" the right to keep and use weapons in the home for self-defense is "off the table." Given the presumption that most citizens are law abiding, and the reality that the need to defend oneself may suddenly arise in a host of locations outside the home, I fear that the District's policy choice may well be just the first of an unknown number of dominoes to be knocked off the table.[39]

[Today's decision] will surely give rise to a far more active judicial role in making vitally important national policy decisions than was envisioned at any time in the 18th, 19th, or 20th centuries.

The Court properly disclaims any interest in evaluating the wisdom of the specific policy choice challenged in this case, but it fails to pay heed to a far more important policy choice — the choice made by the Framers themselves. The Court would have us believe that over 200 years ago, the Framers made a choice to limit the tools available to elected officials wishing to regulate civilian

---

39. It was just a few years after the decision in *Miller* that Justice Frankfurter (by any measure a true judicial conservative) warned of the perils that would attend this Court's entry into the "political thicket" of legislative districting. *Colegrove v. Green,* 328 U.S. 549 (1946) (plurality opinion). The equally controversial political thicket that the Court has decided to enter today is qualitatively different from the one that concerned Justice Frankfurter: While our entry into that thicket was justified because the political process was manifestly unable to solve the problem of unequal districts, no one has suggested that the political process is not working exactly as it should in mediating the debate between the advocates and opponents of gun control. What impact the Court's unjustified entry into *this* thicket will have on that ongoing debate — or indeed on the Court itself — is a matter that future historians will no doubt discuss at length. It is, however, clear to me that adherence to a policy of judicial restraint would be far wiser than the bold decision announced today.

uses of weapons, and to authorize this Court to use the common-law process of case-by-case judicial lawmaking to define the contours of acceptable gun control policy. Absent compelling evidence that is nowhere to be found in the Court's opinion, I could not possibly conclude that the Framers made such a choice.

For these reasons, I respectfully dissent.

JUSTICE BREYER, with whom JUSTICE STEVENS, JUSTICE SOUTER, and JUSTICE GINSBURG join, dissenting.

. . . .

I

The majority's conclusion is wrong for two independent reasons. The first reason is that set forth by Justice Stevens — namely, that the Second Amendment protects militia-related, not self-defense-related, interests. . . .

The second independent reason is that the protection the Amendment provides is not absolute. The Amendment permits government to regulate the interests that it serves. Thus, irrespective of what those interests are — whether they do or do not include an independent interest in self-defense — the majority's view cannot be correct unless it can show that the District's regulation is unreasonable or inappropriate in Second Amendment terms. This the majority cannot do. . . .

II

. . . .

[C]olonial history itself offers important examples of the kinds of gun regulation that citizens would then have thought compatible with the "right to keep and bear arms," whether embodied in Federal or State Constitutions, or the background common law. And those examples include substantial regulation of firearms in urban areas, including regulations that imposed obstacles to the use of firearms for the protection of the home. . . .

This historical evidence demonstrates that a self-defense assumption is the *beginning*, rather than the *end*, of any constitutional inquiry. That the District law impacts self-defense merely raises *questions* about the law's constitutionality. . . . There are no purely logical or conceptual answers to such questions. All of which to say that to raise a self-defense question is not to answer it.

III

I therefore begin by asking a process-based question: How is a court to determine whether a particular firearm regulation (here, the District's restriction on handguns) is consistent with the Second Amendment? What kind of constitutional standard should the court use? How high a protective hurdle does the Amendment erect?

The question matters. The majority is wrong when it says that the District's law is unconstitutional "[u]nder any of the standards of scrutiny that we have applied to enumerated constitutional rights." How could that be? It certainly would not be unconstitutional under, for example, a "rational basis" standard, which requires a court to uphold regulation so long as it bears a "rational relationship" to a "legitimate governmental purpose." The law at issue here, which in part seeks to prevent gun-related accidents, at least bears a "rational relationship" to that "legitimate" life-saving objective....

Respondent proposes that the Court adopt a "strict scrutiny" test, which would require reviewing with care each gun law to determine whether it is "narrowly tailored to achieve a compelling governmental interest." But the majority implicitly, and appropriately, rejects that suggestion by broadly approving a set of laws — prohibitions on concealed weapons, forfeiture by criminals of the Second Amendment right, prohibitions on firearms in certain locales, and governmental regulation of commercial firearm sales — whose constitutionality under a strict scrutiny standard would be far from clear.

Indeed, adoption of a true strict-scrutiny standard for evaluating gun regulations would be impossible. That is because almost every gun-control regulation will seek to advance (as the one here does) a "primary concern of every government — a concern for the safety and indeed the lives of its citizens." *United States v. Salerno*, 481 U.S. 739 (1987). The Court has deemed that interest, as well as "the Government's general interest in preventing crime," to be "compelling," and the Court has in a wide variety of constitutional contexts found such public-safety concerns sufficiently forceful to justify restrictions on individual liberties, see *e.g.*, *Brandenburg v. Ohio*, 395 U.S. 444 (1969) (per curiam) (First Amendment free speech rights); *Sherbert v. Verner*, 374 U.S. 398 (1963) (First Amendment religious rights); *Brigham City v. Stuart*, 547 U.S. 398 (2006) (Fourth Amendment protection of the home); *New York v. Quarles*, 467 U.S. 649 (1984) (Fifth Amendment rights under *Miranda v. Arizona*); *Salerno*, *supra* (Eighth Amendment bail rights). Thus, any attempt *in theory* to apply strict scrutiny to gun regulations will *in practice* turn into an interest-balancing inquiry, with the interests protected by the Second Amendment on one side and the governmental public-safety concerns on the other, the only question being whether the regulation at issue impermissibly burdens the former in the course of advancing the latter.

I would simply adopt such an interest-balancing inquiry explicitly....

In applying this kind of standard the Court normally defers to a legislature's empirical judgment in matters where a legislature is likely to have greater expertise and greater institutional factfinding capacity....

30

The above-described approach seems preferable to a more rigid approach here for a further reason. Experience as much as logic has led the Court to decide that in one area of constitutional law or another the interests are likely to prove stronger on one side of a typical constitutional case than on the other. Here, we have little prior experience. Courts that *do* have experience in these matters have uniformly taken an approach that treats empirically-based legislative judgment with a degree of deference....

IV

....

[Justice Breyer turns now to the constitutionality of the District's ban on handguns.]

A

No one doubts the constitutional importance of the statute's basic objective, saving lives. But there is considerable debate about whether the District's statute helps to achieve that objective. I begin by reviewing the statute's tendency to secure that objective from the perspective of (1) the legislature (namely, the Council of the District of Columbia) that enacted the statute in 1976, and (2) a court that seeks to evaluate the Council's decision today.

1

First, consider the facts as the legislature saw them when it adopted the District statute. As stated by the local council committee that recommended its adoption, the major substantive goal of the District's handgun restriction is "to reduce the potentiality for gun-related crimes and gun-related deaths from occurring within the District of Columbia." The committee concluded, on the basis of "extensive public hearings" and "lengthy research," that "[t]he easy availability of firearms in the United States has been a major factor contributing to the drastic increase in gun-related violence and crime over the past 40 years." It reported to the Council "startling statistics," regarding gun-related crime, accidents, and deaths, focusing particularly on the relation between handguns and crime and the proliferation of handguns within the District.

The committee informed the Council that guns were "responsible for 69 deaths in this country each day," for a total of "[a]pproximately 25,000 gun-deaths...each year," along with an additional 200,000 gun-related injuries. Three thousand of these deaths, the report stated, were accidental. A quarter of the victims in those accidental deaths were children under the age of 14. And according to the committee, "[f]or every intruder stopped by a homeowner with a firearm, there are 4 gun-related accidents within the home."

In respect to local crime, the committee observed that there were 285 murders in the District during 1974 — a record number. The committee also stated that, "[c]ontrary to popular opinion on the subject, firearms are more frequently involved in deaths and violence among relatives and friends than in premeditated criminal activities." Citing an article from the American Journal of Psychiatry, the committee reported that "[m]ost murders are committed by previously law-abiding citizens, in situations where spontaneous violence is generated by anger, passion or intoxication, and where the killer and victim are acquainted." "Twenty-five percent of these murders," the committee informed the Council, "occur within families."

The committee report furthermore presented statistics strongly correlating handguns with crime. Of the 285 murders in the District in 1974, 155 were committed with handguns. This did not appear to be an aberration, as the report revealed that "handguns [had been] used in roughly 54% of all murders" (and 87% of murders of law enforcement officers) nationwide over the preceding several years. Nor were handguns only linked to murders, as statistics showed that they were used in roughly 60% of robberies and 26% of assaults. "A crime committed with a pistol," the committee reported, "is 7 times more likely to be lethal than a crime committed with any other weapon." ...

The District's special focus on handguns thus reflects the fact that the committee report found them to have a particularly strong link to undesirable activities in the District's exclusively urban environment. The District did not seek to prohibit possession of other sorts of weapons deemed more suitable for an "urban area."

2

Next, consider the facts as a court must consider them looking at the matter as of today. Petitioners, and their *amici,* have presented us with more recent statistics that tell much the same story that the committee report told 30 years ago. At the least, they present nothing that would permit us to second-guess the Council in respect to the numbers of gun crimes, injuries, and deaths, or the role of handguns.

From 1993 to 1997, there were 180,533 firearm-related deaths in the United States, an average of over 36,000 per year. Fifty-one percent were suicides, 44% were homicides, 1% were legal interventions, 3% were unintentional accidents, and 1% were of undetermined causes. Over that same period there were an additional 411,800 nonfatal firearm-related injuries treated in U.S. hospitals, an average of over 82,000 per year. Of these, 62% resulted from assaults, 17% were unintentional, 6% were suicide attempts, 1% were legal interventions, and 13% were of unknown causes.

The statistics are particularly striking in respect to children and adolescents. In over one in every eight firearm-related deaths in 1997, the victim was someone under the age of 20. Firearm-related deaths account for 22.5% of all injury deaths between the ages of 1 and 19. More male teenagers die from firearms than from all natural causes combined.

Handguns are involved in a majority of firearm deaths and injuries in the United States. From 1993 to 1997, 81% of firearm-homicide victims were killed by handgun. In the same period, for the 41% of firearm injuries for which the weapon type is known, 82% of them were from handguns. And among children under the age of 20, handguns account for approximately 70% of all unintentional firearm-related injuries and deaths....

Handguns also appear to be a very popular weapon among criminals. In a 1997 survey of inmates who were armed during the crime for which they were incarcerated, 83.2% of state inmates and 86.7% of federal inmates said that they were armed with a handgun. And handguns are not only popular tools for crime, but popular objects of it as well: the FBI received on average over 274,000 reports of stolen guns for each year between 1985 and 1994, and almost 60% of stolen guns are handguns. Department of Justice studies have concluded that stolen handguns in particular are an important source of weapons for both adult and juvenile offenders.

Statistics further suggest that urban areas, such as the District, have different experiences with gun-related death, injury, and crime, than do less densely populated rural areas. A disproportionate amount of violent and property crimes occur in urban areas, and urban criminals are more likely than other offenders to use a firearm during the commission of a violent crime....

3

Respondent and his many *amici* for the most part do not disagree about the *figures* set forth in the preceding subsection, but they do disagree strongly with the District's *predictive judgment* that a ban on handguns will help solve the crime and accident problems that those figures disclose....

First, they point out that, since the ban took effect, violent crime in the District has increased, not decreased. Indeed, a comparison with 49 other major cities reveals that the District's homicide rate is actually substantially *higher* relative to these other cities than it was before the handgun restriction went into effect.

Second, respondent's *amici* point to a statistical analysis that regresses murder rates against the presence or absence of strict gun laws in 20 European nations. That analysis concludes that strict gun laws are correlated with *more* murders, not fewer. They further argue that handgun bans do not reduce suicide rates, or rates of accidents, even those involving children.

Third, they point to evidence indicating that firearm ownership does have a beneficial self-defense effect. Based on a 1993 survey, the authors of one study estimated that there were 2.2-to-2.5 million defensive uses of guns (mostly brandishing, about a quarter involving the actual firing of a gun) annually. Another study estimated that for a period of 12 months ending in 1994, there were 503,481 incidents in which a burglar found himself confronted by an armed homeowner, and that in 497,646 (98.8%) of them, the intruder was successfully scared away. A third study suggests that gun-armed victims are substantially less likely than non-gun-armed victims to be injured in resisting robbery or assault. And additional evidence suggests that criminals are likely to be deterred from burglary and other crimes if they know the victim is likely to have a gun.

Fourth, respondent's *amici* argue that laws criminalizing gun possession are self-defeating, as evidence suggests that they will have the effect only of restricting law-abiding citizens, but not criminals, from acquiring guns. . . .

These empirically based arguments may have proved strong enough to convince many legislatures, as a matter of legislative policy, not to adopt total handgun bans. But the question here is whether they are strong enough to destroy judicial confidence in the reasonableness of a legislature that rejects them. And that they are not. For one thing, they can lead us more deeply into the uncertainties that surround any effort to reduce crime, but they cannot prove either that handgun possession diminishes crime or that handgun bans are ineffective. The statistics do show a soaring District crime rate. And the District's crime rate went up after the District adopted its handgun ban. But, as students of elementary logic know, *after it* does not mean *because of it*. What would the District's crime rate have looked like without the ban? Higher? Lower? The same? Experts differ; and we, as judges, cannot say.

What about the fact that foreign nations with strict gun laws have higher crime rates? Which is the cause and which the effect? The proposition that strict gun laws *cause* crime is harder to accept than the proposition that strict gun laws in part grow out of the fact that a nation already has a higher crime rate. And we are then left with the same question as before: What would have happened to crime without the gun laws — a question that respondent and his *amici* do not convincingly answer.

Further, suppose that respondent's *amici* are right when they say that householders' possession of loaded handguns help to frighten away intruders. On that assumption, one must still ask whether that benefit is worth the potential death-related cost. And that is a question without a directly provable answer.

Finally, consider the claim of respondent's *amici* that handgun bans *cannot* work; there are simply too many illegal guns already in existence for a ban on legal guns to make a difference. In a word, they claim that, given the urban sea of pre-existing legal guns, criminals can readily find arms regardless. Nonetheless, a legislature might respond, we want to make an effort to try to dry up that urban sea, drop by drop. And none of the studies can show that effort is not worthwhile.

34

In a word, the studies to which respondent's *amici* point raise policy-related questions. They succeed in proving that the District's predictive judgments are controversial. But they do not by themselves show that those judgments are incorrect; nor do they demonstrate a consensus, academic or otherwise, supporting that conclusion.

Thus, it is not surprising that the District and its *amici* support the District's handgun restriction with studies of their own. One in particular suggests that, statistically speaking, the District's law has indeed had positive life-saving effects. Others suggest that firearm restrictions as a general matter reduce homicides, suicides, and accidents in the home. Still others suggest that the defensive uses of handguns are not as great in number as respondent's *amici* claim....

The upshot is a set of studies and counterstudies that, at most, could leave a judge uncertain about the proper policy conclusion. But from respondent's perspective any such uncertainty is not good enough. That is because legislators, not judges, have primary responsibility for drawing policy conclusions from empirical fact. And, given that constitutional allocation of decisionmaking responsibility, the empirical evidence presented here is sufficient to allow a judge to reach a firm *legal* conclusion....

[T]he District's decision represents the kind of empirically based judgment that legislatures, not courts, are best suited to make. In fact, deference to legislative judgment seems particularly appropriate here, where the judgment has been made by a local legislature, with particular knowledge of local problems and insight into appropriate local solutions....

B

I next assess the extent to which the District's law burdens the interests that the Second Amendment seeks to protect....

1

The District's statute burdens the Amendment's first and primary objective [of protecting the militia] hardly at all....

To begin with, the present case has nothing to do with *actual* military service.... I am aware of no indication that the District either now or in the recent past has called up its citizenry to serve in a militia, that it has any inkling of doing so anytime in the foreseeable future, or that this law must be construed to prevent the use of handguns during legitimate militia activities....

[T]he District's law does not seriously affect military training interests. The law permits residents to engage in activities that will increase their familiarity with firearms. They may register (and thus possess in their homes) weapons other than handguns, such as rifles and shotguns. See D. C. Code §§ 7-2502.01, 7-2502.02(a) (only weapons that cannot be registered are sawed-off shotguns, machine guns, short-barreled rifles, and pistols not registered before 1976) ....

And while the District law prevents citizens from training with handguns *within the District*, the District consists of only 61.4 square miles of urban area. The adjacent States do permit the use of handguns for target practice, and those States are only a brief subway ride away.…

Of course, a subway rider must buy a ticket, and the ride takes time. It also costs money to store a pistol, say, at a target range, outside the District. But given the costs already associated with gun ownership and firearms training, I cannot say that a subway ticket and a short subway ride (and storage costs) create more than a minimal burden. Compare *Crawford v. Marion County Election Bd.*, 553 U.S. ____ (2008) (Breyer, J., dissenting) (acknowledging travel burdens on indigent persons in the context of voting where public transportation options were limited).…

2

The majority briefly suggests that the "right to keep and bear Arms" might encompass an interest in hunting. But in enacting the present provisions, the District sought "to take nothing away from sportsmen." And any inability of District residents to hunt near where they live has much to do with the jurisdiction's exclusively urban character and little to do with the District's firearm laws.…

3

The District's law does prevent a resident from keeping a loaded handgun in his home. And it consequently makes it more difficult for the householder to use the handgun for self-defense in the home against intruders, such as burglars. [S]tatistics suggest that handguns are the most popular weapon for self defense. And there are some legitimate reasons why that would be the case… To that extent the law burdens to some degree an interest in self-defense that for present purposes I have assumed the Amendment seeks to further.

C

In weighing needs and burdens, we must take account of the possibility that there are reasonable, but less restrictive alternatives. Are there *other* potential measures that might similarly promote the same goals while imposing lesser restrictions? Here I see none.

The reason there is no clearly superior, less restrictive alternative to the District's handgun ban is that the ban's very objective is to reduce significantly the number of handguns in the District, say, for example, by allowing a law enforcement officer immediately to assume that *any* handgun he sees is an *illegal* handgun. And there is no plausible way to achieve that objective other than to ban the guns.…

[A]ny measure less restrictive in respect to the use of handguns for self-defense will, to that same extent, prove less effective in preventing the use of handguns for illicit purposes. If a resident has a handgun in the home that he can use for self-defense, then he has a handgun in the home that he can use to commit suicide or engage in acts of domestic violence....

Licensing restrictions would not similarly reduce the handgun population, and the District may reasonably fear that even if guns are initially restricted to law-abiding citizens, they might be stolen and thereby placed in the hands of criminals....

The absence of equally effective alternatives to a complete prohibition finds support in the empirical fact that other States and urban centers prohibit particular types of weapons....

D

The upshot is that the District's objectives are compelling; its predictive judgments as to its law's tendency to achieve those objectives are adequately supported; the law does impose a burden upon any self-defense interest that the Amendment seeks to secure; and there is no clear less restrictive alternative. I turn now to the final portion of the "permissible regulation" question: Does the District's law *disproportionately* burden Amendment-protected interests? Several considerations, taken together, convince me that it does not.

First, the District law is tailored to the life-threatening problems it attempts to address. The law concerns one class of weapons, handguns, leaving residents free to possess shotguns and rifles, along with ammunition. The area that falls within its scope is totally urban.

Second, the self-defense interest in maintaining loaded handguns in the home to shoot intruders is not the *primary* interest, but at most a subsidiary interest, that the Second Amendment seeks to serve....

Further, any self-defense interest at the time of the Framing could not have focused exclusively upon urban-crime related dangers. Two hundred years ago, most Americans, many living on the frontier, would likely have thought of self-defense primarily in terms of outbreaks of fighting with Indian tribes, rebellions such as Shays' Rebellion, marauders, and crime-related dangers to travelers on the roads, on footpaths, or along waterways. Insofar as the Framers focused at all on the tiny fraction of the population living in large cities, they would have been aware that these city dwellers were subject to firearm restrictions that their rural counterparts were not. They are unlikely then to have thought of a right to keep loaded handguns in homes to confront intruders in urban settings as *central*....

Nor, for that matter, am I aware of any evidence that *handguns* in particular were central to the Framers' conception of the Second Amendment. The lists of militia-related weapons in the late 18th-century state statutes appear primarily to refer to other sorts of weapons, muskets in particular....

Third, irrespective of what the Framers *could have thought,* we know what they *did think.* Samuel Adams, who lived in Boston, advocated a constitutional amendment that would have precluded the Constitution from ever being "construed" to "prevent the people of the United States, who are peaceable citizens, from keeping their own arms." Samuel Adams doubtless knew that the Massachusetts Constitution contained somewhat similar protection. And he doubtless knew that Massachusetts law prohibited Bostonians from keeping loaded guns in the house. So how could Samuel Adams have advocated such protection *unless* he thought that the protection was *consistent* with local regulation that seriously impeded urban residents from using their arms against intruders? It seems unlikely that he meant to deprive the Federal Government of power (to enact Boston-type weapons regulation) that he know Boston had and (as far as we know) he would have thought constitutional under the Massachusetts Constitution....

Fourth, a contrary view, as embodied in today's decision, will have unfortunate consequences. The decision will encourage legal challenges to gun regulation throughout the Nation. Because it says little about the standards used to evaluate regulatory decisions, it will leave the Nation without clear standards for resolving those challenges. And litigation over the course of many years, or the mere specter of such litigation, threatens to leave cities without effective protection against gun violence and accidents during that time....

V

The majority derides my approach as "judge-empowering." I take this criticism seriously, but I do not think it accurate....

The majority's methodology is, in my view, substantially less transparent than mine. At a minimum, I find it difficult to understand the reasoning that seems to underlie certain conclusions that it reaches.

The majority spends the first 54 pages of its opinion attempting to rebut Justice Stevens' evidence that the Amendment was enacted with a purely militia-related purpose. In the majority's view, the Amendment also protects an interest in armed personal self-defense, at least to some degree. But the majority does not tell us precisely what that interest is. "Putting all of [the Second Amendment's] textual elements together," the majority says, "we find that they guarantee the individual right to possess and carry weapons in case of confrontation." Then, three pages later, it says that "we do not read the Second Amendment to permit citizens to carry arms for *any sort* of confrontation." Yet, with one critical exception, it does not explain which confrontations count. It simply leaves that question unanswered.

The majority does, however, point to one type of confrontation that counts, for it describes the Amendment as "elevat[ing] above all other interests the right of law-abiding, responsible citizens to use arms in defense of hearth and home." What is its basis for finding that to be the core of the Second Amendment right? The only historical sources identified by the majority that even appear to touch upon that specific matter consist of an 1866 newspaper editorial discussing the Freedmen's Bureau Act, two quotations from that 1866 Act's legislative history, and a 1980 state court opinion saying that in colonial times the same were used to defend the home as to maintain the militia. How can citations such as these support the far-reaching proposition that the Second Amendment's primary concern is not its stated concern about the militia, but rather a right to keep loaded weapons at one's bedside to shoot intruders?

Nor is it at all clear to me how the majority decides *which* loaded "arms" a homeowner may keep. The majority says that that Amendment protects those weapons "typically possessed by law-abiding citizens for lawful purposes." This definition conveniently excludes machineguns, but permits handguns, which the majority describes as "the most popular weapon chosen by Americans for self-defense in the home." But what sense does this approach make? According to the majority's reasoning, if Congress and the States lift restrictions on the possession and use of machineguns, and people buy machineguns to protect their homes, the Court will have to reverse course and find that the Second Amendment *does*, in fact, protect the individual self-defense-related right to possess a machinegun. On the majority's reasoning, if tomorrow someone invents a particularly useful, highly dangerous self-defense weapon, Congress and the States had better ban it immediately, for once it becomes popular Congress will no longer possess the constitutional authority to do so. In essence, the majority determines what regulations are permissible by looking to see what existing regulations permit. There is no basis for believing that the Framers intended such circular reasoning.

I am similarly puzzled by the majority's list, in Part III of its opinion, of provisions that in its view would survive Second Amendment scrutiny. These consist of (1) "prohibitions on carrying concealed weapons"; (2) "prohibitions on the possession of firearms by felons"; (3) "prohibitions on the possession of firearms by... the mentally ill"; (4) "laws forbidding the carrying of firearms in sensitive places such as schools and government buildings"; and (5) government "conditions and qualifications" attached "to the commercial sale of arms." Why these? Is it that similar restrictions existed in the late 18th century? The majority fails to cite any colonial analogues....

At the same time the majority ignores a more important question: Given the purposes for which the Framers enacted the Second Amendment, how should it be applied to modern-day circumstances that they could not have anticipated? Assume, for argument's sake, that the Framers did intend the Amendment to offer a degree of self-defense protection. Does that mean that the Framers also intended to guarantee a right to possess a loaded gun near swimming pools, parks, and playgrounds? That they would not have cared about the children who might pick up a loaded gun on their parents' bedside table? That they (who certainly showed concern for the risk of fire) would have lacked concern for the risk of accidental deaths or suicides that readily accessible loaded handguns in urban areas might bring? Unless we believe that they intended future generations to ignore such matters, answering questions such as the questions in this case requires judgment—judicial judgment exercised within a framework for constitutional analysis that guides that judgment and which makes its exercise transparent. One cannot answer those questions by combining inconclusive historical research with judicial *ipse dixit.*...

B. The Origins of the U.S. Constitution

Page 26. At the end of the Note, add the following:

For a general treatment of the document, with an emphasis on this point, see A. Amar, America's Constitution: A Biography (2005).

C. The Basic Framework

Page 48. At the end of section 2b of the Note, add the following:

For a sophisticated argument on behalf of judicial deference to democratic processes, see A. Vermeule, Judging Under Uncertainty (2006). For an emphasis on the political nature of constitutional law, and a corresponding plea for judicial deference to political majorities, see Posner, The Political Court, 119 Harv. L. Rev. 31 (2005).

Page 49. Before the first paragraph on this page of section 2e of the Note, add the following:

For an exploration of the possible role of constitutions and courts in protecting "capabilities" rather than rights, see Nussbaum, Constitutions and Capabilities: "Perception" Against Lofty Formalism, 121 Harv. L. Rev. 4 (2007).

Page 49.   At the end of section 2e of the Note, add the following:

Is it so clear, in any case, that the argument for judicial review depends on claims about comparative advantages of courts and judges? See Fallon, The Core of An Uneasy Case *For* Judicial Review, 121 Harv. L. Rev. 1693 (2008). Fallon argues that even if courts are no better than legislatures in identifying rights, it is important to see that judicial review might result in a situation in which rights are overprotected rather than underprotected — and that that situation might be better than the opposite. If judicial review serves to prevent errors in only one direction, involving failures to protect rights adequately, such review might be justified even if courts are not better than legislatures at identifying rights correctly.

Page 85.   At the end of section 2 of the Note, add the following:

In Boumediene v. Bush, 128 S. Ct. 2229 (2008), the Supreme Court addressed the Military Commissions Act of 2006 (MCA), a law passed in response to the Court's earlier decisions holding that the federal habeas statute gave federal courts jurisdiction to address claims by foreign nationals detained at the U.S. Naval Station at Guantanamo Bay, Cuba. Section 7 amended the federal habeas statute to provide that "No court, justice, or judge shall have jurisdiction to hear or consider an application for a writ of habeas corpus filed by or on behalf of an alien detained by the United States who has been determined by the United States to have been properly detained as an enemy combatant or is awaiting such determination." The Court, in an opinion by Justice Kennedy, that "acknowledge[d]" the "litigation history that prompted Congress to enact the MCA," concluded that section 7 constituted a "clear statement of congressional intent to strip the federal courts of jurisdiction in pending cases."

Having found that the MCA stripped federal courts of jurisdiction, the Court then held that the MCA violated the Suspension Clause of Art. I, § 9, cl. 2 (which provides that "[t]he privilege of the Writ of Habeas Corpus shall not be suspended unless when in Cases of Rebellion or Invasion the public Safety may require it") because the petitioners fell within the historic scope of the writ and the procedures Congress had provided in lieu of access to habeas were an inadequate substitute. The Court concluded:

Officials charged with daily operational responsibility for our security may consider a judicial discourse on the history of the Habeas Corpus Act of 1679 and like matters to be far removed from the Nation's present, urgent concerns. Established legal doctrine, however, must be consulted for its teaching. Remote in time it may be; irrelevant to the present it is not. Security depends upon a sophisticated intelligence apparatus and the ability of our Armed Forces to act and to interdict. There are further considerations, however. Security subsists, too, in fidelity to freedom's first principles. Chief among these are freedom from arbitrary and unlawful restraint and the personal liberty that is secured by adherence to the separation of powers. It is from these principles that the judicial authority to consider petitions for habeas corpus relief derives.

Our opinion does not undermine the Executive's powers as Commander in Chief. On the contrary, the exercise of those powers is vindicated, not eroded, when confirmed by the Judicial Branch. Within the Constitution's separation-of-powers structure, few exercises of judicial power are as legitimate or as necessary as the responsibility to hear challenges to the authority of the Executive to imprison a person. . . .

The several concurring and dissenting opinions all proceeded from the premise that the MCA had stripped federal courts of their habeas jurisdiction, addressing only the questions whether the constitutional habeas jurisdiction extended to individuals in petitioners' situation and whether Congress had provided sufficient process to such individuals (if any process was in fact required.)

F. "Case or Controversy" Requirements and the Passive Virtues

Page 105. After Lujan and before the Note, add the following:

MASSACHUSETTS v. EPA

549 U.S. 497 (2007)

JUSTICE STEVENS delivered the opinion of the Court.

A well-documented rise in global temperatures has coincided with a significant increase in the concentration of carbon dioxide in the atmosphere. Respected scientists believe the two trends are related. For when carbon dioxide is released into the atmosphere, it acts like the ceiling of a greenhouse, trapping solar energy and retarding the escape of reflected heat. It is therefore a species — the most important species — of a "greenhouse gas."

Calling global warming "the most pressing environmental challenge of our time," a group of States, local governments, and private organizations, alleged in a petition for certiorari that the Environmental Protection Agency (EPA) has abdicated its responsibility under the Clean Air Act to regulate the emissions of four greenhouse gases, including carbon dioxide. Specifically, petitioners asked us to answer two questions concerning the meaning of § 202(a)(1) of the Act: whether EPA has the statutory authority to regulate greenhouse gas emissions from new motor vehicles; and if so, whether its stated reasons for refusing to do so are consistent with the statute.
. . .

I

Section 202(a)(1) of the Clean Air Act, provides:

> The [EPA] Administrator shall by regulation prescribe (and from time to time revise) in accordance with the provisions of this section, standards applicable to the emission of any air pollutant from any class or classes of new motor vehicles or new motor vehicle engines, which in his judgment cause, or contribute to, air pollution which may reasonably be anticipated to endanger public health or welfare. . . .

The Act defines "air pollutant" to include "any air pollution agent or combination of such agents, including any physical, chemical, biological, radioactive . . . substance or matter which is emitted into or otherwise enters the ambient air." § 7602(g). "Welfare" is also defined broadly: among other things, it includes "effects on . . . weather . . . and climate." § 7602(h).
. . .

IV

Article III of the Constitution limits federal-court jurisdiction to "Cases" and "Controversies." . . .

The parties' dispute turns on the proper construction of a congressional statute, a question eminently suitable to resolution in federal court. Congress has moreover authorized this type of challenge to EPA action. That authorization is of critical importance to the standing inquiry: "Congress has the power to define injuries and articulate chains of causation that will give rise to a case or controversy where none existed before." *Lujan*, 504 U.S., at 580 (Kennedy, J., concurring in part and concurring in judgment). "In exercising this power, however, Congress must at the very least identify the injury it seeks to vindicate and relate the injury to the class of persons entitled to bring suit." We will not, therefore, "entertain citizen suits to vindicate the public's nonconcrete interest in the proper administration of the laws."

EPA maintains that because greenhouse gas emissions inflict widespread harm, the doctrine of standing presents an insuperable jurisdictional obstacle. We do not agree....

To ensure the proper adversarial presentation, *Lujan* holds that a litigant must demonstrate that it has suffered a concrete and particularized injury that is either actual or imminent, that the injury is fairly traceable to the defendant, and that it is likely that a favorable decision will redress that injury. However, a litigant to whom Congress has "accorded a procedural right to protect his concrete interests," — here, the right to challenge agency action unlawfully withheld, § 7607(b)(1) — "can assert that right without meeting all the normal standards for redressability and immediacy." When a litigant is vested with a procedural right, that litigant has standing if there is some possibility that the requested relief will prompt the injury-causing party to reconsider the decision that allegedly harmed the litigant. Ibid.; see also Sugar Cane Growers Cooperative of Fla. v. Veneman, 289 F.3d 89, 94-95 (C.A.D.C.2002) ("A [litigant] who alleges a deprivation of a procedural protection to which he is entitled never has to prove that if he had received the procedure the substantive result would have been altered. All that is necessary is to show that the procedural step was connected to the substantive result").

Only one of the petitioners needs to have standing to permit us to consider the petition for review. We stress here, as did Judge Tatel below, the special position and interest of Massachusetts. It is of considerable relevance that the party seeking review here is a sovereign State and not, as it was in *Lujan,* a private individual.

Well before the creation of the modern administrative state, we recognized that States are not normal litigants for the purposes of invoking federal jurisdiction. As Justice Holmes explained in Georgia v. Tennessee Copper Co., 206 U.S. 230, 237 (1907), a case in which Georgia sought to protect its citizens from air pollution originating outside its borders:

> "The case has been argued largely as if it were one between two private parties; but it is not. The very elements that would be relied upon in a suit between fellow-citizens as a ground for equitable relief are wanting here. The State owns very little of the territory alleged to be affected, and the damage to it capable of estimate in money, possibly, at least, is small. This is a suit by a State for an injury to it in its capacity of *quasi*-sovereign. In that capacity the State has an interest independent of and behind the titles of its citizens, in all the earth and air within its domain. It has the last word as to whether its mountains shall be stripped of their forests and its inhabitants shall breathe pure air."

Just as Georgia's "independent interest... in all the earth and air within its domain" supported federal jurisdiction a century ago, so too does Massachusetts' well-founded desire to preserve its sovereign territory today. That Massachusetts does in fact own a great deal of the "territory alleged to be affected" only reinforces the conclusion that its stake in the outcome of this case is sufficiently concrete to warrant the exercise of federal judicial power. [Given] [its] procedural right and Massachusetts' stake in protecting its quasi-sovereign interests, the Commonwealth is entitled to special solicitude in our standing analysis.

With that in mind, it is clear that petitioners' submissions as they pertain to Massachusetts have satisfied the most demanding standards of the adversarial process. EPA's steadfast refusal to regulate greenhouse gas emissions presents a risk of harm to Massachusetts that is both "actual" and "imminent." [*Lujan*, 504 U.S., at 560 (internal quotation marks omitted).]

There is, moreover, a "substantial likelihood that the judicial relief requested" will prompt EPA to take steps to reduce that risk.

The Injury

The harms associated with climate change are serious and well recognized. Indeed, the NRC Report itself — which EPA regards as an "objective and independent assessment of the relevant science" — identifies a number of environmental changes that have already inflicted significant harms, including "the global retreat of mountain glaciers, reduction in snow-cover extent, the earlier spring melting of rivers and lakes, [and] the accelerated rate of rise of sea levels during the 20th century relative to the past few thousand years...." NRC Report 16.

Petitioners allege that this only hints at the environmental damage yet to come. According to the climate scientist Michael MacCracken, "qualified scientific experts involved in climate change research" have reached a "strong consensus" that global warming threatens (among other things) a precipitate rise in sea levels by the end of the century, "severe and irreversible changes to natural ecosystems," a "significant reduction in water storage in winter snow-pack in mountainous regions with direct and important economic consequences," and an increase in the spread of disease. He also observes that rising ocean temperatures may contribute to the ferocity of hurricanes.

That these climate-change risks are "widely shared" does not minimize Massachusetts' interest in the outcome of this litigation. See Federal Election Comm'n v. Akins, 524 U.S. 11, 24 (1998) ("[W]here a harm is concrete, though widely shared, the Court has found 'njury in fact' "). According to petitioners' unchallenged affidavits, global sea levels rose somewhere between 10 and 20 centimeters over the 20th century as a result of global warming. These rising seas have already begun to swallow Massachusetts' coastal land. Because the Commonwealth "owns a substantial portion of the state's coastal property," it has alleged a particularized injury in its capacity as a landowner. The severity of

45

that injury will only increase over the course of the next century: If sea levels continue to rise as predicted, one Massachusetts official believes that a significant fraction of coastal property will be "either permanently lost through inundation or temporarily lost through periodic storm surge and flooding events." Remediation costs alone, petitioners allege, could run well into the hundreds of millions of dollars.

Causation

EPA does not dispute the existence of a causal connection between manmade greenhouse gas emissions and global warming. At a minimum, therefore, EPA's refusal to regulate such emissions "contributes" to Massachusetts' injuries.

EPA nevertheless maintains that its decision not to regulate greenhouse gas emissions from new motor vehicles contributes so insignificantly to petitioners' injuries that the agency cannot be haled into federal court to answer for them. For the same reason, EPA does not believe that any realistic possibility exists that the relief petitioners seek would mitigate global climate change and remedy their injuries. That is especially so because predicted increases in greenhouse gas emissions from developing nations, particularly China and India, are likely to offset any marginal domestic decrease.

But EPA overstates its case. Its argument rests on the erroneous assumption that a small incremental step, because it is incremental, can never be attacked in a federal judicial forum. Yet accepting that premise would doom most challenges to regulatory action. Agencies, like legislatures, do not generally resolve massive problems in one fell regulatory swoop. They instead whittle away at them over time, refining their preferred approach as circumstances change and as they develop a more-nuanced understanding of how best to proceed. That a first step might be tentative does not by itself support the notion that federal courts lack jurisdiction to determine whether that step conforms to law.

And reducing domestic automobile emissions is hardly a tentative step. Even leaving aside the other greenhouse gases, the United States transportation sector emits an enormous quantity of carbon dioxide into the atmosphere-according to the MacCracken affidavit, more than 1.7 billion metric tons in 1999 alone. That accounts for more than 6% of worldwide carbon dioxide emissions. To put this in perspective: Considering just emissions from the transportation sector, which represent less than one-third of this country's total carbon dioxide emissions, the United States would still rank as the third-largest emitter of carbon dioxide in the world, outpaced only by the European Union and China. Judged by any standard, U.S. motor-vehicle emissions make a meaningful contribution to greenhouse gas concentrations and hence, according to petitioners, to global warming.

The Remedy

While it may be true that regulating motor-vehicle emissions will not by itself *reverse* global warming, it by no means follows that we lack jurisdiction to decide whether EPA has a duty to take steps to *slow* or *reduce* it. Because of the enormity of the potential consequences associated with man-made climate change, the fact that the effectiveness of a remedy might be delayed during the (relatively short) time it takes for a new motor-vehicle fleet to replace an older one is essentially irrelevant. Nor is it dispositive that developing countries such as China and India are poised to increase greenhouse gas emissions substantially over the next century: A reduction in domestic emissions would slow the pace of global emissions increases, no matter what happens elsewhere.

We moreover attach considerable significance to EPA's "agree[ment] with the President that 'we must address the issue of global climate change,'" (quoting remarks announcing Clear Skies and Global Climate Initiatives, 2002 Public Papers of George W. Bush, Vol. 1, Feb. 14, p. 227 (2004)), and to EPA's ardent support for various voluntary emission-reduction programs,...

In sum—at least according to petitioners' uncontested affidavits—the rise in sea levels associated with global warming has already harmed and will continue to harm Massachusetts. The risk of catastrophic harm, though remote, is nevertheless real. That risk would be reduced to some extent if petitioners received the relief they seek. We therefore hold that petitioners have standing to challenge the EPA's denial of their rulemaking petition.

...

[On the merits, the Court ruled that the EPA does have statutory authority to regulate greenhouse gases and that it would be required on remand to ground any decision not to take regulatory action in the text of the relevant statute.]

VIII

The judgment of the Court of Appeals is reversed, and the case is remanded for further proceedings consistent with this opinion

It is so ordered.

CHIEF JUSTICE ROBERTS, with whom JUSTICE SCALIA, JUSTICE THOMAS, and JUSTICE ALITO join, dissenting.

Global warming may be a "crisis," even "the most pressing environmental problem of our time." Indeed, it may ultimately affect nearly everyone on the planet in some potentially adverse way, and it may be that governments have done too little to address it. It is not a problem, however, that has escaped the attention of policymakers in the Executive and Legislative Branches of our Government, who continue to consider regulatory, legislative, and treaty-based means of addressing global climate change.

Apparently dissatisfied with the pace of progress on this issue in the elected branches, petitioners have come to the courts claiming broad-ranging injury, and attempting to tie that injury to the Government's alleged failure to comply with a rather narrow statutory provision. I would reject these challenges as nonjusticiable....

I

...

[Petitioners] bear the burden of alleging an injury that is fairly traceable to the Environmental Protection Agency's failure to promulgate new motor vehicle greenhouse gas emission standards, and that is likely to be redressed by the prospective issuance of such standards.

Before determining whether petitioners can meet this familiar test, however, the Court changes the rules. It asserts that "States are not normal litigants for the purposes of invoking federal jurisdiction," and that given "Massachusetts' stake in protecting its quasi-sovereign interests, the Commonwealth is entitled to *special solicitude* in our standing analysis."

Relaxing Article III standing requirements because asserted injuries are pressed by a State, however, has no basis in our jurisprudence, and support for any such "special solicitude" is conspicuously absent from the Court's opinion. [The] Court has to go back a full century in an attempt to justify its novel standing rule, but even there it comes up short. The Court's analysis hinges on Georgia v. Tennessee Copper Co., 206 U.S. 230 (1907) — a case that did indeed draw a distinction between a State and private litigants, but solely with respect to available remedies. The case had nothing to do with Article III standing....

In contrast to the present case, there was no question in *Tennessee Copper* about Article III injury. There was certainly no suggestion that the State could show standing where the private parties could not; there was no dispute, after all, that the private landowners had "an action at law." *Tennessee Copper* has since stood for nothing more than a State's right, in an original jurisdiction action, to sue in a representative capacity as *parens patriae*. Nothing about a State's ability to sue in that capacity dilutes the bedrock requirement of showing injury, causation, and redressability to satisfy Article III.

[Far] from being a substitute for Article III injury, *parens patriae* actions raise an additional hurdle for a state litigant: the articulation of a "quasi-sovereign interest" "*apart* from the interests of particular private parties." Just as an association suing on behalf of its members must show not only that it represents the members but that at least one satisfies Article III requirements, so too a State asserting quasi-sovereign interests as *parens patriae* must still show that its citizens satisfy Article III. Focusing on Massachusetts's interests as quasi-sovereign makes the required showing here harder, not easier.

...

II

It is not at all clear how the Court's "special solicitude" for Massachusetts plays out in the standing analysis, except as an implicit concession that petitioners cannot establish standing on traditional terms. But the status of Massachusetts as a State cannot compensate for petitioners' failure to demonstrate injury in fact, causation, and redressability.

[If] petitioners rely on loss of land as the Article III injury,... they must ground the rest of the standing analysis in that specific injury.... The very concept of global warming seems inconsistent with this particularization requirement. Global warming is a phenomenon "harmful to humanity at large," 415 F.3d, at 60 (Sentelle, J., dissenting in part and concurring in judgment), and the redress petitioners seek is focused no more on them than on the public generally — it is literally to change the atmosphere around the world.

If petitioners' particularized injury is loss of coastal land, it is also that injury that must be "actual or imminent, not conjectural or hypothetical."

As to "actual" injury, the Court observes that "global sea levels rose somewhere between 10 and 20 centimeters over the 20th century as a result of global warming" and that "[t]hese rising seas have already begun to swallow Massachusetts' coastal land." But none of petitioners' declarations supports that connection. One declaration states that "a rise in sea level due to climate change is occurring on the coast of Massachusetts, in the metropolitan Boston area," but there is no elaboration. And the declarant goes on to identify a "significan[t]" *non*-global-warming cause of Boston's rising sea level: land subsidence. Thus, aside from a single conclusory statement, there is nothing in petitioners' 43 standing declarations and accompanying exhibits to support an inference of actual loss of Massachusetts coastal land from 20th century global sea level increases. It is pure conjecture.

The Court's attempts to identify "imminent" or "certainly impending" loss of Massachusetts coastal land fares no better. One of petitioners' declarants predicts global warming will cause sea level to rise by 20 to 70 centimeters *by the year 2100*. Another uses a computer modeling program to map the Commonwealth's coastal land and its current elevation, and calculates that the high-end estimate of sea level rise would result in the loss of significant state-owned coastal land. But the computer modeling program has a conceded average error of about 30 centimeters and a maximum observed error of 70 centimeters. As an initial matter, if it is possible that the model underrepresents the elevation of coastal land to an extent equal to or in excess of the projected sea level rise, it is difficult to put much stock in the predicted loss of land. But even placing that problem to the side, accepting a century-long time horizon and a series of compounded estimates renders requirements of imminence and immediacy utterly toothless....

III

Petitioners' reliance on Massachusetts's loss of coastal land as their injury in fact for standing purposes creates insurmountable problems for them with respect to causation and redressability. To establish standing, petitioners must show a causal connection between that specific injury and the lack of new motor vehicle greenhouse gas emission standards, and that the promulgation of such standards would likely redress that injury.... And importantly, when a party is challenging the Government's allegedly unlawful regulation, or lack of regulation, of a third party, satisfying the causation and redressability requirements becomes "substantially more difficult."

Petitioners view the relationship between their injuries and EPA's failure to promulgate new motor vehicle greenhouse gas emission standards as simple and direct: Domestic motor vehicles emit carbon dioxide and other greenhouse gases. Worldwide emissions of greenhouse gases contribute to global warming and therefore also to petitioner' alleged injuries. Without the new vehicle standards, greenhouse gas emissions — and therefore global warming and its attendant harms — have been higher than they otherwise would have been; once EPA changes course, the trend will be reversed.

The Court ignores the complexities of global warming, and does so by now disregarding the "particularized" injury it relied on in step one, and using the dire nature of global warming itself as a bootstrap for finding causation and redressability. First, it is important to recognize the extent of the emissions at issue here. Because local greenhouse gas emissions disperse throughout the atmosphere and remain there for anywhere from 50 to 200 years, it is global emissions data that are relevant. According to one of petitioners' declarations, domestic motor vehicles contribute about 6 percent of global carbon dioxide emissions and 4 percent of global greenhouse gas emissions. The amount of global emissions at issue here is smaller still; § 202(a)(1) of the Clean Air Act covers only *new* motor vehicles and *new* motor vehicle engines, so petitioners' desired emission standards might reduce only a fraction of 4 percent of global emissions.

This gets us only to the relevant greenhouse gas emissions; linking them to global warming and ultimately to petitioners' alleged injuries next requires consideration of further complexities. As EPA explained in its denial of petitioners' request for rulemaking,

"predicting future climate change necessarily involves a complex web of economic and physical factors including: our ability to predict future global anthropogenic emissions of [greenhouse gases] and aerosols; the fate of these emissions once they enter the atmosphere (e.g., what percentage are absorbed by vegetation or are taken up by the oceans); the impact of those emissions that remain in the atmosphere on the radiative properties of the atmosphere;

changes in critically important climate feedbacks (e.g., changes in cloud cover and ocean circulation); changes in temperature characteristics (e.g., average temperatures, shifts in daytime and evening temperatures); changes in other climatic parameters (e.g., shifts in precipitation, storms); and ultimately the impact of such changes on human health and welfare (e.g., increases or decreases in agricultural productivity, human health impacts)."

Petitioners are never able to trace their alleged injuries back through this complex web to the fractional amount of global emissions that might have been limited with EPA standards. In light of the bit-part domestic new motor vehicle greenhouse gas emissions have played in what petitioners describe as a 150-year global phenomenon, and the myriad additional factors bearing on petitioners' alleged injury — the loss of Massachusetts coastal land — the connection is far too speculative to establish causation.

IV

Redressability is even more problematic. To the tenuous link between petitioners' alleged injury and the indeterminate fractional domestic emissions at issue here, add the fact that petitioners cannot meaningfully predict what will come of the 80 percent of global greenhouse gas emissions that originate outside the United States. As the Court acknowledges, "developing countries such as China and India are poised to increase greenhouse gas emissions substantially over the next century," so the domestic emissions at issue here may become an increasingly marginal portion of global emissions, and any decreases produced by petitioners' desired standards are likely to be overwhelmed many times over by emissions increases elsewhere in the world.

Petitioners offer declarations attempting to address this uncertainty, contending that "[i]f the U.S. takes steps to reduce motor vehicle emissions, other countries are very likely to take similar actions regarding their own motor vehicles using technology developed in response to the U.S. program." In other words, do not worry that other countries will contribute far more to global warming than will U.S. automobile emissions; someone is bound to invent something, and places like the People's Republic of China or India will surely require use of the new technology, regardless of cost. The Court previously has explained that when the existence of an element of standing "depends on the unfettered choices made by independent actors not before the courts and whose exercise of broad and legitimate discretion the courts cannot presume either to control or to predict," a party must present facts supporting an assertion that the actor will proceed in such a manner. The declarations' conclusory (not to say fanciful) statements do not even come close.

No matter, the Court reasons, because *any* decrease in domestic emissions will "slow the pace of global emissions increases, no matter what happens elsewhere." Every little bit helps, so Massachusetts can sue over any little bit.

The Court's sleight-of-hand is in failing to link up the different elements of the three-part standing test. What must be *likely* to be redressed is the particular injury in fact. The injury the Court looks to is the asserted loss of land. The Court contends that regulating domestic motor vehicle emissions will reduce carbon dioxide in the atmosphere, *and therefore* redress Massachusett's injury. But even if regulation *does* reduce emissions-to some indeterminate degree, given events elsewhere in the world, the Court never explains why that makes it *likely* that the injury in fact — the loss of land — will be redressed. School-children know that a kingdom might be lost "all for the want of a horseshoe nail," but "likely" redressability is a different matter. The realities make it pure conjecture to suppose that EPA regulation of new automobile emissions will *likely* prevent the loss of Massachusetts coastal land.

V

Petitioners' difficulty in demonstrating causation and redressability is not surprising given the evident mismatch between the source of their alleged injury — catastrophic global warming — and the narrow subject matter of the Clean Air Act provision at issue in this suit. The mismatch suggests that petitioners' true goal for this litigation may be more symbolic than anything else. The constitutional role of the courts, however, is to decide concrete cases — not to serve as a convenient forum for policy debates.

[The] good news is that the Court's "special solicitude" for Massachusetts limits the future applicability of the diluted standing requirements applied in this case. The bad news is that the Court's self-professed relaxation of those Article III requirements has caused us to transgress "the proper — and properly limited — role of the courts in a democratic society."

I respectfully dissent.

* * *

For an illuminating discussion of various issues in the case, see Freeman & Vermeule, Massachusetts v. EPA: From Politics to Expertise, 2007 Supreme Court Review 51.

Page 110. At the end of the second full paragraph, add the following:

In Hein v. Freedom from Religion Foundation, 127 S. Ct. 2553 (2007), the Court essentially confined *Flast* to its facts. *Hein* involved a challenge to

President Bush's Faith-Based and Community Initiatives Program. Taxpayers complained that the executive branch had used public money to fund conferences with the purpose and effect of promoting religion. They contended that the resulting expenditures violated the Establishment Clause. Justice Alito, writing for himself, Chief Justice Roberts, and Justice Kennedy, said that *Flast* meant only that taxpayers could challenge an explicit congressional decision to use taxpayer funds for arguably religious purposes. If the executive branch used a general appropriation to promote religion, taxpayers could not bring suit. Justice Scalia, writing for himself and Justice Thomas, contended that *Flast* was an anomaly and should be overruled. Justice Souter, joined by Justices Stevens, Ginsburg, and Breyer, contended that for purposes of standing, there was no relevant distinction between a specific congressional appropriation and the executive's use of taxpayer funds for religious purposes.

In DaimlerChrysler Corp. v. Cuno, 547 U.S. 33 (2006), the Supreme Court held that municipal taxpayers in Toledo, Ohio, lacked standing to challenge a state tax credit offered to DaimlerChrysler as an incentive for it to expand its operations in the city. The taxpayers alleged that the tax breaks, which they asserted violated the Commerce Clause, would increase their own tax burdens. The Court held that "affording state taxpayers standing to press such challenges simply because their tax burden gives them an interest in the state treasury would interpose the federal courts as 'virtually continuing monitors of the wisdom and soundness' of state fiscal administration, contrary to the more modest role Article III envisions for federal courts."

Page 132.   After section 4 of the Note, add the following:

4a. *Climate change and the environment.* Suppose that a state sues a number of automobile manufacturers for a public nuisance, claiming that their emissions contribute to climate change, in a way that endangers American citizens. Does this suit present a political question? Does it matter if under standard common law principles, a nuisance is presented, because the risk is unreasonable? For a rejection of such an argument on political question grounds, see California v. GMC, 2007 U.S. Dist. LEXIS 68547 (N.D. Cal. 2007). Would the case come out differently if it had been brought against power plant companies?

Now suppose that a suit is brought by a large number of ordinary citizens against oil and gas companies, seeking tort damages for causing erosion to coastal wetlands by dredging canals and laying pipelines over a course of years, which led to the loss of a natural buffer against hurricane winds and storm surges which, in turn, damaged the residents' properties and directly caused personal injuries and deaths. Does this claim present a political question? For a negative answer, see Barasich v. Columbia Gulf Transmission Co., 467 F. Supp. 2d 676 (E.D. La. 2006).

Can the two problems be distinguished? Consider the view that the climate change problem implicates difficult issues of international relations, as most environmental problems do not. Does that point fit with the analysis in *Baker v. Carr*?

Page 153.   After section 1 of the Note, add the following:

1a. *Continued gridlock over the justiciability of partisan gerrymandering.* In League of United Latin Am. Citizens v. Perry, 548 U.S. 399 (2006), the Court once again confronted a claim of unconstitutional partisan gerrymandering and once again found itself unable to generate a controlling opinion. The case involved a challenge to Texas's mid-decade congressional redistricting, a redistricting undertaken with the express purpose of favoring Republican candidates. Justice Scalia, joined by Justice Thomas, reiterated his position in *Vieth* that political gerrymanders are nonjusticiable. Justice Kennedy did not "revisit the justiciability holding" in *Vieth*, but found that appellants had failed to "offer the Court a manageable, reliable measure of fairness for determining whether a partisan gerrymander violates the Constitution." In particular, he rejected their claim that the decision to conduct a mid-decade redistricting rendered the plan unconstitutional.

Chief Justice Roberts, joined by Justice Alito — both of whom had joined the Court after the decision in *Vieth* — agreed with Justice Kennedy's conclusion that the challengers "ha[d] not provided 'a reliable standard for identifying unconstitutional political gerrymanders,' " and asserted, somewhat surprisingly in light of the fact that the Supreme Court had remanded an earlier appeal in the Texas case to the trial court with directions to reconsider its decision in light of *Vieth*, that "[t]he question whether any such standard exists — that is, whether a challenge to a political gerrymander presents a justiciable case or controversy — has not been argued in these cases." He therefore took "no position on that question, which has divided the Court," and joined the Court's disposition of the political gerrymandering claims "without specifying whether appellants have failed to state a claim on which relief can be granted, or have failed to present a justiciable controversy."

The other four Justices all reiterated their view that claims of unconstitutional political gerrymandering are justiciable. Justices Stevens and Breyer would have reached the merits of the challengers' claims and struck down the plan. In light of the Court's continued division, Justice Souter, joined by Justice Ginsburg, "[saw] nothing to be gained by working through these cases on the standard I would have applied in [*Vieth,*] because here as in *Vieth* we have no majority for any single criterion of impermissible gerrymander." He would "therefore [have] treat[ed] the broad issue of gerrymander much as the subject of an improvident grant of certiorari."

G. The Jurisdiction of the Supreme Court

Page 161.   Before the fourth full paragraph, add the following:

Normally, the Court provides no reason for its denial of a petition for certiorari, although Justices who voted to hear the case will on occasion dissent from the denial of certiorari, explaining why they thought the petition should have been granted.

Far less often, Justices who voted to deny the petition for certiorari will explain their reasons. In Padilla v. Hanft, 547 U.S. 1062 (2006), the Supreme Court addressed a petition for certiorari by Jose Padilla, an American citizen arrested inside the United States and held by the President as an enemy combatant because of his alleged ties to al Qaeda. In an earlier proceeding, discussed on pages 394-95 of the main volume, the Court had held that Padilla had filed his first petition for habeas corpus in the wrong venue. Padilla then refiled his petition for habeas corpus in the appropriate venue, and when that petition was denied by the court of appeals, sought review by the Supreme Court.

Three justices — Justices Souter, Ginsburg, and Breyer — would have heard Padilla's case. Three other justices — Justices Scalia, Thomas, and Alito — gave no indication of their position, but clearly had voted to deny the petition (since otherwise there would have been four votes to grant certiorari). A final group of three — Justice Kennedy, joined by the Chief Justice and Justice Stevens — issued a concurrence in the denial of certiorari:

> The Court's decision to deny the petition for writ of certiorari is, in my view, a proper exercise of its discretion in light of the circumstances of the case. The history of petitioner Jose Padilla's detention, however, does require this brief explanatory statement....
>
> [On June 9, 2002,] the President issued an order to the Secretary of Defense designating Padilla an enemy combatant and ordering his military detention....

After Padilla sought certiorari in this Court, the Government obtained an indictment charging him with various federal crimes. The President ordered that Padilla be released from military custody and transferred to the control of the Attorney General to face criminal charges ... The Government also filed a brief in opposition to certiorari, arguing, among other things, that Padilla's petition should be denied as moot.

The Government's mootness argument is based on the premise that Padilla, now having been charged with crimes and released from military custody, has received the principal relief he sought. Padilla responds that his case was not mooted by the Government's voluntary actions because there remains a possibility that he will be redesignated and redetained as an enemy combatant.

Whatever the ultimate merits of the parties' mootness arguments, there are strong prudential considerations disfavoring the exercise of the Court's certiorari power. Even if the Court were to rule in Padilla's favor, his present custody status would be unaffected. Padilla is scheduled to be tried on criminal charges. Any consideration of what rights he might be able to assert if he were returned to military custody would be hypothetical, and to no effect, at this stage of the proceedings.

In light of the previous changes in his custody status and the fact that nearly four years have passed since he first was detained, Padilla, it must be acknowledged, has a continuing concern that his status might be altered again. That concern, however, can be addressed if the necessity arises. Padilla is now being held pursuant to the control and supervision of the United States District Court for the Southern District of Florida, pending trial of the criminal case. In the course of its supervision over Padilla's custody and trial the District Court will be obliged to afford him the protection, including the right to a speedy trial, guaranteed to all federal criminal defendants. Were the Government to seek to change the status or conditions of Padilla's custody, that court would be in a position to rule quickly on any responsive filings submitted by Padilla....

That Padilla's claims raise fundamental issues respecting the separation of powers, including consideration of the role and function of the courts, also counsels against addressing those claims when the course of legal proceedings has made them, at least for now, hypothetical. This is especially true given that Padilla's current custody is part of the relief he sought, and that its lawfulness is uncontested.

2

FEDERALISM AT WORK: CONGRESS AND THE NATIONAL ECONOMY

C. The Evolution of Commerce Clause Doctrine: The Lessons (?) of History

Page 225. After section 2 of the Note, add the following:

2a. Wickard *revisited.* Gonzales v. Raich, 545 U.S. 1 (2005), upheld the constitutionality of a comprehensive federal ban on the private cultivation and use of marijuana, as applied to marijuana grown at a person's home and intended solely for use by that person or a person for whom the grower was a caretaker, legal under state law, as a medical treatment. Justice Stevens, writing for the Court, cited *Wickard* for the proposition that "Congress can regulate purely intrastate activity that is not itself 'commercial,' in that it is not produced for sale, if it concludes that failure to regulate that class of activity would undercut the regulation of the interstate market in that commodity." Congress "had a rational basis for concluding [that] the high demand in the interstate market will draw such marijuana into that market."

The marijuana growers pointed to three factual differences between their case and *Wickard:* The statute in *Wickard* exempted small farming operations, *Wickard* "involved a 'quintessential economic activity' — a commercial farm — whereas respondents do not sell marijuana," and the record in *Wickard* "made it clear that the aggregate production of wheat for use on farms had a significant impact on market prices." The Court agreed that these differences were accurate, but concluded that they were irrelevant. The statutory exemption was a matter of policy discretion that had not affected the substance of *Wickard's* analysis; the Court did not treat the activity on which Wickard premised his challenge, "the cultivation of wheat for home consumption," as "part of his commercial farming operation," and Congress had made findings that production of marijuana for local use had a significant impact on the national market.

Justice Scalia concurred in the judgment, with a separate opinion emphasizing that the congressional prohibition was constitutionally permissible as a necessary and proper means of executing the power to regulate interstate commerce in marijuana. "The regulation of an intrastate activity may be essential to a comprehensive regulation of interstate commerce even though the intrastate activity does not itself 'substantially affect' interstate commerce." He indicated that the Necessary and Proper Clause might impose greater limits on congressional power than the Court's analysis did.

Justice O'Connor wrote a dissent, joined by Chief Justice Rehnquist and in large part by Justice Thomas, who also wrote a separate dissent. Justice O'Connor concluded that "[there] is simply no evidence that homegrown medicinal marijuana users constitute, in the aggregate, a sizable enough class to have a discernable, let alone substantial, impact on the national illicit drug market—or otherwise to threaten the [overall regulatory] regime." On the commerce clause issue, Justice Thomas's dissent restated his position in *Lopez*.

Page 225. At the end of section 2a of the Note, add the following:

After *Raich*, might the Gun Free School Zones Act be upheld as an integral part of a larger scheme for regulating gun *sales*? Might the civil remedy provision of the Violence Against Women Act be upheld as an integral part of a larger scheme for regulating safety at educational institutions, places of public accommodations, and workplaces? Note that Justice Breyer in *Morrison* suggested an analysis along those lines, arguing that the *Morrison* decision simply counseled Congress to draft its statutes more carefully. How should the Court address a constitutional challenge to a provision enacted "on its own," but which could be understood *either* as part of a larger scheme assembled statute-by-statute *or* as a free-standing statute?

For a collection of comments, mostly critical, on *Raich*, see Symposium, Federalism After *Gonzalez v. Raich*, 9 Lewis & Clark L. Rev. 743-934 (2005).

2b. Guillen. Pierce County v. Guillen, 537 U.S. 129 (2003), upheld under the commerce clause a federal statute protecting reports and surveys compiled by state agencies as part of a federal program to identify potential accident sites from discovery in lawsuits in state and federal courts. "Congress could reasonably believe that adopting a measure eliminating an unforeseen side effect of the information-gathering requirement [would] result in more diligent efforts to collect the relevant information [and], ultimately, greater safety on our Nation's roads." The statute was "aimed at improving safety in the channels of commerce and increasing protection for the instrumentalities of interstate commerce." Berman, *Guillen* and Gullibility: Piercing the Surface of Commerce Clause Doctrine, 89 Iowa L. Rev. 1487, 1502 (2004), points out that the decision invokes the first and second categories identified in *Lopez*, and that the federal statute is not itself a regulation of the channels or instrumentalities of interstate commerce, but is rather "a regulation *of* judicial procedure adopted (purportedly) *for the purpose* of protecting instrumentalities and channels." Berman asks whether such a rule is consistent with *Lopez* and *Morrison*, and suggests that it is because the Court regarded the assertedly commerce-protecting purposes of the statutes in those cases as "pretextual."

Page 226. At the end of section 3 of the Note, add the following:

In *Raich*, the Court defined "economic" activities as those involving "the production, distribution, and consumption of commodities." Justice O'Connor's dissent observed, "It will not do to say that Congress may regulate noncommercial activity simply because it [can substitute] for commercial activity. Most commercial goods or services have some sort of privately producible analogue. [To] draw the line wherever private activity affects the demand for market goods is to draw no line at all, and to declare everything economic." Do the transactions described by Ides and Choper involve economic activities under the *Raich* definition?

Page 226. At the end of section 4 of the Note, add the following:

In *Raich*, the Court found that the statute regulating drugs was "at the opposite end of the regulatory spectrum" from the one at issue in *Lopez*. Could the statute in *Lopez* be upheld on theory that it was one component of a coordinated national strategy to control the transfer of guns? Is making it a crime to possess a gun near a school a rational component of such a strategy? Dissenting in *Raich*, Justice O'Connor wrote: "If the Court is right, then *Lopez* stands for nothing more than a drafting guide: Congress should have described the relevant crime as 'transfer or possession of a firearm anywhere in the nation' — thus including commercial and noncommercial activity, and clearly encompassing some activity with assuredly substantial effect on interstate commerce." Is it correct to describe the proposed statute as one involving a (mere?) drafting question?

Justice O'Connor emphasized that the growers were producing a good that their physicians had concluded would provide them medical benefits, and that their activity was legal under local law. Should this be construed as an argument that the statute was unconstitutional as applied to Raich's activities? Is such an argument consistent with the proposition that Congress can regulate intrastate activities as part of a comprehensive regulatory system? Justice O'Connor argued that her analysis went beyond an as-applied challenge because it invoked "objective markers" that demonstrated why Raich's activities fell within a larger class of activities that Congress could not reach.

On the question of "objective markers," the Court responded that the first "rationale logically extends to place *any* federal regulation [of] *any* locally cultivated and possessed controlled substance for *any* purpose" beyond the scope of congressional power. "One need not have a degree in economics to understand why a nationwide exemption for the vast quantity of marijuana (or other drugs) locally cultivated for personal use [may] have a substantial impact on the interstate market for this extraordinarily popular substance." The second argument was inconsistent with the Supremacy Clause: "[State] action cannot circumscribe Congress' plenary commerce power."

D. State Regulation of Interstate Commerce

Page 245.   At the end of section 1 of the Note, add the following:

1a. *The Scope of* Carbone. United Haulers Ass'n v. Oneida-Herkimer Solid Waste Management Auth., 127 S. Ct. 1786 (2007), involved "flow control" ordinances like that in *Carbone*, but in *United Haulers* the facility to which solid waste was required to be sent was owned by a public agency. This was sufficient to distinguish the case from *Carbone*.

Unlike private enterprise, government is vested with the responsibility of protecting the health, safety, and welfare of its citizens. These important responsibilities set state and local government apart from a typical private business.

Given these differences, it does not make sense to regard laws favoring local government and laws favoring private industry with equal skepticism. [Laws] favoring local government [may] be directed toward any number of legitimate goals unrelated to protectionism.

[The] contrary approach [would] lead to unprecedented and unbounded interference by the courts with state and local government. The dormant Commerce Clause is not a roving license for federal courts to decide what activities are appropriate for state and local government to undertake, and what activities must be the province of private market competition. [It] is not the province of the Commerce Clause to control the decision of the voters on whether government or the private sector should provide waste management services.

Chief Justice Roberts's opinion observed that "the most palpable harm imposed by the ordinances — more expensive trash removal — is likely to fall upon the very people who voted for the laws. [There] is no reason to [hand] local businesses a victory they could not obtain through the political process." (Writing for a plurality, Chief Justice Roberts also found that the ordinances did not impose an excessive burden that was disproportionate to its benefits. Justice Scalia did not join this portion of the opinion.)

Justice Thomas concurred in the judgment, stating that, although he had joined *Carbone*, he "no longer believe[d] it was correctly decided," because the "negative Commerce Clause has no basis in the Constitution has provide unworkable in practice." Justice Alito, joined by Justices Stevens and Kennedy, dissented, arguing that the case was indistinguishable from *Carbone*.

Department of Revenue of Kentucky v. Davis, 128 S. Ct. 1801 (2008), relied on *United Haulers* to uphold a state law that imposed taxes on income from state and municipal bonds issued by states other than Kentucky, but exempted income from bonds issued by Kentucky itself, its cities, and other Kentucky governmental units.

Page 273. At the end of Note 4, add the following:

In Department of Revenue of Kentucky v. Davis, 128 S. Ct. 1801 (2008), Justice Souter made similar comments about the limited capacity of the courts to engage in "cost-benefit analysis":

What is most significant about these cost-benefit questions is not even the difficulty of answering them or the inevitable uncertainty of the predictions that might be made in trying to come up with answers, but the unsuitability of the judicial process and judicial forums for making whatever predictions and reaching whatever answers are possible at all. While it is not our business to suggest that the current system be reconsidered, if it is to be placed in question a congressional forum has two advantages. Congress has some hope of acquiring more complete information than adversary trials may produce, and an elected legislature is the preferable institution for incurring the economic risks of any alteration in the way things have traditionally been done.

3

THE SCOPE OF CONGRESS'S POWERS: TAXING AND SPENDING, WAR POWERS, INDIVIDUAL RIGHTS, AND STATE AUTONOMY

A. Regulation Through Taxing, Spending, and the War Power

Page 294.   At the end of section 4 of the Note, add the following:

c. Do general principles of federalism impose any independent constraints on congressional spending power, particularly if Congress is using its spending power to impose restrictions that would otherwise exceed its power? In this light, consider Cutter v. Wilkinson, 544 U.S. 709 (2005). The case concerned section 3 of the Religious Land Use and Institutionalized Persons Act of 2000 (RLUIPA), 42 U.S.C. §2000cc-1(a)(1)-(2). That section provided, with respect to "a program or activity that receives Federal financial assistance," that "[n]o government shall impose a substantial burden on the religious exercise of a person residing in or confined to an institution," unless the burden furthers "a compelling governmental interest," and does so by "the least restrictive means." RLUIPA was passed in response to the Supreme

Court's decision in City of Boerne v. Flores, 521 U.S. 507 (1997), which had struck down provisions of the Religious Freedom Restoration Act of 1993, 42 U.S.C. §2000bb et seq., that had imposed a similar prohibition without any spending clause underpinning, as exceeding Congress's power under section 5 of the Fourteenth Amendment. (*City of Boerne* is excerpted on page 306 of the main volume.)

Cutter involved a lawsuit by current and former inmates of Ohio state prisons, alleging that prison officials violated section 3 by failing to accommodate the exercise of their "nonmainstream" religions. The officials claimed that section 3 improperly advanced religion in violation of the establishment clause of the First Amendment. The Supreme Court, in an opinion by Justice Ginsburg, which observed that every state accepts federal funding for its prisons (and is therefore subject to section 3), unanimously rejected that claim. The Court, noting that the court of appeals had struck down RLUIPA on establishment clause grounds without reaching the officials' arguments that it also violating the spending clause and the Tenth Amendment, declined to consider those challenges. But Justice Thomas, in concurrence, suggested that section 3 might exceed Congress's authority under the spending clause absent some showing that there was "some obvious, simple, and direct relation" between RLUIPA's requirements and the expenditures. Nevertheless, he observed that "while Congress' condition stands, the States subject themselves to that condition by voluntarily accepting federal funds. The States' voluntary acceptance of Congress' condition undercuts Ohio's argument that Congress is encroaching on its turf."

Page 296. At the end of Note 6, add the following:

In Arlington Central School Dist. Bd. of Educ. v. Murphy, 548 U.S. 291 (2006), the Supreme Court used this principle to construe a provision of the Individuals with Disabilities Education Act (IDEA) that provides attorney's fees to parents who successfully challenge a school district's failure to provide their disabled child with appropriate educational services. The Court construed the provision not to permit recovery of fees charged by experts in IDEA proceedings. The Court noted that IDEA had been passed pursuant to Congress's spending power and stated that "[i]n a Spending Clause case, the key is ... what the States are clearly told regarding the conditions that go along with the acceptance of those funds." In this case, the fact that the Court had held in earlier cases regarding other attorney's fees and costs provisions that expert fees were not recoverable meant that recipients of federal funds could not be said to have had "the requisite fair notice" that accepting the federal funds would subject them to this particular liability.

In Winkelman v. Parma City School Dist., 127 S. Ct. 1994 (2007), another IDEA case, the Supreme Court held that the statute grants parents an independent enforceable right to bring suit seeking an appropriate education for their children. It rejected the school district's claim that *Arlington Central School Dist.* required that IDEA unambiguously accord parents such a right in order to satisfy the "clear notice" requirement for statutes passed pursuant to the spending power: *Arlington* involved the question "whether IDEA 'furnishes clear notice regarding the liability at issue'"; by contrast, the Winkelmans' lawsuit "does not impose any substantive condition or obligation on States they would not otherwise be required by law to observe. The basic measure of monetary recovery, moreover, is not expanded by recognizing that some rights repose in both the parent and the child. ... A determination by the Court that some distinct class of people has independent, enforceable rights might result in a change to the States' statutory obligations. But that is not the case here."

Page 299. Before Section B, add the following:

To what extent does the First Amendment constrain Congress's use of its spending and war powers? The question of government-funded speech itself is treated in Chapter 7, at pages 1348-1367. But consider in this light the constitutionality of the Solomon Amendment, 10 U.S.C. §983(b)(1). That provision withholds federal funds from institutions of higher education that deny military recruiters the same access to campuses and students that they provide to other employers. For many years, the American Association of Law Schools (AALS) has required its members to withhold "any form of placement assistance or use of the school's facilities" from employers who discriminate on the basis of sexual orientation or other specified criteria. The AALS concluded that the military runs afoul of that policy because of congressional policies that limit the right of gay people to serve in the military. Nonetheless, following enactment of the Solomon Amendment, the AALS permitted its members to allow military recruiters to use their facilities as long as the schools took steps to "ameliorate" the impact of military recruiting on the student body. In response, most law schools allowed military recruiters to enter their campuses, but many schools refused to provide military recruiters with the same access that they offered to other employers. The Department of Defense subsequently notified schools that the failure to provide equal access could jeopardize their federal funds.

In Rumsfeld v. FAIR, 547 U.S. 47 (2006), the Supreme Court upheld the Amendment against a First Amendment challenge. The Court's First Amendment analysis is discussed in Chapter 7 of this Supplement. Before the Court reached the question whether the First Amendment limited Congress's power, however, it addressed the antecedent question of Congress's general power to obtain access for military recruiters in the first place. In a unanimous opinion by Chief Justice Roberts, the Court identified two complementary sources of congressional power:

> The Constitution grants Congress the power to "provide for the common Defence," "[t]o raise and support Armies," and "[t]o provide and maintain a Navy." Art. I, § 8, cls. 1, 12-13. Congress' power in this area "is broad and sweeping," and there is no dispute in this case that it includes the authority to require campus access for military recruiters. That is, of course, unless Congress exceeds constitutional limitations on its power in enacting such legislation. But the fact that legislation that raises armies is subject to First Amendment constraints does not mean that we ignore the purpose of this legislation when determining its constitutionality; as we recognized in Rostker [v. Goldberg, 453 U.S. 57, 70 (1981)], "judicial deference . . . is at its apogee" when Congress legislates under its authority to raise and support armies.
>
> Although Congress has broad authority to legislate on matters of military recruiting, it nonetheless chose to secure campus access for military recruiters indirectly, through its Spending Clause power. The Solomon Amendment gives universities a choice: Either allow military recruiters the same access to students afforded any other recruiter or forgo certain federal funds. Congress' decision to proceed indirectly does not reduce the deference given to Congress in the area of military affairs. Congress' choice to promote its goal by creating a funding condition deserves at least as deferential treatment as if Congress had imposed a mandate on universities.
>
> Congress' power to regulate military recruiting under the Solomon Amendment is arguably greater because universities are free to decline the federal funds. In Grove City College v. Bell, 465 U.S. 555, 575-76 (1984), we rejected a private college's claim that conditioning federal funds on its compliance with Title IX of the Education Amendments of 1972 [which forbids sex discrimination by institutions receiving federal funds] violated the First Amendment. We thought this argument "warrant[ed] only brief consideration" because "Congress is free to attach reasonable and unambiguous conditions to federal financial assistance that educational institutions are not obligated to accept." We concluded that no First Amendment violation had occurred — without reviewing the substance of the First Amendment claims — because Grove City could decline the Government's funds.

Given contemporary realities in higher education, are institutions actually free to decline federal funds? Is that factual question even relevant to the constitutional inquiry? Consider also whether the government bears any factual burden regarding whether the Solomon Amendment actually contributes to effective military recruiting.

B. Congress's Enforcement Power Under the Reconstruction Amendments

Page 327.   At the end of section 4 of the Note, add the following:

The scope of the Court's decision in *Lane* has already sparked extensive litigation in the lower federal courts regarding the question of what other uses of Title II involve permissible abrogation of state sovereign immunity. Compare, e.g., Constantine v. Rectors & Visitors of George Mason University 411 F.3d 474 (4th Cir. 2005) (holding that Title II is valid section 5 legislation with respect to claims of discrimination in public higher education); Association for Disabled Americans, Inc. v. Florida International University, 405 F.3d 954 (11th Cir. 2005) (same); Bill M. v. Nebraska Department of Health & Human Services, Finance & Support, 408 F. 3d 1096 (8th Cir. 2005) (holding that section 5 does not permit abrogation of states' sovereign immunity with respect to claims of discrimination in the provision of certain health-care services), vacated, 547 U.S. 1067 (2006).

Note also that a large proportion of state agencies are covered by section 504 of the Rehabilitation Act of 1973, which provides in pertinent part that "[n]o otherwise qualified individual with a disability ... shall, solely by reason of her or his disability, be excluded from the participation in, be denied the benefits of, or be subjected to discrimination under any program or activity receiving Federal financial assistance." Federal law provides that states "shall not be immune under the Eleventh Amendment of the Constitution of the United States from suit in Federal court for a violation of section 504 ... or the provisions of any other Federal statute prohibiting discrimination by recipients of Federal financial assistance." 42 U.S.C. § 2000d-7. And section 504 is enforceable through private causes of action. See Barnes v. Gorman, 536 U.S. 181 (2002). The courts of appeals that have addressed the issue have held that prohibitions on discrimination are sufficiently related to the purposes for which the federal funds are being spent to make such conditions appropriate under the spending clause. See also Lau v. Nichols, 414 U.S. 563 (1974) (upholding the ban on race discrimination in federally funded programs under Title VI of the Civil Rights Act); Sabri v. United States, 541 U.S. 600 (2004) (upholding a ban on bribery of state, local, and tribal officials of entities that receive federal funds, even without a requirement that the alleged bribe be related to specific federal funds). As long as the Supreme Court permits Congress to condition federal funds on states' waiver of their sovereign immunity, does the Eleventh Amendment actually impose much of a practical constraint on congressional abrogation of sovereign immunity?

In United States v. Georgia, 546 U.S. 151 (2006), the Court refined its analysis of congressional power under section 5. Goodman, an inmate in a Georgia prison, sued various state defendants challenging the conditions of his confinement. Among other things, he sought money damages under Title II of the ADA, claiming that the state's failure to accommodate his disabilities — he was a paraplegic and was often left for hours at a time in his wheelchair in a cell where he could neither turn around nor reach the toilet facilities — violated the Act. The state asserted sovereign immunity, but the Supreme Court rejected that claim. In a unanimous opinion written by Justice Scalia, the Court noted that

> While the Members of this Court have disagreed regarding the scope of Congress's "prophylactic" enforcement powers under §5 of the Fourteenth Amendment, no one doubts that §5 grants Congress the power to "enforce ... the provisions" of the Amendment by creating private remedies against the States for *actual* violations of those provisions.... This enforcement power includes the power to abrogate state sovereign immunity by authorizing private suits for damages against the States. Thus, insofar as Title II creates a private cause of action for damages against the States for conduct that *actually* violates the Fourteenth Amendment, Title II validly abrogates state sovereign immunity. The Eleventh Circuit erred in dismissing those of Goodman's Title II claims that were based on such unconstitutional conduct.

C. The Tenth Amendment as a Federalism-Based Limitation on Congressional Power

Page 352. At the end of section 2 of the Note, add the following:

MEDELLIN v. TEXAS, 128 S. CT. 1346 (2008). Medellin, a Mexican national who had lived in the United States since his early childhood, was arrested, charged, and convicted of capital murder and sentenced to death. A central piece of evidence in the state's case was his detailed confession. Medellin gave the confession after being provided with his *Miranda* warnings, but without being informed of his right under Article 36(1)(b) of the Vienna Convention on Consular Relations (to which the United States is a signatory) to notify the Mexican consulate of his detention.

Medellin did not raise his Vienna Convention claim until state postconviction proceedings. The Texas state courts held that the claim was therefore procedurally defaulted and declined to address it. Medellin then sought federal habeas review. While his habeas petition was pending, the International Court of Justice (ICJ) decided the *Case Concerning Avena and Other Mexican Nationals (Mex. v. U.S.)*, 2004 I. C. J. 12. (Medellin was one of the other Mexican nationals named in the decision). The ICJ held that the United States had violated Article 36(1)(b) of the Vienna Convention by failing to inform the individuals of their Vienna Convention rights. The ICJ held that the United States was obligated "to provide, by means of its own choosing, review and reconsideration of the convictions and sentences of the [affected] Mexican nationals." Despite the ICJ decision in *Avena*, the court of appeals denied Medellin's claim.

The Supreme Court agreed to hear the case in 2005. While the case was pending, the President issued a memorandum to the Attorney General, announcing, "pursuant to the authority vested in me as President by the Constitution and the laws of the United States of America, that the United States will discharge its international obligations under the decision of the International Court of Justice in [*Avena*], by having State courts give effect to the decision." In light of that memorandum, Medellin filed a second state habeas petition. In light of that petition and the possibility that the Texas courts would resolve Medellin's claim, the Supreme Court dismissed the writ of certiorari as improvidently granted.

On remand, the Texas Court of Criminal Appeals again refused to address the merits of Medellin's claim. It found that neither the *Avena* decision nor the President's memorandum constituted "binding federal law" that overrode its determination of procedural default.

The Supreme Court affirmed. Chief Justice Roberts delivered the opinion of the Court. He rejected Medellin's claim that the ICJ's judgment in *Avena* constituted binding domestic law, such that federal and state courts were obligated to give it effect. The Court recognized that the United States had ratified an optional protocol to the Vienna Convention providing that any disputes under the Convention would "lie within the compulsory jurisdiction of the International Court of Justice" and that Article 94 of the United Nations Charter provided in pertinent part that as a member of the United Nations the United States "undertakes to comply with the decision of the [ICJ] in any case to which it is a party" but held that because the United States had not entered into any "self-executing treaty" obligation, the *Avena* judgment issued by the

ICJ did not "not automatically constitute federal law enforceable in U.S. courts."

"This Court has long recognized the distinction between treaties that automatically have effect as domestic law, and those that — while they constitute international law commitments — do not by themselves function as binding federal law. The distinction was well explained by Chief Justice Marshall's opinion in *Foster v. Neilson*, 27 U.S. 253, 2 Pet. 253 (1829), ... which held that a treaty is 'equivalent to an act of the legislature,'" and hence self-executing, when it 'operates of itself without the aid of any legislative provision.' When, in contrast, '[treaty] stipulations are not self-executing they can only be enforced pursuant to legislation to carry them into effect.' *Whitney v. Robertson*, 124 U.S. 190, 194 (1888). In sum, while treaties 'may comprise international commitments ... they are not domestic law unless Congress has either enacted implementing statutes or the treaty itself conveys an intention that it be "self-executing and is ratified on these terms."'

"A treaty is, of course, 'primarily a compact between independent nations.' It ordinarily 'depends for the enforcement of its provisions on the interest and the honor of the governments which are parties to it'". ...

"[With respect to Article 94, t]he Executive Branch contends that the phrase 'undertakes to comply' is not 'an acknowledgement that an ICJ decision will have immediate legal effect in the courts of U. N. members,' but rather 'a *commitment* on the part of U. N. Members to take *future* action through their political branches to comply with an ICJ decision.'

"We agree with this construction of Article 94. The Article is not a directive to domestic courts. It does not provide that the United States 'shall' or 'must' comply with an ICJ decision, nor indicate that the Senate that ratified the U. N. Charter intended to vest ICJ decisions with immediate legal effect in domestic courts. ...

"The remainder of Article 94 confirms that the U. N. Charter does not contemplate the automatic enforceability of ICJ decisions in domestic courts. Article 94(2) — the enforcement provision — provides the sole remedy for noncompliance: referral to the United Nations Security Council by an aggrieved state.

"The U. N. Charter's provision of an express diplomatic — that is, nonjudicial — remedy is itself evidence that ICJ judgments were not meant to be enforceable in domestic courts. And even this 'quintessentially *international* remed[y]' is not absolute. ... [A]s the President and Senate were undoubtedly aware in subscribing to the U. N. Charter and Optional Protocol, the United States retained the unqualified right to exercise its veto of any Security Council resolution. ...

"If ICJ judgments were instead regarded as automatically enforceable domestic law, they would be immediately and directly binding on state and federal courts pursuant to the Supremacy Clause. Mexico or the ICJ would have no need to proceed to the Security Council to enforce the judgment in this case. Noncompliance with an ICJ judgment through exercise of the Security Council veto — always regarded as an option by the Executive and ratifying Senate during and after consideration of the U. N. Charter, Optional Protocol, and ICJ Statute — would no longer be a viable alternative. There would be nothing to veto. In light of the U. N. Charter's remedial scheme, there is no reason to believe that the President and Senate signed up for such a result.

"In sum, *Medellin's* view that ICJ decisions are automatically enforceable as domestic law is fatally undermined by the enforcement structure established by Article 94. . . .

"The ICJ Statute, incorporated into the U. N. Charter, provides further evidence that the ICJ's judgment in *Avena* does not automatically constitute federal law judicially enforceable in United States courts. . . . [T]he ICJ can hear disputes only between nations, not individuals. . . . Article 59 of the statute provides that '[t]he decision of the [ICJ] has *no binding force except between the parties and in respect of that particular case.*' The dissent does not explain how Medellin, an individual, can be a party to the ICJ proceeding. . . .

"Our Framers established a careful set of procedures that must be followed before federal law can be created under the Constitution — vesting that decision in the political branches, subject to checks and balances. U.S. Const., Art. I, § 7. They also recognized that treaties could create federal law, but again through the political branches, with the President making the treaty and the Senate approving it. Art. II, § 2. . . .

"Our conclusion that *Avena* does not by itself constitute binding federal law is confirmed by the 'postratification understanding' of signatory nations. There are currently 47 nations that are parties to the Optional Protocol and 171 nations that are parties to the Vienna Convention. Yet neither Medellin nor his *amici* have identified a single nation that treats ICJ judgments as binding in domestic courts. . . .

"Our conclusion is further supported by general principles of interpretation . . . . Given that ICJ judgments may interfere with state procedural rules, one would expect the ratifying parties to the relevant treaties to have clearly stated their intent to give those judgments domestic effect, if they had so intended. Here there is no statement in the Optional Protocol, the U. N. Charter, or the ICJ Statute that supports the notion that ICJ judgments displace state procedural rules. . . .

"That the judgment of an international tribunal might not automatically become domestic law hardly means the underlying treaty is 'useless.' Such judgments would still constitute international obligations, the proper subject of political and diplomatic negotiations. And Congress could elect to give them wholesale effect . . . through implementing legislation, as it regularly has. . . .

"[N]either our approach nor our cases require that a treaty provide for self-execution in so many talismanic words; that is a caricature of the Court's opinion. Our cases simply require courts to decide whether a treaty's terms reflect a determination by the President who negotiated it and the Senate that confirmed it that the treaty has domestic effect.

"In addition, Congress is up to the task of implementing non-self-executing treaties, even those involving complex commercial disputes. The judgments of a number of international tribunals enjoy a different status because of implementing legislation enacted by Congress. Such language demonstrates that Congress knows how to accord domestic effect to international obligations when it desires such a result. ...

"In sum, while the ICJ's judgment in *Avena* creates an international law obligation on the part of the United States, it does not of its own force constitute binding federal law that pre-empts state restrictions on the filing of successive habeas petitions. As we noted in [*Sanchez-Llamas v. Oregon*, 548 U.S. 331 (2006)], a contrary conclusion would be extraordinary, given that basic rights guaranteed by our own Constitution do not have the effect of displacing state procedural rules. Nothing in the text, background, negotiating and drafting history, or practice among signatory nations suggests that the President or Senate intended the improbable result of giving the judgments of an international tribunal a higher status than that enjoyed by "many of our most fundamental constitutional protections."

The parts of the Court's opinion that dealt with the legal force of the president's memorandum are excerpted in the section of this supplement dealing with Chapter 4 of the main volume. There, the Court rejected the President's claim that he had inherent authority under the Constitution to require the state to ignore its procedural default rules.

Justice Stevens concurred in the judgment. While he agreed with the majority that the relevant treaties were best read to "contemplat[e] future action by the political branches" and thus to leave "the choice of whether to comply with ICJ judgments, and in what manner, 'to the political, not the judicial department,'" he urged Texas nonetheless to take the treaty obligations into account:

"Under the express terms of the Supremacy Clause, the United States' obligation to 'undertak[e] to comply' with the ICJ's decision falls on each of the States as well as the Federal Government. One consequence of our form of government is that sometimes States must shoulder the primary responsibility for protecting the honor and integrity of the Nation. Texas' duty in this respect is all the greater since it was Texas that—by failing to provide consular notice in accordance with the Vienna Convention—ensnared the United States in the current controversy. Having already put the Nation in breach of one treaty, it is now up to Texas to prevent the breach of another. ...

"The cost to Texas of complying with *Avena* would be minimal, particularly given the remote likelihood that the violation of the Vienna Convention actually prejudiced Jose Ernesto Medellin [without which showing, his conviction and sentence would be affirmed.]. ...

"On the other hand, the costs of refusing to respect the ICJ's judgment are significant. The entire Court and the President agree that breach will jeopardize the United States' 'plainly compelling' interests in 'ensuring the reciprocal observance of the Vienna Convention, protecting relations with foreign governments, and demonstrating commitment to the role of international law.' When the honor of the Nation is balanced against the modest cost of compliance, Texas would do well to recognize that more is at stake than whether judgments of the ICJ, and the principled admonitions of the President of the United States, trump state procedural rules in the absence of implementing legislation.

Justice Breyer, joined by Justices Souter and Ginsburg, dissented.

"[S]elf-executing treaty provisions are not uncommon or peculiar creatures of our domestic law; that they cover a wide range of subjects; ... the *Supremacy Clause* itself answers the self-execution question by applying many, but not all, treaty provisions directly to the States; and ... the Clause answers the self-execution question differently than does the law in many other nations. ...

"The case law provides no simple magic answer to the question whether a particular treaty provision is self-executing. But the case law does make clear that, insofar as today's majority looks for language about 'self-execution' in the treaty itself and insofar as it erects 'clear statement' presumptions designed to help find an answer, it is misguided.

"The many treaty provisions that this Court has found self-executing contain no textual language on the point. Few, if any, of these provisions are clear. ...

"The case law ... suggests practical, context-specific criteria that this Court has previously used to help determine whether, for Supremacy Clause purposes, a treaty provision is self-executing. The provision's text matters very much. ... Drafting history is also relevant. But, again, that is not because it will explicitly address the relevant question. Instead text and history, along with subject matter and related characteristics will help our courts determine whether, as Chief Justice Marshall put it, the treaty provision 'addresses itself to the political ... department[s]' for further action or to 'the judicial department' for direct enforcement.

"In making this determination, this Court has found the provision's subject matter of particular importance. Does the treaty provision declare peace? Does it promise not to engage in hostilities? If so, it addresses itself to the political branches. Alternatively, does it concern the adjudication of traditional private legal rights such as rights to own property, to conduct a business, or to obtain civil tort recovery? If so, it may well address itself to the Judiciary. Enforcing such rights and setting their boundaries is the bread-and-butter work of the courts.

"One might also ask whether the treaty provision confers specific, detailed individual legal rights. Does it set forth definite standards that judges can readily enforce? Other things being equal, where rights are specific and readily enforceable, the treaty provision more likely 'addresses' the judiciary.

"Alternatively, would direct enforcement require the courts to create a new cause of action? Would such enforcement engender constitutional controversy? Would it create constitutionally undesirable conflict with the other branches? In such circumstances, it is not likely that the provision contemplates direct judicial enforcement ...

"Applying the approach just described, I would find the relevant treaty provisions self-executing as applied to the ICJ judgment before us (giving that judgment domestic legal effect) for the following reasons, taken together.

"First, the language of the relevant treaties strongly supports direct judicial enforceability, at least of judgments of the kind at issue here. The Optional Protocol bears the title 'Compulsory Settlement of Disputes,' thereby emphasizing the mandatory and binding nature of the procedures it sets forth. ...

"True, neither the Protocol nor the Charter explicitly states that the obligation to comply with an ICJ judgment automatically binds a party *as a matter of domestic law* without further domestic legislation. *But how could the language of those documents do otherwise?* The treaties are multilateral. And, as I have explained, some signatories follow British further-legislation-always-needed principles, others follow United States Supremacy Clause principles, and still others, *e.g.*, the Netherlands, can directly incorporate treaty provisions into their domestic law in particular circumstances. ...

"*Second*, the Optional Protocol here applies to a dispute about the meaning of a Vienna Convention provision that is itself self-executing and judicially enforceable. [The majority left that question open, finding it unnecessary to decide the issue.] The Convention provision is about an individual's 'rights,' namely, his right upon being arrested to be informed of his separate right to contact his nation's consul. ... The dispute arises at the intersection of an individual right with ordinary rules of criminal procedure; it consequently concerns the kind of matter with which judges are familiar. The provisions contain judicially enforceable standards. ...

"*Fourth*, the majority's very different approach has seriously negative practical implications. The United States has entered into at least 70 treaties that contain provisions for ICJ dispute settlement similar to the Protocol before us. ... [T]he consequence is to undermine longstanding efforts in those treaties to create an effective international system for interpreting and applying many, often commercial, self-executing treaty provisions.

"*Fifth*, other factors, related to the particular judgment here at issue, make that judgment well suited to direct judicial enforcement. ... Courts frequently work with criminal procedure and related prejudice. Legislatures do not. Judicial standards are readily available for working in this technical area. Legislative standards are not readily available. Judges typically determine such matters, deciding, for example, whether further hearings are necessary, after reviewing a record in an individual case. Congress does not normally legislate in respect to individual cases. ...

"*Sixth*, to find the United States' treaty obligations self-executing as applied to the ICJ judgment (and consequently to find that judgment enforceable) does not threaten constitutional conflict with other branches; it does not require us to engage in nonjudicial activity; and it does not require us to create a new cause of action. ...

"*Seventh*, neither the President nor Congress has expressed concern about direct judicial enforcement of the ICJ decision. To the contrary, the President favors enforcement of this judgment. Thus, insofar as foreign policy impact, the interrelation of treaty provisions, or any other matter within the President's special treaty, military, and foreign affairs responsibilities might prove relevant, such factors *favor*, rather than militate against, enforcement of the judgment before us. ...

Page 352.   At the end of section 3 of the Note, add the following:

Siegel, Commandeering and Its Alternatives: A Federalism Perspective, 59 Vand. L. Rev. 1629, 1634-35 (2006), argues that the anticommandeering decisions "vindicate federalism values [by] requiring the federal government to internalize more of the costs of federal regulation [but undermine] federalism values when the (clearly constitutional) alternative of preemption is reasonably available." He proposes that commandeering should be presumptively unconstitutional "when preemption is not a feasible alternative in the short run, the federal mandate is unfunded and expensive, and the federal government makes little effective effort to alleviate reasonable accountability concerns," but should be constitutional "when preemption constitutes a feasible alternative in the short run and such preemption would reduce state regulatory [control], the federal mandate is fully funded or relatively [inexpensive], and the federal government takes effective measures to maintain lines of accountability." Applying these principles, Siegel concludes that the statute in *New York v. United States* should have been upheld because preemption there "was reasonably available (and indeed had already been threatened)," and that *Printz* is a closer case. Does this approach provide standards that courts can in practice apply in a principled manner?

3a. *The scope of the decisions: the war on terror.* Consider the implications of these decisions for efforts by the national government to gain assistance from (sometimes reluctant) state and local governments in identifying and interrogating people in connection with investigations of alleged terrorist activities. Do the following observations justify the application of these decisions in that context?

> [Federalism], in particular the autonomy protected by the anti-commandeering doctrine, can protect constitutional rights better than the direct assertion of claims based on those rights. State and local government officials exert pressure on the federal government that works differently from constitutional rights. Claims of autonomy [can] arise out of strong interpretations of constitutional rights. These interpretations may be drastically overstated or naively idealistic and, consequently, quite unlikely to move courts to rein in the federal government as it pursues national security. But state and local government autonomy can exert pressure on the federal government to moderate its efforts and take care not to offend constitutional rights, even rights that the courts would not now be willing to enforce. To carry out its programs, the national government will need to inspire the confidence of the vast numbers of police and other personnel employed at the state and, especially, local government level.
>
> Because state and local government autonomy can work as a safeguard for the rights of the people, the anti-commandeering doctrine should remain in place, in full force, unmodified by any sort of emergency exception. [It] is true that this autonomy deprives the national government of a means to carry out programs that may be vitally important. But in cases of the "direst emergency and peril," the great majority of persons employed at the state and local level of government can be expected to respond without objection. Where there are pockets of noncompliance, the federal government can send in its own personnel, including the military. The different levels of government will exert pressure on each other. State and local government will tend to resist only when the emergency is not dire and when the actions of the federal government offend local beliefs, often idealistic beliefs about constitutional rights. The federal government will want to win compliance and will take steps to inspire cooperation, such as offering ample funding and framing demands that take account of ideas about individual rights. Remove the anti-commandeering doctrine, or temper it with an emergency exception, and this beneficial interaction is lost.

Althouse, The Vigor of Anti-Commandeering Doctrine in Times of Terror, 69 Brook. L. Rev. 1231, 1274-1275 (2004).

Consider also the views expressed in Young, Welcome to the Dark Side: Liberals Rediscover Federalism in the Wake of the War on Terror, 69 Brook. L. Rev. 1277, 1311 (2004):

> Federalism is about dividing power; nothing much depends on what the power in question is being used for. It is also about providing institutional space for a diversity of political views. As such, it should surprise no one that a commitment to state and local autonomy would take on the hue of political opposition to the prevailing orthodoxy at the center, whatever that orthodoxy happens to be. Relatively few people are likely to embrace federalism for its own [sake]. Rather, support for state autonomy vis-à-vis national power on both Left and Right has ebbed and flowed throughout our history, according to the dynamics of whatever political issue is most salient at any given time.

3b. *The Tenth Amendment and the inflection of statutory interpretation.* In Gonzales v. Oregon, 546 U.S. 243 (2006), the Supreme Court was faced with a challenge to the Attorney General's interpretation of the federal Controlled Substances Act (CSA), which regulates the distribution of various drugs. After Oregon passed a Death with Dignity Act that exempted physicians from civil or criminal liability for prescribing lethal doses of various drugs to terminally ill patients under defined circumstances, the Attorney General issued an Interpretive Rule declaring that using controlled substances to assist suicide is not a legitimate medical practice and that dispensing or prescribing them for this purpose would be unlawful under the CSA and would subject physicians to loss of their prescribing privileges.

By a 6-3 vote, the Court rejected the Attorney General's position. The Court did not question whether Congress would have the ability, using its commerce power, to forbid doctor-assisted suicide. (The answer to that question is at least suggested by the Court's decision the previous Term in Gonzales v. Raich, 545 U.S. 1 (2005), holding that a federal ban on the cultivation and use of marijuana also contained in the CSA overrode California's Compassionate Use statute). Rather, the question was whether the Attorney General's interpretation of the CSA to forbid physician-assisted suicide was a permissible interpretation of the Act. Much of Justice Kennedy's opinion for the Court was taken up with conventional administrative law analysis. But his opinion also relied on the traditional role of the states in regulating medical practice as an interpretive aid:

> The structure and operation of the CSA presume and rely upon a functioning medical profession regulated under the States' police powers. The Attorney General can register a physician to dispense controlled substances "if the applicant is authorized to dispense ... controlled substances under

the laws of the State in which he practices." 21 U.S.C. §823(f) . When considering whether to revoke a physician's registration, the Attorney General looks not just to violations of federal drug laws; but he "shall" also consider "the recommendation of the appropriate state licensing board or professional disciplinary authority" and the registrant's compliance with state and local drug laws. The very definition of a "practitioner" eligible to prescribe includes physicians "licensed, registered, or otherwise permitted, by the United States or the jurisdiction in which he practices" to dispense controlled substances. §802(21). Further cautioning against the conclusion that the CSA effectively displaces the States' general regulation of medical practice is the Act's pre-emption provision, which indicates that, absent a positive conflict, none of the Act's provisions should be "construed as indicating an intent on the part of the Congress to occupy the field in which that provision operates . . . to the exclusion of any State law on the same subject matter which would otherwise be within the authority of the State."

Oregon's regime is an example of the state regulation of medical practice that the CSA presupposes. Rather than simply decriminalizing assisted suicide, ODWDA limits its exercise to the attending physicians of terminally ill patients, physicians who must be licensed by Oregon's Board of Medical Examiners. The statute gives attending physicians a central role, requiring them to provide prognoses and prescriptions, give information about palliative alternatives and counseling, and ensure patients are competent and acting voluntarily. Any eligible patient must also get a second opinion from another registered physician, and the statute's safeguards require physicians to keep and submit to inspection detailed records of their actions.

Even though regulation of health and safety is "primarily, and historically, a matter of local concern," Hillsborough County v. Automated Medical Laboratories, Inc., 471 U.S. 707, 719 (1985), there is no question that the Federal Government can set uniform national standards in these areas. See *Raich. . . .*

In the face of the CSA's silence on the practice of medicine generally and its recognition of state regulation of the medical profession it is difficult to defend the Attorney General's declaration that the statute impliedly criminalizes physician-assisted suicide. . . . [The Government] points to the teachings of Hippocrates, the positions of prominent medical organizations, the Federal Government, and the judgment of the 49 States that have not legalized physician-assisted suicide as further support for the proposition that the practice is not legitimate medicine.

On its own, this understanding of medicine's boundaries is at least reasonable. The primary problem with the Government's argument, however, is its assumption that the CSA impliedly authorizes an Executive officer to bar a use simply because it may be inconsistent with one reasonable understanding of medical practice. Viewed alone, the prescription requirement may support such an understanding, but statutes "should not be read as a series of unrelated and isolated provisions." The CSA's substantive provisions and their arrangement undermine this assertion of an expansive federal authority to regulate medicine. . . .

The Government's interpretation of the prescription requirement also fails under the objection that the Attorney General is an unlikely recipient of such broad authority, given the Secretary [of Health and Human Service]'s primacy in shaping medical policy under the CSA, and the statute's otherwise careful allocation of decisionmaking powers. Just as the conventions of expression indicate that Congress is unlikely to alter a statute's obvious scope and division of authority through muffled hints, the background principles of our federal system also belie the notion that Congress would use such an obscure grant of authority to regulate areas traditionally supervised by the States' police power. It is unnecessary even to consider the application of clear statement requirements, or presumptions against pre-emption to reach this commonsense conclusion. For all these reasons, we conclude the CSA's prescription requirement does not authorize the Attorney General to bar dispensing controlled substances for assisted suicide in the face of a state medical regime permitting such conduct.

The Chief Justice and Justices Scalia and Thomas dissented. After explaining why he thought the Attorney General's interpretation of the CSA was justifiable, Justice Scalia, joined by the other two dissenters remarked:

The Court's decision today is perhaps driven by a feeling that the subject of assisted suicide is none of the Federal Government's business. It is easy to sympathize with that position. The prohibition or deterrence of assisted suicide is certainly not among the enumerated powers conferred on the United States by the Constitution, and it is within the realm of public morality *(bonos mores)* traditionally addressed by the so-called police power of the States. But then, neither is prohibiting the recreational use of drugs or discouraging drug addiction among the enumerated powers. From an early time in our national history, the Federal Government has used its enumerated powers, such as its power to regulate interstate commerce, for the purpose of protecting public morality — for example, by banning the interstate shipment of lottery tickets, or the interstate transport of women for immoral purposes. Unless we are to repudiate a long and well-established principle of our jurisprudence, using the federal commerce power to prevent assisted suicide is unquestionably permissible. The question before us is not whether Congress *can* do this, or even whether Congress *should* do this; but simply whether Congress *has* done this in the CSA. I think there is no doubt that it has.

Justice Thomas, in a solo dissent, argued that, in light of *Raich*, the "principles of federalism and our constitutional structure" on which the majority had relied were "water over the dam" and observed that "[t]he Court's reliance upon the constitutional principles that it rejected in *Raich* — albeit under the guise of statutory interpretation — is perplexing to say the least."

Page 355.   At the end of section 7 of the Note, add the following:

In Watters v. Wachovia Bank, N.A., 127 S. Ct. 1559 (2007), the Supreme Court held that Michigan's attempt to regulate the bank's mortgage business was preempted by the National Bank Act and various regulations promulgated by the Office of the Comptroller of the Currency. Relying on *New York*, the Court rejected Michigan's tenth amendment-based challenge, stating that "if a power is delegated to Congress in the Constitution" — as the power to regulate the operations of nationally chartered banks is conferred by the commerce and necessary and proper clauses — then "the Tenth Amendment expressly disclaims any reservation of that power to the States."

Page 356.   At the conclusion of the Note, add the following.

Consider this summary:

[The] historic progression of the various models of federalism [reflects] a pendulum-like attempt to achieve the proper balance between underlying federalism values, each model perhaps overcompensating for the excesses of its predecessor. After the Great Depression crippled the capacity of state and local governments to cope with unprecedented levels of social and economic despair, the Supreme Court adopted a model of federalism that exalted the problem-solving value at the expense of the check-and-balance value to approve pragmatic New Deal legislative programs. [Cooperative] federalism [recovers] some of the balance through a partnership-based approach to regulation in areas of interjurisdictional overlap, allowing state and federal governments to take responsibility for interlocking components of a collaborative regulatory regime. [Cooperative] federalism has [been] criticized as an overly pragmatic model that insufficiently protects anti-tyranny values. [The] New Federalism reestablishes the supremacy of the check-and-balance value over all others in order to bolster the line between state and federal authority against pressures [that] would blur the boundary. [But] the New Federalism's focus on preserving bright-line boundaries [renders it unable to effectively mediate the competition between federalism values, contributing to a governmental ethos that obstructs even desirable regulatory activity in the interjurisdictional gray area (such as federal initiative that might have been taken in the aftermath of Hurricane Katrina). [In] this ironic respect, the New Federalism simply does what New Deal federalism did in the opposite direction — shortchanging the problem-solving value in the name of the check-and-balance value, which it mistakes for federalism generally.

Ryan, Federalism and the Tug of War Within: Seeking Checks and Balances in the Interjurisdictional Gray Area, 66 Md. L. Rev. 503, 511-12 (2007).

4

THE DISTRIBUTION OF NATIONAL POWERS

B. A Case Study: Presidential Seizure

Page 375. After section 2 of the Note, add the following:

3. *A "completion" power?* Consider the proposition that *Dames & Moore* illustrates an executive power "to prescribe incidental details needed to carry into execution a legislative scheme, even in the absence of any congressional authorization to complete the scheme." Goldsmith & Manning, The President's Completion Power, 115 Yale L. J. 2280, 2282 (2006). As Professors Goldsmith and Manning describe the power, "Congress can limit it, for example, by denying the President the authority to complete a statute through certain means or by specifying the manner in which a statute must be implemented. But in the absence of such affirmative legislative limitation or specification, courts and Presidents have recognized an Article II power of some uncertain scope to complete a legislative scheme." Compare Koh, Setting the World Right, 115 Yale L. J. 2350, 2368-70 (2006):

Upon examination, [the] completion power is just another term for an implied Necessary and Proper Clause for the President, a power that [the] Framers chose to give Congress, not the President....

The recent constitutional debate over presidential signing statements has raged precisely because the President has claimed an unenumerated Article

II power to interpret a statutory scheme faithfully not to Congress's intent, but rather to his own reading of what that scheme's goals might be.

Page 375.   Before Section C, insert the following:

MEDELLIN v. TEXAS, 128 S. Ct. 1346 (2008). The United States is a signatory of the Vienna Convention on Consular Relations. The Convention obligates signatories to inform detained foreign nationals of the right to request assistance from the consul of their states. At the time that this case arose, the United States was also a signatory of an Optional Protocol providing that the International Court of Justice (IJC) would have jurisdiction to resolve disputes arising out of the interpretation or application of the Convention.

Medellin, a citizen of Mexico, was convicted of murder in state court and sentenced to death. In his application for state postconviction relief, he claimed that he had not been informed of his consular rights in violation of the Convention. Both the state and federal courts rejected his request for relief on the ground that he had failed to raise the claim earlier.

Meanwhile, the IJC rendered a decision involving Medellin and 50 other foreign national held in the United States, all of whom claimed that they had not been informed of their consular rights. The IJC held that the United States was obligated "to provide, by means of its own choosing, review and reconsideration of the convictions and sentences" of the affected parties without regard to state procedural default rules.

The Supreme Court granted certiorari to review the lower court decision denying Medellin's claim. While the case was pending, President Bush issued a Memorandum to the United States Attorney General, which provided that he had "determined pursuant to the authority vested in me as President by the Constitution and laws of the United States of America, that the United States will discharge its international obligations under the decision of the [ICJ] by having State courts give effect to the decision." Medellin then filed a second application for post-conviction relief in state court, and the United States Supreme Court dismissed the petition for certiorari as improvidently granted in order to allow the state proceedings to go forward. When the state again denied relief, the Supreme Court granted certiorari for a second time.

Chief Justice Roberts delivered the opinion of the Court. In the first part of his opinion, excerpted in the section of this supplement dealing with Chapter 3 of the main volume, the Court held that the Convention was not "self-executing" and, therefore was not binding on state and federal courts as a matter of domestic law. In the second portion of the opinion, the Court turned to the legal effect of the President's memorandum.

"The United States maintains that the President's constitutional role uniquely qualifies' him to resolve the sensitive foreign policy decision that bear on compliance with an ICJ decision and to do so expeditiously.' [We] do not question these propositions. [In] this case, the President seeks to vindicate United States interests in ensuring the reciprocal observance of the Vienna Convention, protecting relations with foreign governments and demonstrating commitment to the role of international law. These interests are plainly compelling.

"Such considerations, however, do not allow us to set aside first principles. The President's authority to act, as with the exercise of any governmental power, must stem either from an act of Congress or from the Constitution itself.' [*Youngstown*; *Dames & Moore*]....

"The President has an array of political and diplomatic means available to enforce international obligations, but unilaterally converting a non-self-executing treaty into a self-executing one is not among them. The responsibility for transforming an international obligation arising from a non-self-executing treaty into domestic law falls to Congress....

"Once a treaty is ratified without provisions clearly according it domestic effect, [whether] the treaty will ever have such effect is governed by the fundamental constitutional principle that '"[t]he power to make the necessary laws is in Congress; the power to execute in the President"' [*Hamdan*, quoting Ex parte Milligan, 4 Wall. 2, 139 (1866)....

"A non-self-executing treaty, by definition, is one that was ratified with the understanding that it is not to have domestic effect of its own force. That understanding precludes the assertion that Congress has implicitly authorized the President — acting on his own — to achieve precisely the same result....

"When the President asserts the power to enforce' a non-self-executing treaty by unilaterally creating domestic law, he acts in conflict with the implicit understanding of the ratifying Senate. His assertion of authority, insofar as it is based on the pertinent non-self-executing treaties, is therefore within Justice Jackson's third category, not the first or even the second....

"The United States nonetheless maintains that the President's Memorandum should be given effect as domestic law because this case involves a valid Presidential action in the context of Congressional "acquiescence."' Under the *Youngstown* tripartite framework, congressional acquiescence is pertinent when the President's action falls within the second [category]. Here, however, as we have explained the President's effort to accord domestic effect to the [ICJ] judgment does not meet that prerequisite.

"In any event, even if we were persuaded that congressional acquiescence could support the President's asserted authority to create domestic law pursuant to a non-self-executing treaty, such acquiescence does not exist here....

"We [turn] to the United States' claim that — independent of the United States' treaty obligations — the Memorandum is a valid exercise of the

85

President's foreign affairs authority to resolve claims disputes with foreign nations. [The Court cites *Dames & Moore* among other cases].

"The claims-settlement cases involve a narrow set of circumstances: the making of executive agreements to settle civil claims between American citizens and foreign governments or foreign nationals. They are based on the view that 'a systematic, unbroken, executive practice, long pursued to the knowledge of the Congress and never before questioned,' can 'raise a presumption that the [action] had been [taken] pursuant to its consent.' [*Dames & Moore*]....

"The President's Memorandum is not supported by a 'particularly longstanding practice' of congressional acquiescence, but rather is what the United States itself has described as 'unprecedented action.' Indeed, the Government has not identified a single instance in which the President as attempted (or Congress has acquiesced in) a Presidential directive issued to state courts, much less one that reaches deep into the heart of the State's police powers and compels state courts to reopen final criminal judgments and set aside neutrally applicable state laws....

"Medellin argues that the President's Memorandum is a valid exercise of his 'Take Care' power. [This] authority allows the President to execute the laws, not make them. For the reasons we have stated, the [ICJ] judgment is not domestic law; accordingly, the President cannot rely on his Take Care powers here."

Justice Stevens concurred in the judgment. Justice Breyer, joined by Justices Souter and Ginsburg, dissented. In the first part of his opinion, Justice Breyer concluded that the Convention was self-executing and, hence, binding on the states. He then turned to the President's Memorandum: "It is difficult to believe that in the exercise of his Article II powers pursuant to a ratified treaty, the President can *never* take action that would result in setting aside state law. Suppose that the President believes it necessary that he implement a treaty provision requiring a prisoner exchange involving someone in state custody in order to avoid a proven military threat. Or suppose he believes it necessary to secure a foreign consul's treaty-based rights to move freely or to contact an arrested foreign national. Does the Constitution require the President in each and every such instance to obtain a special statute authorizing his action? On the other hand, the Constitution must impose significant restrictions upon the President's ability, by invoking Article II treaty-implementation authority, to circumvent ordinary legislative processes and to pre-empt state law as he does so.

"Given the Court's comparative lack of expertise in foreign affairs; given the importance of the Nation's foreign relations; given the difficulty of finding the proper constitutional balance among state and federal, executive and legislative, powers in such matters; and given the likely future importance of this Court's efforts to do so, I would very much hesitate before concluding that the Constitution implicitly sets forth broad prohibitions (or permissions) in this area....

"I would thus be content to leave the matter in the constitutional shade from which it has emerged. Given my view of this case, I need not answer the question."

C. Foreign Affairs

Page 383. At the end of the Note, add the following:

For an effort to answer many of the questions posed in this Note regarding the "war" against terrorism, see Bradley & Goldsmith, Congressional Authorization and the War on Terrorism, 118 Harv. L. Rev. 2047 (2005). The authors argue that the Resolution confers full power on the President to prosecute war even though it is not a formal declaration of war. They claim that

> [The] international law role for declarations of war has largely disappeared. [This] is the principal reason why, despite hundreds of armed conflicts around the world during this period, [it] appears that no nation has declared war since the late 1940's....
>
> [In] light of the longstanding political branch practice of initiating war without a formal declaration of war, consistent judicial approval of this practice, changes in international law that render war declaration less relevant, and general scholarly consensus, it seems clear that Congress need not issue a formal declaration of war in order to provide its full authorization for the President to prosecute a war.

Id. at 2061-62.

With regard to the "enemy" covered by the Resolution, Bradley and Goldsmith argue that it includes not just "nations, organizations or persons" who participated in the September 11 attack, but also at least some "terrorist organizations that are affiliated with al Qaeda in its conflict with the United States, but that did not aid al Qaeda in the September 11 attacks or harbor its [members]." Id. at 2107.

With regard to the end of the war, the authors acknowledge that the "potentially indefinite length of the authorized conflict raises difficult questions about how long the United States may detain a captured terrorist enemy combatant." Id. at 2120. They conclude that "with respect to the power to detain terrorist combatants outside the conflict in Afghanistan, the end of the conflict should be viewed in individual rather than group-based terms. Under this approach, the question is [whether] hostilities have, in essence, ceased with the individual because he no longer poses a substantial danger of rejoining hostilities." Id. at 2125.

Page 395. At the bottom of the page, add the following:

But see Cleveland, Hamdi Meets Youngstown: Justice Jackson's Wartime Security Jurisprudence and the Detention of "Enemy Combatants," 68 Albany L. Rev. 1127 (2005) (arguing that the Court should have "rigorously scrutinized claims that Congress had authorized such detentions"); Chemerinsky, Enemy Combatants and Separation of Powers, 1 J. Natl. Sec. L. & P. 73, 84 (2005) ("Justice O'Connor's conclusion [that the AUMF] permits the detention of enemy combatants is inconsistent with the many decisions holding that preclusion of meaningful judicial review must be explicit, not implied."). Cf. Sunstein, Administrative Law Goes to War, 118 Harv. L. Rev. 2663 (2005) (using administrative law principles to conclude that the issue posed by indefinite detention of a citizen arrested in the United States on the ground that he aided the September 11 attack is "extremely difficult").

Page 397. At the end of section 3 of the Note, add the following:

For an examination of the background facts relating to *Quirin*, concluding that the case involved "a process and a decision with so many deficiencies that it should be remembered as a precedent not worth repeating," see Fisher, Military Commissions: Problems of Authority and Practice, 24 B. U. Int'l. L. J 15 (2006). Fisher points out that the Roosevelt administration decided not to proceed against the saboteurs in civilian court because "it feared that a public trial would reveal that the eight men were captured not as a result of uncanny FBI skills, but rather because [one of the saboteurs] turned himself in" and because "[by] concealing [this] assistance, the administration might discourage future attempts at sabotage." Id. at 35. Chief Justice Stone wrote the opinion in the case despite the fact that his son was a member of the defense team, and Justice Frankfurter also participated even though he had previously advised the administration on how the tribunial should be set up. Id. at 37-38. The Court issued a one-page per curiam order ruling for the government shortly after oral argument, but did not issue is full opinion until nearly three months later, at which point six of the eight defendants had been executed. Id. at 38-39. Justice Frankfurter later referred to *Quirin* as "not a happy precedent," and Justice Douglas, who also participated in the case, later commented that the case indicated that "it is extremely undesireable to announce a decision on the merits without an opinion accompanying it. Because once the search for the grounds, the examination of the grounds that had been advanced is made, sometimes those grounds crumble." Id. at 40.

Page 397. After section 3 of the Note, add the following:

HAMDAN V. RUMSFELD
548 U.S. 557 (2006)

JUSTICE STEVENS announced the judgment of the Court and delivered the opinion of the Court with respect to Parts I through IV, Parts VI through VI-D-iii, Part VI-D-v, and Part VII, and an opinion with respect to Parts V and VI-D-iv, in which JUSTICE SOUTER, JUSTICE GINSBURG, and JUSTICE BREYER join.

[Hamdan was captured in November, 2001, during the war with the Taliban and held at Guantanamo Bay. A year after his capture, the President deemed him eligible for trial by a military commission on unspecified charges. A year after that, he was charged with conspiracy "to commit offenses triable by military commission." He filed a writ of habeas corpus, alleging that the military commission lacked authority to try him because neither an act of Congress nor the common law of war allowed a trial for conspiracy and because the procedures that the President had adopted violated military and international law, including the principle that a defendant must be permitted to see and hear evidence against him.]

For the reasons that follow, we conclude that the military commission convened to try Hamdan lacks power to proceed because its structure and procedures violate both the [Uniform Code of Military Justice (UCMJ)] and the Geneva Conventions. Four of us also conclude that the offense with which Hamdan has been charged is not an "offens[e] that by ... the law of war may be tried by military commissions." 10 U.S.C. § 821.

I

[O]n November 13, 2001, while the United States was still engaged in active combat with the Taliban, the President issued a comprehensive military order intended to govern the "Detention, Treatment, and Trial of Certain Non-Citizens in the War Against Terrorism," 66 Fed. Reg. 57833 (hereinafter November 13 Order or Order). Those subject to the November 13 Order include any noncitizen for whom the President determines "there is reason to believe" that he or she (1) "is or was" a member of al Qaeda or (2) has engaged or participated in terrorist activities aimed at or harmful to the United States. Any such individual "shall, when tried, be tried by military commission for any and all offenses triable by military commission that such individual is alleged to have committed, and may be punished in accordance with the penalties provided under applicable law, including imprisonment or death."...

On July 3, 2003, the President announced his determination that Hamdan and five other detainees at Guantanamo Bay were subject to the November 13 Order and thus triable by military commission. [The] charging document, which is unsigned, contains 13 numbered paragraphs. The first two paragraphs recite the asserted bases for the military commission's jurisdiction—namely, the November 13 Order and the President's July 3, 2003, declaration that Hamdan is eligible for trial by military commission. The next nine paragraphs, collectively entitled "General Allegations," describe al Qaeda's activities from its inception in 1989 through 2001 and identify Osama bin Laden as the group's leader. Hamdan is not mentioned in these paragraphs.

Only the final two paragraphs, entitled "Charge: Conspiracy," contain allegations against Hamdan. Paragraph 12 charges that "from on or about February 1996 to on or about November 24, 2001," Hamdan "willfully and knowingly joined an enterprise of persons who shared a common criminal purpose and conspired and agreed with [named members of al Qaeda] to commit the following offenses triable by military commission: attacking civilians; attacking civilian objects; murder by an unprivileged belligerent; and terrorism." There is no allegation that Hamdan had any command responsibilities, played a leadership role, or participated in the planning of any activity.

Paragraph 13 lists four "overt acts" that Hamdan is alleged to have committed sometime between 1996 and November 2001 in furtherance of the "enterprise and conspiracy": (1) he acted as Osama bin Laden's "bodyguard and personal driver," "believ[ing]" all the while that bin Laden "and his associates were involved in" terrorist acts prior to and including the attacks of September 11, 2001; (2) he arranged for transportation of, and actually transported, weapons used by al Qaeda members and by bin Laden's bodyguards (Hamdan among them); (3) he "drove or accompanied [O]sama bin Laden to various al Qaida-sponsored training camps, press conferences, or lectures," at which bin Laden encouraged attacks against Americans; and (4) he received weapons training at al Qaeda-sponsored camps.....

On November 8, 2004 [the] District Court granted Hamdan's petition for habeas corpus and stayed the commission's proceedings....

The Court of Appeals for the District of Columbia Circuit reversed. [Chief Justice Roberts participated in the Court of Appeals decision (which was rendered before his appointment to the Supreme Court) and therefore disqualified himself from participation in the Supreme Court decision]. . . . [1]

IV

The military commission, a tribunal neither mentioned in the Constitution nor created by statute, was born of military necessity. . . .

Exigency alone, of course, will not justify the establishment and use of penal tribunals not contemplated by Article I, § 8 and Article III, § 1 of the Constitution unless some other part of that document authorizes a response to the felt need. And that authority, if it exists, can derive only from the powers granted jointly to the President and Congress in time of war. . . .

Whether [the] President may constitutionally convene military commissions "without the sanction of Congress" in cases of "controlling necessity" is a question this Court has not answered definitively, and need not answer today. For we held in *Quirin* that Congress had, through Article of War 15, sanctioned the use of military commissions in such circumstances. Article 21 of the UCMJ, the language of which is substantially identical to the old Article 15 and was preserved by Congress after World War II, reads as follows:

> "Jurisdiction of courts-martial not exclusive.
> "The provisions of this code conferring jurisdiction upon courts-martial shall not be construed as depriving military commissions, provost courts, or other military tribunals of concurrent jurisdiction in respect of offenders or offenses that by statute or by the law of war may be tried by such military commissions, provost courts, or other military tribunals."

We have no occasion to revisit *Quirin*'s controversial characterization of Article of War 15 as congressional authorization for military commissions. Contrary to the Government's assertion, however, even *Quirin* did not view the authorization as a sweeping mandate for the President to "invoke military commissions when he deems them necessary." Rather, the *Quirin* Court recognized that Congress had simply preserved what power, under the Constitution and the common law of war, the President had had before 1916 to convene military commissions — with the express condition that the President and those under his command

---

1. In portions of its opinion not reprinted here, the Court rejected on statutory construction grounds the Government's argument that the Detainee Treatment Act (DTA), enacted while the Hamdan case was pending, deprived the Court of jurisdiction and rejected the Government's argument that it should delay decision in the case until the final outcome of the military proceedings. — EDS.

comply with the law of war.[23] That much is evidenced by the Court's inquiry, *following* its conclusion that Congress had authorized military commissions, into whether the law of war had indeed been complied with in that case.

The Government would have us dispense with the inquiry that the *Quirin* Court undertook and find in either the [Authorization for the Use of Military Force(AUMF) enacted in the immediate wake of the bombing of the World Trade Center] or the DTA specific, overriding authorization for the very commission that has been convened to try Hamdan. Neither of these congressional Acts, however, expands the President's authority to convene military commissions. First, while we assume that the AUMF activated the President's war powers, see [*Hamdi*] and that those powers include the authority to convene military commissions in appropriate circumstances, there is nothing in the text or legislative history of the AUMF even hinting that Congress intended to expand or alter the authorization set forth in Article 21 of the UCMJ.

Likewise, the DTA cannot be read to authorize this commission. Although the DTA, unlike either Article 21 or the AUMF, was enacted after the President had convened Hamdan's commission, it contains no language authorizing that tribunal or any other at Guantanamo Bay....

Together, the UCMJ, the AUMF, and the DTA at most acknowledge a general Presidential authority to convene military commissions in circumstances where justified under the "Constitution and laws," including the law of war. Absent a more specific congressional authorization, the task of this Court is, as it was in *Quirin,* to decide whether Hamdan's military commission is so justified. It is to that inquiry we now turn.

V

[The plurality examines the history of military commissions and concludes that they are used (1) when martial law has been declared; (2) as part of a temporary military government over occupied enemy territory or territory regained from an enemy where civilian government does not function; and (3) "as an incident to the conduct of war" when necessary "to seize and subject to disciplinary measures those enemies who in their attempt to thwart or impede our military effort have violated the law of war."]

Quirin is the model the Government invokes most frequently to defend the commission convened to try Hamdan. That is both appropriate and unsurprising.

---

23. Whether or not the President has independent power, absent congressional authorization, to convene military commissions, he may not disregard limitations that Congress has, in proper exercise of its own war powers, placed on his powers. See [*Youngstown,*] (Jackson, J., concurring). The Government does not argue otherwise.

Since Guantanamo Bay is neither enemy-occupied territory nor under martial law, the law-of-war commission is the only model available. At the same time, no more robust model of executive power exists; *Quirin* represents the high-water mark of military power to try enemy combatants for war crimes....

The charge against Hamdan [alleges] a conspiracy extending over a number of years, from 1996 to November 2001. All but two months of that more than 5-year-long period preceded the attacks of September 11, 2001, and the enactment of the AUMF—the Act of Congress on which the Government relies for exercise of its war powers and thus for its authority to convene military commissions. Neither the purported agreement with Osama bin Laden and others to commit war crimes, nor a single overt act, is alleged to have occurred in a theater of war or on any specified date after September 11, 2001. None of the overt acts that Hamdan is alleged to have committed violates the law of war.

These facts alone cast doubt on the legality of the charge and, hence, the [commission]. But the deficiencies in the time and place allegations also underscore—indeed are symptomatic of—the most serious defect of this charge: The offense it alleges is not triable by law-of-war military commission.

There is no suggestion that Congress has, in exercise of its constitutional authority to "define and punish... Offences against the Law of Nations," U.S. Const., Art. I, § 8, cl. 10, positively identified "conspiracy" as a war crime. As we explained in *Quirin,* that is not necessarily fatal to the Government's claim of authority to try the alleged offense by military commission; Congress, through Article 21 of the UCMJ, has "incorporated by reference" the common law of war, which may render triable by military commission certain offenses not defined by statute. When, however, neither the elements of the offense nor the range of permissible punishments is defined by statute or treaty, the precedent must be plain and unambiguous. To demand any less would be to risk concentrating in military hands a degree of adjudicative and punitive power in excess of that contemplated either by statute or by the Constitution....

[That] burden is far from satisfied here. The crime of "conspiracy" has rarely if ever been tried as such in this country by any law-of-war military commission not exercising some other form of jurisdiction, and does not appear in either the Geneva Conventions or the Hague Conventions—the major treaties on the law of war.... [The plurality's lengthy discussion of the historical precedent is omitted].

The charge's shortcomings are not merely formal, but are indicative of a broader inability on the Executive's part here to satisfy the most basic precondition—at least in the absence of specific congressional authorization—for establishment of military commissions: military necessity. Hamdan's tribunal was appointed not by a military commander in the field of battle, but by a retired major general stationed away from any active hostilities. Hamdan is charged not with an overt act for which he was caught redhanded in a theater of war and which military efficiency demands be tried expeditiously, but with an *agreement* the inception of which long predated the attacks of September 11, 2001 and the AUMF. That may well be a crime,[41] but it is not an offense that "by the law of war may be tried by military commissio[n]." None of the overt acts alleged to have been committed in furtherance of the agreement is itself a war crime, or even necessarily occurred during time of, or in a theater of, war. Any urgent need for imposition or execution of judgment is utterly belied by the record; Hamdan was arrested in November 2001 and he was not charged until mid-2004. These simply are not the circumstances in which, by any stretch of the historical evidence or this Court's precedents, a military commission established by Executive Order under the authority of Article 21 of the UCMJ may lawfully try a person and subject him to punishment.

VI

Whether or not the Government has charged Hamdan with an offense against the law of war cognizable by military commission, the commission lacks power to proceed. The UCMJ conditions the President's use of military commissions on compliance not only with the American common law of war, but also with the rest of the UCMJ itself, insofar as applicable, and with the "rules and precepts of the law of nations," including, *inter alia,* the four Geneva Conventions signed in 1949. The procedures that the Government has decreed will govern Hamdan's trial by commission violate these laws.

A

[Under Commission Order No. 1, the rights of the the accused] are subject [to] one glaring condition: The accused and his civilian counsel may be excluded from, and precluded from ever learning, what evidence was presented during any part of the proceeding that either the Appointing Authority or the presiding officer decides to "close." Grounds for such closure "include the protection of information classified or classifiable... ; information protected by law or rule from unauthorized disclosure; the physical safety of participants in Commission proceedings, including prospective witnesses; intelligence and law enforcement sources, methods, or activities; and other national security interests." Appointed military defense counsel must be privy to these closed sessions, but may, at the

---

41. Justice Thomas' suggestion that our conclusion precludes the Government from bringing to justice those who conspire to commit acts of terrorism is therefore wide of the mark. That conspiracy is not a violation of the law of war triable by military commission does not mean the Government may not, for example, prosecute by court-martial or in federal court those caught "plotting terrorist atrocities like the bombing of the Khobar Towers."

presiding officer's discretion, be forbidden to reveal to his or her client what took place therein.

Another striking feature of the rules governing Hamdan's commission is that they permit the admission of *any* evidence that, in the opinion of the presiding officer, "would have probative value to a reasonable person." Under this test, not only is testimonial hearsay and evidence obtained through coercion fully admissible, but neither live testimony nor witnesses' written statements need be sworn. Moreover, the accused and his civilian counsel may be denied access to evidence in the form of "protected information" [which includes classified information as well as "information protected by law or rule from unauthorized disclosure" and "information concerning other national security interests,"] so long as the presiding officer concludes that the evidence is "probative" [and] that its admission without the accused's knowledge would not "result in the denial of a full and fair trial." Finally, a presiding officer's determination that evidence "would not have probative value to a reasonable person" may be overridden by a majority of the other commission members.

Once all the evidence is in, the commission members (not including the presiding officer) must vote on the accused's guilt. A two-thirds vote will suffice for both a verdict of guilty and for imposition of any sentence not including death (the imposition of which requires a unanimous vote). Any appeal is taken to a three-member review panel composed of military officers and designated by the Secretary of Defense, only one member of which need have experience as a judge. The review panel is directed to "disregard any variance from procedures specified in this Order or elsewhere that would not materially have affected the outcome of the trial before the Commission." Once the panel makes its recommendation to the Secretary of Defense, the Secretary can either remand for further proceedings or forward the record to the President with his recommendation as to final disposition. The President then, unless he has delegated the task to the Secretary, makes the "final decision." He may change the commission's findings or sentence only in a manner favorable to the accused.....

C

In part because the difference between military commissions and courts-martial originally was a difference of jurisdiction alone, and in part to protect against abuse and ensure evenhandedness under the pressures of war, the procedures governing trials by military commission historically have been the same as those governing courts-martial....

There is a glaring historical exception to this general rule. The procedures and evidentiary rules used to try General Yamashita near the end of World War II deviated in significant respects from those then governing courts-martial. The force of that precedent, however, has been seriously undermined by post-World War II developments....

The procedures and rules of evidence employed during Yamashita's trial departed so far from those used in courts-martial that they generated an unusually long and vociferous critique from two Members of this Court [citing the dissenting opinion of Justice Rutledge, joined by Justice Murphy, in In re Yamashita, 327 U.S. 1 (1946)]. Among the dissenters' primary concerns was that the commission had free rein to consider all evidence "which in the commission's opinion 'would be of assistance in proving or disproving the charge,' without any of the usual modes of authentication."

The majority, however, did not pass on the merits of Yamashita's procedural challenges because it concluded that his status disentitled him to any protection under the Articles of War (specifically, those set forth in Article 38, which would become Article 36 of the UCMJ) or the Geneva Convention of 1929. The Court explained that Yamashita was neither a "person made subject to the Articles of War by Article 2" thereof, nor a protected prisoner of war being tried for crimes committed during his detention.

At least partially in response to subsequent criticism of General Yamashita's trial, the UCMJ's codification of the Articles of War after World War II expanded the category of persons subject thereto to include defendants in Yamashita's (and Hamdan's) position, and the Third Geneva Convention of 1949 extended prisoner-of-war protections to individuals tried for crimes committed before their capture. The most notorious exception to the principle of uniformity, then, has been stripped of its precedential value.

The uniformity principle is not an inflexible one; it does not preclude all departures from the procedures dictated for use by courts-martial. But any departure must be tailored to the exigency that necessitates it. That understanding is reflected in Article 36 of the UCMJ, which provides:

> "(a) The procedure, including modes of proof, in cases before courts-martial, courts of inquiry, military commissions, and other military tribunals may be prescribed by the President by regulations which shall, so far as he considers practicable, apply the principles of law and the rules of evidence generally recognized in the trial of criminal cases in the United States district courts, but which may not be contrary to or inconsistent with this chapter.
> "(b) All rules and regulations made under this article shall be uniform insofar as practicable and shall be reported to Congress."...

[Without] reaching the question whether any provision of Commission Order No. 1 is strictly "contrary to or inconsistent with" other provisions of the UCMJ, we conclude that the "practicability" determination the President has made is insufficient to justify variances from the procedures governing courts-martial....

The President here has determined, pursuant to subsection (a), that it is impracticable to apply the rules and principles of law that govern "the trial of criminal cases in the United States district courts," § 836(a), to Hamdan's commission. We assume that complete deference is owed that determination. The President has not, however, made a similar official determination that it is impracticable to apply the rules for courts-martial. And even if subsection (b)'s requirements may be satisfied without such an official determination, the requirements of that subsection are not satisfied here.

Nothing in the record before us demonstrates that it would be impracticable to apply court-martial rules in this case. . . .

The absence of any showing of impracticability is particularly disturbing when considered in light of the clear and admitted failure to apply one of the most fundamental protections afforded not just by the Manual for Courts-Martial but also by the UCMJ itself: the right to be present. Whether or not that departure technically is "contrary to or inconsistent with" the terms of the UCMJ, 10 U.S.C. § 836(a), the jettisoning of so basic a right cannot lightly be excused as "practicable."

Under the circumstances, then, the rules applicable in courts-martial must apply. Since it is undisputed that Commission Order No. 1 deviates in many significant respects from those rules, it necessarily violates Article 36(b).

The Government's objection that requiring compliance with the court-martial rules imposes an undue burden both ignores the plain meaning of Article 36(b) and misunderstands the purpose and the history of military commissions. The military commission was not born of a desire to dispense a more summary form of justice than is afforded by courts-martial; it developed, rather, as a tribunal of necessity to be employed when courts-martial lacked jurisdiction over either the accused or the subject matter. Exigency lent the commission its legitimacy, but did not further justify the wholesale jettisoning of procedural protections. . . .

D

The procedures adopted to try Hamdan also violate the Geneva Conventions. . . .

i

The Court of Appeals relied on Johnson v. Eisentrager, 339 U.S. 763 (1950) to hold that Hamdan could not invoke the Geneva Conventions to challenge the Government's plan to prosecute him in accordance with Commission Order No. 1. *Eisentrager* involved a challenge by 21 German nationals to their 1945 convictions for war crimes by a military tribunal convened in Nanking, China, and to their subsequent imprisonment in occupied Germany. The petitioners

97

argued, *inter alia,* that the 1929 Geneva Convention rendered illegal some of the procedures employed during their trials, which they said deviated impermissibly from the procedures used by courts-martial to try American soldiers. We rejected that claim on the merits because the petitioners (unlike Hamdan here) had failed to identify any prejudicial disparity "between the Commission that tried [them] and those that would try an offending soldier of the American forces of like rank," and in any event could claim no protection, under the 1929 Convention, during trials for crimes that occurred before their confinement as prisoners of war.

Buried in a footnote of the opinion, however, is this curious statement suggesting that the Court lacked power even to consider the merits of the Geneva Convention argument:

> "We are not holding that these prisoners have no right which the military authorities are bound to respect. The United States, by the Geneva Convention of July 27, 1929, concluded with forty-six other countries, including the German Reich, an agreement upon the treatment to be accorded captives. These prisoners claim to be and are entitled to its protection. It is, however, the obvious scheme of the Agreement that responsibility for observance and enforcement of these rights is upon political and military authorities. Rights of alien enemies are vindicated under it only through protests and intervention of protecting powers as the rights of our citizens against foreign governments are vindicated only by Presidential intervention."

The Court of Appeals, on the strength of this footnote, held that "the 1949 Geneva Convention does not confer upon Hamdan a right to enforce its provisions in court."

Whatever else might be said about the *Eisentrager* footnote, it does not control this case. [For], regardless of the nature of the rights conferred on Hamdan, they are, as the Government does not dispute, part of the law of war. And compliance with the law of war is the condition upon which the authority set forth in Article 21 is granted.

ii

[A]s an alternative to its holding that Hamdan could not invoke the Geneva Conventions at all, the Court of Appeals concluded that the Conventions did not in any event apply to the armed conflict during which Hamdan was captured....

Article 3, often referred to as Common Article 3 because, like Article 2, it appears in all four Geneva Conventions, provides that in a "conflict not of an international character occurring in the territory of one of the High Contracting Parties, each Party to the conflict shall be bound to apply, as a minimum," certain provisions protecting "[p]ersons taking no active part in the hostilities, including members of armed forces who have laid down their arms and those placed *hors de combat* by ?. . detention." One such provision prohibits "the passing of sentences and the carrying out of executions without previous judgment pronounced by a regularly constituted court affording all the judicial guarantees which are recognized as indispensable by civilized peoples."

The Court of Appeals thought, and the Government asserts, that Common Article 3 does not apply to Hamdan because the conflict with al Qaeda, being " 'international in scope,' " does not qualify as a ' "conflict not of an international character." ' That reasoning is erroneous. The term "conflict not of an international character" is used here in contradistinction to a conflict between nations. So much is demonstrated by the "fundamental logic [of] the Convention's provisions on its application." Common Article 2 provides that "the present Convention shall apply to all cases of declared war or of any other armed conflict which may arise between two or more of the High Contracting Parties." [Common] Article 3, by contrast, affords some minimal protection, falling short of full protection under the Conventions, to individuals associated with neither a signatory nor even a nonsignatory "Power" who are involved in a conflict "in the territory of" a signatory. The latter kind of conflict is distinguishable from the conflict described in Common Article 2 chiefly because it does not involve a clash between nations whether signatories or not. In context, then, the phrase "not of an international character" bears its literal meaning. . . .

iii

Common Article 3, then, is applicable here and, as indicated above, requires that Hamdan be tried by a "regularly constituted court affording all the judicial guarantees which are recognized as indispensable by civilized peoples." While the term "regularly constituted court" is not specifically defined in either Common Article 3 or its accompanying commentary, other sources disclose its core meaning. The commentary accompanying a provision of the Fourth Geneva Convention, for example, defines " 'regularly constituted' " tribunals to include "ordinary military courts" and "definitely exclud[e] all special tribunals." . . .

The Government offers only a cursory defense of Hamdan's military commission in light of Common Article 3. As Justice Kennedy explains, that defense fails because "[t]he regular military courts in our system are the courts-martial established by congressional statutes." At a minimum, a military commission "can be 'regularly constituted' by the standards of our military justice system only if some practical need explains deviations from court-martial practice." As we have explained, see Part VI-C, *supra,* no such need has been demonstrated here.

iv

[This portion of Justice Stevens' opinion is joined only by Justices Souter, Ginsburg, and Breyer].

Inextricably intertwined with the question of regular constitution is the evaluation of the procedures governing the tribunal and whether they afford "all the judicial guarantees which are recognized as indispensable by civilized peoples." Like the phrase "regularly constituted court," this phrase is not defined in the text of the Geneva Conventions. But it must be understood to incorporate at least the barest of those trial protections that have been recognized by customary international law. Many of these are described in Article 75 of Protocol I to the Geneva Conventions of 1949, adopted in 1977 (Protocol I). Although the United States declined to ratify Protocol I, its objections were not to Article 75 thereof. Indeed, it appears that the Government "regard[s] the provisions of Article 75 as an articulation of safeguards to which all persons in the hands of an enemy are entitled. Among the rights set forth in Article 75 is the "right to be tried in [one's] presence."

We agree with Justice Kennedy that the procedures adopted to try Hamdan deviate from those governing courts-martial in ways not justified by any "evident practical need," and for that reason, at least, fail to afford the requisite guarantees. We add only that, as noted in Part VI-A, *supra,* various provisions of Commission Order No. 1 dispense with the principles, articulated in Article 75 and indisputably part of the customary international law, that an accused must, absent disruptive conduct or consent, be present for his trial and must be privy to the evidence against him. That the Government has a compelling interest in denying Hamdan access to certain sensitive information is not doubted. But, at least absent express statutory provision to the contrary, information used to convict a person of a crime must be disclosed to him....

VII

We have assumed, as we must, that the allegations made in the Government's charge against Hamdan are true. We have assumed, moreover, the truth of the message implicit in that charge — viz., that Hamdan is a dangerous individual whose beliefs, if acted upon, would cause great harm and even death to innocent civilians, and who would act upon those beliefs if given the opportunity. It bears emphasizing that Hamdan does not challenge, and we do not today address, the Government's power to detain him for the duration of active hostilities in order to prevent such harm. But in undertaking to try Hamdan and subject him to criminal punishment, the Executive is bound to comply with the Rule of Law that prevails in this jurisdiction.

The judgment of the Court of Appeals is reversed, and the case is remanded for further proceedings.

It is so ordered.

JUSTICE BREYER, with whom JUSTICE KENNEDY, JUSTICE SOUTER, and JUSTICE GINSBURG join, concurring.

The dissenters say that today's decision would "sorely hamper the President's ability to confront and defeat a new and deadly enemy." They suggest that it undermines our Nation's ability to "preven[t] future attacks" of the grievous sort that we have already suffered. That claim leads me to state briefly what I believe the majority sets forth both explicitly and implicitly at greater length. The Court's conclusion ultimately rests upon a single ground: Congress has not issued the Executive a "blank check." Cf. [*Hamdi* (plurality opinion)]. Indeed, Congress has denied the President the legislative authority to create military commissions of the kind at issue here. Nothing prevents the President from returning to Congress to seek the authority he believes necessary.

Where, as here, no emergency prevents consultation with Congress, judicial insistence upon that consultation does not weaken our Nation's ability to deal with danger. To the contrary, that insistence strengthens the Nation's ability to determine — through democratic means — how best to do so. The Constitution places its faith in those democratic means. Our Court today simply does the same.

JUSTICE KENNEDY, with whom JUSTICE SOUTER, JUSTICE GINSBURG, and JUSTICE BREYER join as to Parts I and II, concurring in part.

Military Commission Order No. 1, which governs the military commission established to try petitioner Salim Hamdan for war crimes, exceeds limits that certain statutes, duly enacted by Congress, have placed on the President's authority to convene military courts. This is not a case, then, where the Executive can assert some unilateral authority to fill a void left by congressional inaction. It is a case where Congress, in the proper exercise of its powers as an independent branch of government, and as part of a long tradition of legislative involvement in matters of military justice, has considered the subject of military tribunals and set limits on the President's authority. Where a statute provides the conditions for the exercise of governmental power, its requirements are the result of a deliberative and reflective process engaging both of the political branches. Respect for laws derived from the customary operation of the Executive and Legislative Branches gives some assurance of stability in time of crisis. The Constitution is best preserved by reliance on standards tested over time and insulated from the pressures of the moment.

These principles seem vindicated here, for a case that may be of extraordinary importance is resolved by ordinary rules. The rules of most relevance here are those pertaining to the authority of Congress and the interpretation of its enactments.

It seems appropriate to recite these rather fundamental points because the Court refers, as it should in its exposition of the case, to the requirement of the Geneva Conventions of 1949 that military tribunals be "regularly constituted" — a requirement that controls here, if for no other reason, because Congress requires that military commissions like the ones at issue conform to the "law of war." Whatever the substance and content of the term "regularly constituted" as interpreted in this and any later cases, there seems little doubt that it relies upon the importance of standards deliberated upon and chosen in advance of crisis, under a system where the single power of the Executive is checked by other constitutional mechanisms. All of which returns us to the point of beginning — that domestic statutes control this case. If Congress, after due consideration, deems it appropriate to change the controlling statutes, in conformance with the Constitution and other laws, it has the power and prerogative to do so....

I

Trial by military commission raises separation-of-powers concerns of the highest order. Located within a single branch, these courts carry the risk that offenses will be defined, prosecuted, and adjudicated by executive officials without independent review. Concentration of power puts personal liberty in peril of arbitrary action by officials, an incursion the Constitution's three-part system is designed to avoid. It is imperative, then, that when military tribunals are established, full and proper authority exists for the Presidential directive.

The proper framework for assessing whether Executive actions are authorized is the three-part scheme used by Justice Jackson in his opinion in [*Youngstown.*] "When the President acts pursuant to an express or implied authorization of Congress, his authority is at its maximum, for it includes all that he possesses in his own right plus all that Congress can delegate." "When the President acts in absence of either a congressional grant or denial of authority, he can only rely upon his own independent powers, but there is a zone of twilight in which he and Congress may have concurrent authority, or in which its distribution is uncertain." And "[w]hen the President takes measures incompatible with the expressed or implied will of Congress, his power is at its lowest ebb."

In this case, as the Court observes, the President has acted in a field with a history of congressional participation and regulation. [The] UCMJ as a whole establishes an intricate system of military justice. [While] these laws provide authority for certain forms of military courts, they also impose limitations, at least two of which control this case. If the President has exceeded these limits, this becomes a case of conflict between Presidential and congressional action — a case within Justice Jackson's third category, not the second or first....

[In the next part of his opinion, Justice Kennedy argued that the military commissions violate the UCMJ requirement that "insofar as practicable" all rules and regulations must be uniform and the requirement that military commissions comport with statutes and the laws of war].

Assuming the President has authority to establish a special military commission to try Hamdan, the commission must satisfy Common Article 3's requirement of a "regularly constituted court affording all the judicial guarantees which are recognized as indispensable by civilized people." The terms of this general standard are yet to be elaborated and further defined, but Congress has required compliance with it by referring to the "law of war" in § 821. The Court correctly concludes that the military commission here does not comply with this provision.

Common Article 3's standard of a "regularly constituted court affording all the judicial guarantees which are recognized as indispensable by civilized peoples," supports, at the least, a uniformity principle similar to that codified in § 836(b). The concept of a "regularly constituted court" providing "indispensable" judicial guarantees requires consideration of the system of justice under which the commission is established, though no doubt certain minimum standards are applicable.

The regular military courts in our system are the courts-martial established by congressional statutes. Acts of Congress confer on those courts the jurisdiction to try "any person" subject to war crimes prosecution. 10 U.S.C. § 818. As the Court explains, moreover, while special military commissions have been convened in previous armed conflicts — a practice recognized in § 821 — those military commissions generally have adopted the structure and procedure of courts-martial....

In addition, whether or not the possibility, contemplated by the regulations here, of midtrial procedural changes could by itself render a military commission impermissibly irregular, an acceptable degree of independence from the Executive is necessary to render a commission "regularly constituted" by the standards of our Nation's system of justice. And any suggestion of Executive power to interfere with an ongoing judicial process raises concerns about the proceedings' fairness....

At a minimum a military commission like the one at issue — a commission specially convened by the President to try specific persons without express congressional authorization — can be "regularly constituted" by the standards of our military justice system only if some practical need explains deviations from court-martial practice....

II

[The] circumstances of Hamdan's trial present no exigency requiring special speed or precluding careful consideration of evidence. For roughly four years, Hamdan has been detained at a permanent United States military base in Guantanamo Bay, Cuba. And regardless of the outcome of the criminal proceedings at issue, the Government claims authority to continue to detain him based on his status as an enemy combatant....

In sum, as presently structured, Hamdan's military commission exceeds the bounds Congress has placed on the President's authority in §§ 836 and 821 of the UCMJ. Because Congress has prescribed these limits, Congress can change them, requiring a new analysis consistent with the Constitution and other governing laws. At this time, however, we must apply the standards Congress has provided. By those standards the military commission is deficient.

III

In light of the conclusion that the military commission here is unauthorized under the UCMJ, I see no need to consider several further issues addressed in the plurality opinion by Justice Stevens and the dissent by Justice Thomas.

First, I would not decide whether Common Article 3's standard — a "regularly constituted court affording all the judicial guarantees which are recognized as indispensable by civilized peoples" — necessarily requires that the accused have the right to be present at all stages of a criminal trial...

I likewise see no need to address the validity of the conspiracy charge against [Hamdan]....

Finally, [I] express no view on the merits of other limitations on military commissions described as elements of the common law of war in Part V of Justice Stevens' opinion....

[Justice Scalia wrote a dissenting opinion, joined by Justices Thomas and Alito, which argued that the DTA deprived the Court of jurisdiction.]

JUSTICE THOMAS, with whom JUSTICE SCALIA joins, and with whom JUSTICE ALITO joins in all but Parts I, II-C-1, and III-B-2, dissenting.

[The Court's] opinion openly flouts our well-established duty to respect the Executive's judgment in matters of military operations and foreign affairs. The Court's evident belief that *it* is qualified to pass on the "[m]ilitary necessity" of the Commander in Chief's decision to employ a particular form of force against our enemies is so antithetical to our constitutional structure that it simply cannot go unanswered. I respectfully dissent.

I

Our review of petitioner's claims arises in the context of the President's wartime exercise of his commander-in-chief authority in conjunction with the complete support of Congress. Accordingly, it is important to take measure of the respective roles the Constitution assigns to the three branches of our Government in the conduct of war.

[The] structural advantages attendant to the Executive Branch — namely, the decisiveness, "'activity, secrecy, and dispatch'" that flow from the Executive's "unity'" — led the Founders to conclude that the "President ha[s] primary responsibility — along with the necessary power — to protect the national security and to conduct the Nation's foreign relations." Consistent with this conclusion, the Constitution vests in the President "[t]he executive Power," Art. II, § 1, provides that he "shall be Commander in Chief" of the Armed Forces, § 2, and places in him the power to recognize foreign governments, § 3. This Court has observed that these provisions confer upon the President broad constitutional authority to protect the Nation's security in the manner he deems fit. See, e.g., [the *Prize Cases*].

Congress, to be sure, has a substantial and essential role in both foreign affairs and national security. But "Congress cannot anticipate and legislate with regard to every possible action the President may find it necessary to take or every possible situation in which he might act," and "[s]uch failure of Congress... does not, 'especially... in the areas of foreign policy and national security,' imply 'congressional disapproval' of action taken by the Executive." [*Dames & Moore*]. Rather, in these domains, the fact that Congress has provided the President with broad authorities does not imply — and the Judicial Branch should not infer — that Congress intended to deprive him of particular powers not specifically enumerated. See [*Dames & Moore*].

When "the President acts pursuant to an express or implied authorization from Congress," his actions are ' "supported by the strongest of presumptions and the widest latitude of judicial interpretation, and the burden of persuasion... rest[s] heavily upon any who might attack it." ' Id. [quoting *Youngstown*, Jackson, J., concurring]. Accordingly, in the very context that we address today, this Court has concluded that "the detention and trial of petitioners — ordered by the President in the declared exercise of his powers as Commander in Chief of the Army in time of war and of grave public danger — are not to be set aside by the courts without the clear conviction that they are in conflict with the Constitution or laws of Congress constitutionally enacted." [*Ex parte Quirin.*]

Under this framework, the President's decision to try Hamdan before a military commission for his involvement with al Qaeda is entitled to a heavy measure of deference. In the present conflict, Congress has authorized the President "to use all necessary and appropriate force against those nations, organizations, or persons *he determines* planned, authorized, committed, or aided the terrorist attacks that occurred on September 11, 2001... in order to prevent any future acts of international terrorism against the United States by such nations, organizations or persons." [AUMF, emphasis added]. As a plurality of the Court observed in *Hamdi*, the "capture, detention, and *trial* of unlawful combatants, by 'universal agreement and practice,' are 'important incident[s] of war,' " [emphasis added] and are therefore "an exercise of the 'necessary and appropriate force' Congress has authorized the President to use." [*Hamdi*, Thomas, J., dissenting]....

Although the Court concedes the legitimacy of the President's use of military commissions in certain circumstances, it suggests that the AUMF has no bearing on the scope of the President's power to utilize military commissions in the present conflict. Instead, the Court determines the scope of this power based exclusively on [§ 821]. As I shall discuss below, [§ 821] alone supports the use of commissions here. Nothing in the language of [§ 821], however, suggests that it outlines the entire reach of congressional authorization of military commissions in all conflicts. Accordingly, congressional authorization for military commissions pertaining to the instant conflict derives not only from [§ 821], but also from the more recent, and broader, authorization contained in the AUMF....

II

[In omitted sections of his opinion, Justice Thomas argued that the military commission had jurisdiction over Hamdan and over the offense with which he was charged.]

Today a plurality of this Court would hold that conspiracy to massacre innocent civilians does not violate the laws of war. This determination is unsustainable. The judgment of the political branches that Hamdan, and others like him, must be held accountable before military commissions for their involvement with and membership in an unlawful organization dedicated to inflicting massive civilian casualties is supported by virtually every relevant authority, including all of the authorities invoked by the plurality today. It is also supported by the nature of the present conflict. We are not engaged in a traditional battle with a nation-state, but with a worldwide, hydra-headed enemy, who lurks in the shadows conspiring to reproduce the atrocities of September 11, 2001, and who has boasted of sending suicide bombers into civilian gatherings, has proudly distributed videotapes of beheadings of civilian workers, and has tortured and dismembered captured American soldiers. But according to the plurality, when our Armed Forces capture those who are plotting terrorist atrocities like the bombing of the Khobar Towers, the bombing of the U.S.S. *Cole,* and the attacks of September 11—even if their plots are advanced to the very brink of fulfillment—our military cannot charge those criminals with any offense against the laws of war. Instead, our troops must catch the terrorists "redhanded," in the midst of *the attack itself,* in order to bring them to justice. Not only is this conclusion fundamentally inconsistent with the cardinal principle of the law of war, namely protecting non-combatants, but it would sorely hamper the President's ability to confront and defeat a new and deadly enemy.

After seeing the plurality overturn longstanding precedents in order to seize jurisdiction over this case, and after seeing them disregard the clear prudential counsel that they abstain in these circumstances from using equitable powers, it is no surprise to see them go on to overrule one after another of the President's judgments pertaining to the conduct of an ongoing war. Those Justices who today disregard the commander-in-chief's wartime decisions, only 10 days ago deferred to the judgment of the Corps of Engineers with regard to a matter much more within the competence of lawyers, upholding that agency's wildly implausible conclusion that a storm drain is a tributary of the waters of the United States. See Rapanos v. United States, 547 U.S. _____ (2006) [Justice Thomas' reference is to a case decided earlier in the Term, in which the Court interpreted the words "navigable waters" in the Clean Water Act]. It goes without saying that there is much more at stake here than storm drains. The plurality's willingness to second-guess the determination of the political branches that these conspirators must be brought to justice is both unprecedented and dangerous.

III

The Court holds that even if "the Government has charged Hamdan with an offense against the law of war cognizable by military commission, the commission lacks power to proceed" because of its failure to comply with the terms of the UCMJ and the four Geneva Conventions signed in 1949. This position is untenable.

A

As with the jurisdiction of military commissions, the procedure of such commissions "has [not] been prescribed by statute," but "has been adapted in each instance to the need that called it forth." [Madsen v. Kinsella, 343 U.S. 341 (1952).] Indeed, this Court has concluded that "[i]n the absence of attempts by Congress to limit the President's power, it appears that, as Commander in Chief of the Army and Navy of the United States, he may, in time of war, establish and prescribe the jurisdiction and procedure of military commissions." Id., at 348....

Nothing in the text of Article 36(b) supports the Court's sweeping conclusion that it represents an unprecedented congressional effort to change the nature of military commissions from common-law war courts to tribunals that must presumptively function like courts-martial. And such an interpretation would be strange indeed. The vision of uniformity that motivated the adoption of the UCMJ, embodied specifically in Article 36(b), is nothing more than uniformity across the separate branches of the armed services. There is no indication that the UCMJ was intended to require uniformity in procedure between courts-martial and military commissions, tribunals that the UCMJ itself recognizes are different. To the contrary, the UCMJ expressly recognizes that different tribunals will be constituted in different manners and employ different procedures. See 10 U.S.C. § 866 (providing for three different types of courts-martial — general, special, and summary — constituted in different manners and employing different procedures). Thus, Article 36(b) is best under-stood as establishing that, so far as practicable, the rules and regulations governing tribunals convened by the Navy must be uniform with the rules and regulations governing tribunals convened by the Army. But, consistent with this Court's prior interpretations of Article 21 and over a century of historical practice, it cannot be understood to require the President to con-form the procedures employed by military commissions to those employed by courts-martial.

Even if Article 36(b) could be construed to require procedural uniformity among the various tribunals contemplated by the UCMJ, Hamdan would not be entitled to relief....

The Court provides no explanation why the President's determination that employing court-martial procedures in the military commissions established pursuant to Military Commission Order No. 1 would hamper our war effort is in any way inadequate to satisfy its newly minted "practicability" requirement. On the contrary, this determination is precisely the kind for which the "Judi-ciary has neither aptitude, facilities nor responsibility and which has long been held to belong in the domain of political power not subject to judicial intrusion or inquiry." Chicago & Southern Air Lines, Inc. v. Waterman S.S. Corp., 333 U.S. 103, 111 (1948). And, in the context of the present conflict, it is exactly the kind of determination Congress countenanced when it authorized the President to use all necessary and appropriate force against our enemies....

B

The Court contends that Hamdan's military commission is also unlawful because it violates Common Article 3 of the Geneva Conventions. Furthermore, Hamdan contends that his commission is unlawful because it violates various provisions of the Third Geneva Convention. These contentions are untenable.

1

As an initial matter [both] of Hamdan's Geneva Convention claims are foreclosed by *Eisentrager*. In that case the respondents claimed, *inter alia,* that their military commission lacked jurisdiction because it failed to provide them with certain procedural safeguards that they argued were required under the Geneva Conventions. While this Court rejected the underlying merits of the respondents' Geneva Convention claims, also held, in the alternative, that the respondents could "not assert... that anything in the Geneva Convention makes them immune from prosecution or punishment for war crimes,"...

[The] Court concludes that petitioner may seek judicial enforcement of the provisions of the Geneva Conventions because "they are... part of the law of war. And compliance with the law of war is the condition upon which the authority set forth in Article 21 is granted." But Article 21 authorizes the use of military commissions; it does not purport to render judicially enforceable aspects of the law of war that are not so enforceable of their own accord....

In any event, the Court's argument is too clever by half. The judicial non-enforceability of the Geneva Conventions derives from the fact that those Conventions have exclusive enforcement mechanisms, and this, too, is part of the law of war. The Court's position thus rests on the assumption that Article 21's reference to the "laws of war" selectively incorporates only those aspects of the Geneva Conventions that the Court finds convenient, namely, the substantive requirements of Common Article 3, and not those aspects of the Conventions that the Court, for whatever reason, disfavors, namely the Conventions' exclusive diplomatic enforcement scheme....

Even if the Court were correct that Article 21 of the UCMJ renders judicially enforceable aspects of the law of war that are not so enforceable by their own terms, Article 21 simply cannot be interpreted to render judicially enforceable the particular provision of the law of war at issue here, namely Common Article 3 of the Geneva Conventions. As relevant, Article 21 provides that "[t]he provisions of this chapter conferring jurisdiction upon courts-martial do not deprive military commissions ... of concurrent jurisdiction with respect to *offenders or offenses* that by statute *or by the law of war* may be tried by military commissions" (emphasis added). Thus, to the extent Article 21 can be interpreted as authorizing judicial enforcement of aspects of the law of war that are not otherwise judicially enforceable, that authorization only extends to provisions of the law of war that relate to whether a particular "offender" or a particular "offense" is triable by military commission. Common Article 3 of the Geneva Conventions, the sole provision of the Geneva Conventions relevant to the Court's holding, relates to neither. Rather, it relates exclusively to the particulars of the tribunal itself, namely, whether it is "regularly constituted" and whether it "afford[s] all the judicial guarantees which are recognized as indispensable by civilized peoples."

2

In addition to being foreclosed by *Eisentrager,* Hamdan's claim under Common Article 3 of the Geneva Conventions is meritless. Common Article 3 applies to "armed conflict not of an international character occurring in the territory of one of the High Contracting Parties." "Pursuant to [his] authority as Commander in Chief and Chief Executive of the United States," the President has "accept[ed] the legal conclusion of the Department of Justice ... that common Article 3 of Geneva does not apply to ... al Qaeda ... detainees, because, among other reasons, the relevant conflicts are international in scope and common Article 3 applies only to 'armed conflict not of an international character.'" Under this Court's precedents, "the meaning attributed to treaty provisions by the Government agencies charged with their negotiation and enforcement is entitled to great weight." Sumitomo Shoji America, Inc. v. Avagliano, 457 U.S. 176, 184-185 (1982); United States v. Stuart, 489 U.S. 353, 369 (1989). Our duty to defer to the President's understanding of the provision at issue here is only heightened by the fact that he is acting pursuant to his constitutional authority as Commander in Chief and by the fact that the subject matter of Common Article 3 calls for a judgment about the nature and character of an armed conflict.

The President's interpretation of Common Article 3 is reasonable and should be sustained. The conflict with al Qaeda is international in character in the sense that it is occurring in various nations around the globe. Thus, it is also "occurring in the territory of" more than "one of the High Contracting Parties." The Court does not dispute the President's judgments respecting the nature of our conflict with al Qaeda, nor does it suggest that the President's interpretation of Common Article 3 is implausible or foreclosed by the text of the treaty. Indeed, the Court concedes that Common Article 3 is principally concerned with "furnish[ing] minimal protection to rebels involved in . . . a civil war," precisely the type of conflict the President's interpretation envisions to be subject to Common Article 3. Instead, the Court, without acknowledging its duty to defer to the President, adopts its own, admittedly plausible, reading of Common Article 3. But where, as here, an ambiguous treaty provision ("not of an international character") is susceptible of two plausible, and reasonable, interpretations, our precedents require us to defer to the Executive's interpretation.

3

[I]n any event, Hamdan's military commission complies with the requirements of Common Article 3. It is plainly "regularly constituted" because such commissions have been employed throughout our history to try unlawful combatants for crimes against the law of war. . . .

[The] plurality concludes that Hamdan's commission is unlawful because of the possibility that Hamdan will be barred from proceedings and denied access to evidence that may be used to convict him. But, under the commissions' rules, the Government may not impose such bar or denial on Hamdan if it would render his trial unfair, a question that is clearly within the scope of the appellate review contemplated by regulation and statute.

Moreover, while the Executive is surely not required to offer a particularized defense of these procedures prior to their application, the procedures themselves make clear that Hamdan would only be excluded (other than for disruption) if it were necessary to protect classified (or classifiable) intelligence, including the sources and methods for gathering such intelligence. The Government has explained that "we want to make sure that these proceedings, which are going on in the middle of the war, do not interfere with our war effort and . . . because of the way we would be able to handle interrogations and intelligence information, may actually assist us in promoting our war aims." [This] interest is surely compelling here....

In these circumstances, "civilized peoples" would take into account the context of military commission trials against unlawful combatants in the war on terrorism, including the need to keep certain information secret in the interest of preventing future attacks on our Nation and its foreign installations so long as it did not deprive the accused of a fair trial....

JUSTICE ALITO, with whom JUSTICES SCALIA and THOMAS join in Parts I-III, dissenting....

I

The second element [of Common Article 3, requiring that courts be "regularly constituted"] is the one on which the Court relies, and I interpret this element to require that the court be appointed or established in accordance with the appointing country's domestic law....

In order to determine whether a court has been properly appointed, set up, or established, it is necessary to refer to a body of law that governs such matters. I interpret Common Article 3 as looking to the domestic law of the appointing country because I am not aware of any international law standard regarding the way in which such a court must be appointed, set up, or established, and because different countries with different government structures handle this matter differently. Accordingly, "a regularly constituted court" is a court that has been appointed, set up, or established in accordance with the domestic law of the appointing country.

II

In contrast to this interpretation, the opinions supporting the judgment today hold that the military commission before which petitioner would be tried is not "a regularly constituted court" (a) because "no evident practical need explains" why its "structure and composition... deviate from conventional court-martial standards," and (b) because, contrary to 10 U.S.C. § 836(b), the procedures specified for use in the proceeding before the military commission impermissibly differ from those provided under the Uniform Code of Military Justice (UCMJ) for use by courts-martial, I do not believe that either of these grounds is sound.

A

I see no basis for the Court's holding that a military commission cannot be regarded as "a regularly constituted court" unless it is similar in structure and composition to a regular military court or unless there is an "evident practical need" for the divergence. There is no reason why a court that differs in structure or composition from an ordinary military court must be viewed as having been

111

improperly constituted. Tribunals that vary significantly in structure, composition, and procedures may all be "regularly" or "properly" constituted. Consider, for example, a municipal court, a state trial court of general jurisdiction, an Article I federal trial court, a federal district court, and an international court, such as the International Criminal Tribunal for the Former Yugoslavia. Although these courts are "differently constituted" and differ substantially in many other respects, they are all "regularly constituted." ...

B

I also disagree with the Court's conclusion that petitioner's military commission is "illegal," because its procedures allegedly do not comply with 10 U.S.C. § 836. Even if § 836(b), unlike Common Article 3, does impose at least a limited uniformity requirement amongst the tribunals contemplated by the UCMJ and even if it is assumed for the sake of argument that some of the procedures specified in Military Commission Order No. 1 impermissibly deviate from court-martial procedures, it does not follow that the military commissions created by that order are not "regularly constituted" or that trying petitioner before such a commission would be inconsistent with the law of war. If Congress enacted a statute requiring the federal district courts to follow a procedure that is unconstitutional, the statute would be invalid, but the district courts would not. Likewise, if some of the procedures that may be used in military commission proceedings are improper, the appropriate remedy is to proscribe the use of those particular procedures, not to outlaw the commissions. I see no justification for striking down the entire commission structure simply because it is possible that petitioner's trial might involve the use of some procedure that is improper....

* * *

Congress responded to *Hamdi* and *Hamdan* by enacting the Detainee Treatment Act, 119 Stat. 2739, and the Military Commissions Act, 120 Stat. 2600. The Detainee Treatment Act granted exclusive jurisdiction to the United States Court of Appeals for the District of Columbia Circuit to review decisions made by the Combatant Status Review Tribunal concerning the detention of putative enemy combatants. It limited that court's review to whether the status determination was consistent with procedures established by the Secretary of Defense and "to the extent that the Constitution and laws of the United States are applicable, whether the use of such standards and procedures to make the determination is consistent with the Constitution and laws of the United States." The Military Commissions Act vested the same court with exclusive jurisdiction to review judgments of military tribunals. It restricted this review to "matters of law" and provides that the Court is limited to consideration of "whether the final decision was consistent with the standards and procedures specified in this chapter" and "to the extent applicable, the Constitution and the laws of the United States."

In Boumediene v. Bush, 128 S. Ct. 2229 (2008), a 5-4 decision written by Justice Kennedy, the Supreme Court held that the Detainee Treatment Act unconstitutionally restricted the writ of habeas corpus and that the limited review in the United States Court of Appeals provided for in the Act was not an adequate substitute for habeas. (This portion of the opinion is discussed in the section of the Supplement dealing with Chapter One of the main volume). Some of the Court's language suggested that the due process rights for detainees outlined in *Hamdi* might not provide sufficient protection.

"[The] privilege of habeas corpus entitles the prisoner to a meaningful opportunity to demonstrate that he is being held pursuant to "the erroneous application or interpretation" of relevant law. And the habeas court must have the power to order the conditional release of an [individual]. But, depending on the circumstances, more may be required....

"Petitioners identify what they see as myriad deficiencies in the [Combat Status Review Tribunals (CSRTs)]. The most relevant for our purposes are the constraints upon the detainee's ability to rebut the factual basis for the Government's assertion that he is an enemy combatant. [The] detainee has limited means to find or present evidence to challenge the Government's case against him. He does not have the assistance of counsel and may not be aware of the most critical allegations that the Government relied upon to order his detention. [The] detainee can confront witnesses that testify during the CSRT proceeding. But given that there are in effect no limits on then admission of hearsay evidence [the] detainee's opportunity to question witnesses is likely to be more theoretical than real....

"The Government defends the CSRT process, arguing that it was designed to conform to the procedures suggested by the plurality in *Hamdi*. Setting aside the fact that the relevant language in *Hamdi* did not garner a majority of the Court, it does not control the matter at hand. None of the parties in *Hamdi* argued that there had been a suspension of the writ....

"Even if we were to assume that the CSRTs satisfy due process standards, it would not end our inquiry....

"For the writ of habeas corpus, or its substitute, to function as an effective and proper remedy in this context, the court that conducts the habeas proceeding must have the means to correct errors that occurred during the CSRT proceedings. This includes some authority to assess the sufficiency of the Government's evidence against the detainee. It also must have the authority to admit and consider relevant exculpatory evidence that was not introduced during the earlier proceedings.

Chief Justice Roberts wrote a dissenting opinion, which was joined by Justices Scalia, Thomas and Alito. Justice Scalia also wrote a dissenting opinion, which was joined by Chief Justice Roberts and Justices Thomas and Alito.

Page 397.   At the end of section 4 of the Note, add the following:

In 2006, Congress enacted 42 U.S.C. § 2000dd (the "McCain amendment"), which, in relevant part, provides as follows:

(a) No individual in the custody or under the physical control of the United States Government, regardless of nationality or physical location, shall be subject to cruel, inhuman, or degrading treatment or punishment. . . . .

(d) In this section, the term "cruel, inhuman, or degrading treatment or punishment" means the cruel, unusual, and inhumane treatment or punishment prohibited by the Fifth, Eighth, and Fourteenth Amendments to the Constitution of the United States, as defined in the United States Reservations, Declarations and Understandings to the United Nations Convention Against Torture and Other Forms of Cruel, Inhuman or Degrading Treatment or Punishment done at New York, December 10, 1984.

President Bush signed the measure into law, but made the following statement:

The executive branch shall construe Title X in Division A of the Act, relating to detainees, in a manner consistent with the constitutional authority of the President to supervise the unitary executive branch and as Commander in Chief and consistent with the constitutional limitations on the judicial power, which will assist in achieving the shared objective of the Congress and the President, evidenced in Title X, of protecting the American people from further terrorist attacks.

President's Statement on Signing of H.R. 2863, the "Department of Defense, Emergency Supplemental Appropriations to Address Hurricanes in the Gulf of Mexico, and Pandemic Influenza Act, 2006."

Is the President constitutionally obligated to obey the McCain amendment? In addition to the provisions discussed in *Hamdan*, Common Article 3 of the Geneva Conventions prohibits cruel treatment, torture, and "outrages upon personal dignity, in particular, humiliating and degrading treatment." What effect, if any, does *Hamdan*'s treatment of Common Article 3 have on the President's power with respect to the interrogation of "enemy combatants"?

4a. *Wiretapping.* In 2006, press reports revealed that the National Security Agency engaged in warrantless intercepts of telephone communications between individuals in the United States and individuals located outside the United States in circumstances where at least one participant in the conversation was suspect of terrorist activity. These intercepts appeared to violate the provisions of The Foreign Intelligence Surveillance Act, 50 U.S.C. § 1801 et seq., which set out detailed procedures for obtaining warrants for such searches. The President nonetheless insisted that they were legally permissible because they came within his powers as commander in chief. Relying upon *Hamdi*, he also insisted that the general terms of the AUMF authorized the intercepts, just as the AUMF authorized the detention of "enemy combatants." Do these arguments survive *Hamdan?*

Page 398.   After section 5 of the Note, add the following:

For an argument that the Supreme Court's "war on terror" jurisprudence has focused almost entirely on process without coming to grips with the substantive rights at stake, see Martinez, Process and Substance in the "War on Terror," 108 Colum. L. Rev. 1013 (2008).

6. *Intra-executive separation of powers?* Consider the following proposal:

It is often remarked that "9/11 changed everything"; particularly so in the war on terror, in which Congress has been absent or content to pass vague, open-ended statutes. The result is an executive that subsumes much of the tripartite structure of government....

If major decisions are going to be made by the President, then how might separation of powers be reflected within the executive branch? The first-best concept of "legislative v. executive" checks and balances must be updated to contemplate second-best "executive v. executive divisions."...

A critical mechanism to promote internal separation of powers is bureaucracy....

A well-functioning bureaucracy contains agencies with differing missions and objectives that intentionally overlap to create friction....

The apparatuses are familiar — separate and overlapping cabinet offices, mandatory review of government action by different agencies, civil-service protections for agency workers, reporting requirements to Congress, and an impartial decision-maker to resolve inter-agency conflicts. But these restraints have been informally laid down and inconsistently applied, and in the wake of September 11 they have been decimated. A general framework statute is needed to codify a set of practices. In many ways, the status quo is the worst of all worlds because it creates the facade of external and internal checks when both have withered.

Katyal, Internal Separation of Powers: Checking Today's Most Dangerous Branch from Within, 115 Yale L. J. 2314, 2316-18 (2006).

Page 403. Before the Note, add the following:

For a comprehensive historical study of the power of Congress to control Presidential war making, see Barron & Lederman, The Commander in Chief at the Lowest Ebb — Framing the Problem, Doctrine, and Original Understanding, 121 Harv. L. Rev. 687 (2008), and Barron & Lederman, The Commander in Chief at the Lowest Ebb — A Constitutional History, 121 Harv. L. Rev. 941 (2008). The authors conclude that

> However familiar may be the adage that the legislature may not "interfere[] with the command of the forces and the conduct of campaigns," Congress historically has not acted in accord with it. Throughout its history, Congress has [even] tried to manage the conduct of particular wars once they were under way by enacting statutes that were, in effect, attempts to second-guess or pretermit the President's judgment. [Several] of our most esteemed Presidents — Washington, Lincoln, and both Roosevelts, among others — never invoked the sort of preclusive claims of authority that some modern President appear to embrace without pause. In fact, no Chief Executive did so in any clear way until the onset of the Korean War, even when they confronted problematic restrictions, some of which could not be fully interpreted away and some of which even purported to regulate troop deployments and the actions of troops already deployed.

Id. at 947-48. See also Prakash, Unleashing the Dogs of War: What the Constitution Means by "Declare War," 93 Cornell Law Rev. 45, 50, 120-21 (2007):

> [The] grant of "declare war" power means that only Congress can decide whether the United States will wage war. The President cannot make this crucial decision because the Constitution never grants the Commander in Chief the power to declare war. [As] part of its authority to declare war, Congress may choose what type of war to fight. Congress may authorize a general war — land, sea, and air — against an enemy. Or Congress may authorize only limited offensive measures, such as a sea war only....
>
> In the eighteenth century all sorts of hostile statements and actions were seen as declarations of war. [Individuals] understood as declarations of war the recall or dismissal of ambassadors, the cutting down of another nation's flag, the grant of general letters of reprisal, and the making of a treaty of alliance with a warring nation.

D. Domestic Affairs

Page 430.   Before section 2 of the Note, add the following:

For a detailed historical survey purporting to show that "every president between 1945 and 2004 defended the unitariness of the executive branch with sufficient ardor to rebuff any claims that institutions such as independent counsels and independent agencies have been sanctioned as a matter of constitutional custom or history," see Yoo, Calabresi, & Colangelo, The Unitary Executive in the Modern Era, 1945-2004, 90 Iowa L. Rev. 601 (2005).

5
EQUALITY AND THE CONSTITUTION

A. Race, the Constitution, and Changing Conceptions of Equality

Page 471.   At the end of the carryover paragraph from page 470, add the following:

For more on the NAACP's litigation strategy leading up to *Brown,* including a discussion of litigation as a means of social reform, see M. Tushnet, Some Legacies of *Brown v. Board of Education,* 90 Va. L. Rev. 1693 (2004).

Page 480.   At the end of section 2c of the Note, add the following:

Recall the discussion of the NAACP's attack on "targets of opportunity." Considering Bell's criticisms, was *Brown* an effective target in bringing about institutional change? Consider the view that the decision to push for desegregation reflected the conclusion that a requirement of material equality in separate schools would never be enforced:

The NAACP pushed for integration because it sought to force white-controlled state and local governments to provide a quality education and equal educational opportunity to black schoolchildren. The NAACP had tried for many years to push for educational rights through equalization suits. Equalization suits tried to enforce Plessy v. Ferguson's formula of "separate but equal" by requiring school districts to provide black school-children with educational opportunities and resources as good as those enjoyed by students in all-white schools. [Many] years of frustrating efforts demonstrated that the mandate of equal educational resources was too easy for state governments to evade. Thus, the NAACP sought to integrate the public schools in part on the theory that "green follows white." It believed that the white establishment would expend monetary resources and ensure quality education for black schoolchildren only if blacks were attending the same schools as the children of white parents. Integration would force whites to take into account the social costs that black children suffered from inferior educational opportunities by linking the fates of white and black schoolchildren together.

Balkin, What *Brown* Teaches Us About Constitutional Theory, 90 Va. L. Rev. 1537, 1570-1571 (2004). In retrospect, what strategies were available to the NAACP besides equalization suits and integration?

Page 497.   At the end of section 3e of the Note, add the following:

Too little, too late? Michael Olivas argues that lingering racial divisions in higher education are due in part to courts' historical lack of concern about geographical place in higher education, which Olivas suggests has been empha-sized much more at the elementary and secondary levels.

A large number of life's advantages and opportunities are parceled out by residence, duration, domicile, and location. In higher education, this complex algebra of "place" delegates the statewide coordination of governance of higher education to the institutional boards of trustees and statewide higher education agencies who execute the legislative and corporate requirements to establish and locate colleges. And where a college is located can apportion access in a way that benefits or harms certain citizens.

Olivas, *Brown* and the Desegregative Ideal: Location, Race, and College Atten-dance Policies, 90 Cornell L. Rev. 391 (2005) (examining the effects of college location on the racial composition of attendees, development of surrounding neighborhoods, and black and Hispanic access to higher education).

Page 497.   Before the Note on Final Thoughts, add the following:

PARENTS INVOLVED IN COMMUNITY SCHOOLS v. SEATTLE
SCHOOL DISTRICT NO. 1

127 S. Ct. 2736 (2007)

CHIEF JUSTICE ROBERTS announced the judgment of the Court, and delivered the opinion of the Court with respect to Parts I, II, III-A, and III-C, and an opinion with respect to Parts III-B and IV, in which JUSTICES SCALIA, THOMAS, and ALITO, join.

The school districts in these cases [from Seattle, Washington, and Jefferson County, Kentucky] voluntarily adopted student assignment plans that rely upon race to determine which public schools certain children may attend.... Parents of students denied assignment to particular schools under these plans solely because of their race brought suit, contending that allocating children to different public schools on the basis of race violated the Fourteenth Amendment guarantee of equal protection. The Courts of Appeals below upheld the plans. We granted certiorari, and now reverse.

I

. . .

A

Seattle School District No. 1 operates 10 regular public high schools. In 1998, it adopted the plan at issue in this case for assigning students to these schools. The plan allows incoming ninth graders to choose from among any of the district's high schools, ranking however many schools they wish in order of preference.

Some schools are more popular than others. If too many students list the same school as their first choice, the district employs a series of "tiebreakers" to determine who will fill the open slots at the oversubscribed school. The first tiebreaker selects for admission students who have a sibling currently enrolled in the chosen school. The next tiebreaker depends upon the racial composition of the particular school and the race of the individual student. In the district's public schools approximately 41 percent of enrolled students are white; the remaining 59 percent, comprising all other racial groups, are classified by Seattle for assignment purposes as nonwhite. If an oversubscribed school is not within 10 percentage points of the district's overall white/nonwhite racial balance, it is what the district calls "integration positive," and the district employs a tiebreaker that selects for assignment students whose race "will serve to bring the school into balance." ...

Seattle has never operated segregated schools — legally separate schools for students of different races — nor has it ever been subject to court-ordered desegregation. It nonetheless employs the racial tiebreaker in an attempt to address the effects of racially identifiable housing patterns on school assignments.

...

B

Jefferson County Public Schools operates the public school system in metropolitan Louisville, Kentucky. In 1973 a federal court found that Jefferson County had maintained a segregated school system, and in 1975 the District Court entered a desegregation decree. Jefferson County operated under this decree until 2000, when the District Court dissolved the decree after finding that the district had achieved unitary status by eliminating "to the greatest extent practicable" the vestiges of its prior policy of segregation.

In 2001, after the decree had been dissolved, Jefferson County adopted the voluntary student assignment plan at issue in this case. Approximately 34 percent of the district's 97,000 students are black; most of the remaining 66 percent are white. The plan requires all nonmagnet schools to maintain a minimum black enrollment of 15 percent, and a maximum black enrollment of 50 percent.

At the elementary school level, based on his or her address, each student is designated a "resides" school to which students within a specific geographic area are assigned; elementary resides schools are "grouped into clusters in order to facilitate integration." The district assigns students to nonmagnet schools in one of two ways: Parents of kindergartners, first-graders, and students new to the district may submit an application indicating a first and second choice among the schools within their cluster; students who do not submit such an application are assigned within the cluster by the district. "Decisions to assign students to schools within each cluster are based on available space within the schools and the racial guidelines in the District's current student assignment plan." If a school has reached the "extremes of the racial guidelines," a student whose race would contribute to the school's racial imbalance will not be assigned there. After assignment, students at all grade levels are permitted to apply to transfer between nonmagnet schools in the district. Transfers may be requested for any number of reasons, and may be denied because of lack of available space or on the basis of the racial guidelines.

...

III

A

It is well established that when the government distributes burdens or benefits on the basis of individual racial classifications, that action is reviewed under strict scrutiny. *Johnson* v. *California*, 543 U.S. 499, 505-506 (2005); *Grutter* v. *Bollinger*, 539 U.S. 306, 326 (2003).... In order to satisfy this searching standard of review, the school districts must demonstrate that the use of individual racial classifications in the assignment plans here under review is "narrowly tailored" to achieve a "compelling" government interest.

Without attempting in these cases to set forth all the interests a school district might assert, it suffices to note that our prior cases, in evaluating the use of racial classifications in the school context, have recognized two interests that qualify as compelling. The first is the compelling interest of remedying the effects of past intentional discrimination. See *Freeman* v. *Pitts*, 503 U.S. 467, 494 (1992). Yet the Seattle public schools have not shown that they were ever segregated by law, and were not subject to court-ordered desegregation decrees. The Jefferson County public schools were previously segregated by law and were subject to a desegregation decree entered in 1975. In 2000, the District Court that entered that decree dissolved it, finding that Jefferson County had "eliminated the vestiges associated with the former policy of segregation and its pernicious effects," and thus had achieved "unitary" status Jefferson County accordingly does not rely upon an interest in remedying the effects of past intentional discrimination in defending its present use of race in assigning students.

Nor could it. We have emphasized that the harm being remedied by mandatory desegregation plans is the harm that is traceable to segregation, and that "the Constitution is not violated by racial imbalance in the schools, without more." *Milliken* v. *Bradley*, 433 U.S. 267, 280, n. 14 (1977). Once Jefferson County achieved unitary status, it had remedied the constitutional wrong that allowed race-based assignments. Any continued use of race must be justified on some other basis.

The second government interest we have recognized as compelling for purposes of strict scrutiny is the interest in diversity in higher education upheld in *Grutter*. The specific interest found compelling in *Grutter* was student body diversity "in the context of higher education." The diversity interest was not focused on race alone but encompassed "all factors that may contribute to student body diversity."...

The entire gist of the analysis in *Grutter* was that the admissions program at issue there focused on each applicant as an individual, and not simply as a member of a particular racial group. The classification of applicants by race upheld in *Grutter* was only as part of a "highly individualized, holistic review." ...

In the present cases, by contrast, race is not considered as part of a broader effort to achieve "exposure to widely diverse people, cultures, ideas, and viewpoints"; race, for some students, is determinative standing alone. ...

Even when it comes to race, the plans here employ only a limited notion of diversity, viewing race exclusively in white/nonwhite terms in Seattle and black/"other" terms in Jefferson County. ... The Seattle "Board Statement Reaffirming Diversity Rationale" speaks of the "inherent educational value" in "providing students the opportunity to attend schools with diverse student enrollment." But under the Seattle plan, a school with 50 percent Asian-American students and 50 percent white students but no African-American, Native-American, or Latino students would qualify as balanced, while a school with 30 percent Asian-American, 25 percent African-American, 25 percent Latino, and 20 percent white students would not. It is hard to understand how a plan that could allow these results can be viewed as being concerned with achieving enrollment that is "'broadly diverse.'"

. . .

In upholding the admissions plan in *Grutter*, ... this Court relied upon con-siderations unique to institutions of higher education, noting that in light of "the expansive freedoms of speech and thought associated with the university envir-onment, universities occupy a special niche in our constitutional tradition." ... The present cases are not governed by *Grutter*.

B

Perhaps recognizing that reliance on *Grutter* cannot sustain their plans, both school districts assert additional interests, distinct from the interest upheld in *Grutter*, to justify their race-based assignments. In briefing and argument before this Court, Seattle contends that its use of race helps to reduce racial concentra-tion in schools and to ensure that racially concentrated housing patterns do not prevent nonwhite students from having access to the most desirable schools. Jefferson County has articulated a similar goal, phrasing its interest in terms of educating its students "in a racially integrated environment." Each school district argues that educational and broader socialization benefits flow from a racially diverse learning environment, and each contends that because the diver-sity they seek is racial diversity — not the broader diversity at issue in *Grutter* — it makes sense to promote that interest directly by relying on race alone.

The parties and their *amici* dispute whether racial diversity in schools in fact has a marked impact on test scores and other objective yardsticks or achieves intangible socialization benefits. The debate is not one we need to resolve, however, because it is clear that the racial classifications employed by the districts are not narrowly tailored to the goal of achieving the educational and social benefits asserted to flow from racial diversity. In design and operation, the plans are directed only to racial balance, pure and simple, an objective this Court has repeatedly condemned as illegitimate.

The plans are tied to each district's specific racial demographics, rather than to any pedagogic concept of the level of diversity needed to obtain the asserted educational benefits. In Seattle, the district seeks white enrollment of between 31 and 51 percent (within 10 percent of "the district white average" of 41 percent), and nonwhite enrollment of between 49 and 69 percent (within 10 percent of "the district minority average" of 59 percent). In Jefferson County, by contrast, the district seeks black enrollment of no less than 15 or more than 50 percent.... This comparison makes clear that the racial demographics in each district — whatever they happen to be — drive the required "diversity" numbers....

The districts offer no evidence that the level of racial diversity necessary to achieve the asserted educational benefits happens to coincide with the racial demographics of the respective school districts....

In fact, in each case the extreme measure of relying on race in assignments is unnecessary to achieve the stated goals, even as defined by the districts. For example, at Franklin High School in Seattle, the racial tiebreaker was applied because nonwhite enrollment exceeded 69 percent, and resulted in an incoming ninth-grade class in 2000-2001 that was 30.3 percent Asian-American, 21.9 percent African-American, 6.8 percent Latino, 0.5 percent Native-American, and 40.5 percent Caucasian. Without the racial tiebreaker, the class would have been 39.6 percent Asian-American, 30.2 percent African-American, 8.3 percent Latino, 1.1 percent Native-American, and 20.8 percent Caucasian. When the actual racial breakdown is considered, enrolling students without regard to their race yields a substantially diverse student body under any definition of diversity....

Accepting racial balancing as a compelling state interest would justify the imposition of racial proportionality throughout American society, contrary to our repeated recognition that "at the heart of the Constitution's guarantee of equal protection lies the simple command that the Government must treat citizens as individuals, not as simply components of a racial, religious, sexual or national class." *Miller* v. *Johnson*, 515 U.S. 900, 911 (1995) (quoting *Metro Broadcasting*, 497 U.S., at 602 (O'Connor, J., dissenting); internal quotation marks omitted). Allowing racial balancing as a compelling end in itself would "effectively assure that race will always be relevant in American life, and that the 'ultimate goal' of 'eliminating entirely from governmental decisionmaking such irrelevant factors as a human being's race' will never be achieved." *Croson, supra,* at 495 (plurality opinion of O'Connor, J.) (quoting *Wygant* v. *Jackson Bd. of Ed.,* 476 U.S. 267, 320 (1986) (Stevens, J., dissenting), in turn quoting *Fullilove,* 448 U.S., at 547 (Stevens, J., dissenting); brackets and citation omitted).

...

C

The districts assert, as they must, that the way in which they have employed individual racial classifications is necessary to achieve their stated ends. The minimal effect these classifications have on student assignments, however, suggests that other means would be effective. Seattle's racial tiebreaker results, in the end, only in shifting a small number of students between schools. Approximately 307 student assignments were affected by the racial tiebreaker in 2000-2001; the district was able to track the enrollment status of 293 of these students. Of these, 209 were assigned to a school that was one of their choices, 87 of whom were assigned to the same school to which they would have been assigned without the racial tiebreaker. Eighty-four students were assigned to schools that they did not list as a choice, but 29 of those students would have been assigned to their respective school without the racial tiebreaker, and 3 were able to attend one of the oversubscribed schools due to waitlist and capacity adjustments. In over one-third of the assignments affected by the racial tiebreaker, then, the use of race in the end made no difference, and the district could identify only 52 students who were ultimately affected adversely by the racial tiebreaker in that it resulted in assignment to a school they had not listed as a preference and to which they would not otherwise have been assigned.
. . .

Similarly, Jefferson County's use of racial classifications has only a minimal effect on the assignment of students. Elementary school students are assigned to their first- or second-choice school 95 percent of the time . . . Jefferson County estimates that the racial guidelines account for only 3 percent of assignments. As Jefferson County explains, "the racial guidelines have minimal impact in this process, because they 'mostly influence student assignment in subtle and indirect ways.'"

While we do not suggest that *greater* use of race would be preferable, the minimal impact of the districts' racial classifications on school enrollment casts doubt on the necessity of using racial classifications. In *Grutter*, the consideration of race was viewed as indispensable in more than tripling minority representation at the law school—from 4 to 14.5 percent.
. . .

IV

Justice Breyer's dissent takes a different approach to these cases. . . .

To begin with, Justice Breyer seeks to justify the plans at issue under our precedents recognizing the compelling interest in remedying past intentional discrimination. Not even the school districts go this far, and for good reason. The distinction between segregation by state action and racial imbalance caused by other factors has been central to our jurisprudence in this area for generations.
. . .

Justice Breyer's dissent... relies heavily on dicta from *Swann* v. *Charlotte-Mecklenburg Bd. of Ed.* — far more heavily than the school districts themselves....

Swann addresses only a possible state objective; it says nothing of the permissible *means* — race conscious or otherwise — that a school district might employ to achieve that objective. The reason for this omission is clear enough, since the case did not involve any voluntary means adopted by a school district. The dissent's characterization of *Swann* as recognizing that "the Equal Protection Clause permits local school boards to use race-conscious criteria to achieve positive race-related goals" is — at best a dubious inference. Even if the dicta from *Swann* were entitled to the weight the dissent would give it, and no dicta is, it not only did not address the question presented in *Swann*, it also does not address the question presented in these cases — whether the school districts' use of racial classifications to achieve their stated goals is permissible.

Further, for all the lower court cases Justice Breyer cites as evidence of the "prevailing legal assumption" embodied by *Swann*, very few are pertinent. Most are not. For example, the dissent features *Tometz* v. *Board of Ed., Waukegan City School Dist. No. 61*, 39 Ill. 2d 593, 596-598, 237 N.E.2d 498, 500-502 (1968), an Illinois decision, as evidence that "state and federal courts had considered the matter settled and uncontroversial." But *Tometz* addressed a challenge to a statute requiring race-consciousness in drawing school attendance boundaries — an issue well beyond the scope of the question presented in these cases. Importantly, it considered that issue only under rational-basis review, which even the dissent grudgingly recognizes is an improper standard for evaluating express racial classifications. Other cases cited are similarly inapplicable.... [1]
...

---

1. In fact, all the cases Justice Breyer's dissent cites as evidence of the "prevailing legal assumption," were decided before this Court definitively determined that "all racial classifications... must be analyzed by a reviewing court under strict scrutiny." *Adarand Constructors, Inc.* v. *Pena*, 515 U.S. 200, 227 (1995). Many proceeded under the now-rejected view that classifications seeking to benefit a disadvantaged racial group should be held to a lesser standard of review....

Justice Stevens's reliance on *School Comm. of Boston* v. *Board of Ed.*, 352 Mass. 693, 227 N.E.2d 729 (1967), appeal dism'd, 389 U.S. 572 (1968) *(per curiam)*, is inapposite for the same reason that many of the cases cited by Justice Breyer are inapposite; the case involved a Massachusetts law that required school districts to avoid racial imbalance in schools but did not specify how to achieve this goal — and certainly did not require express racial classifications as the means to do so. The law was upheld under rational-basis review, with the state court explicitly rejecting the suggestion — which is now plainly the law — that "racial group classifications bear a far heavier burden of justification."

At the same time it relies on inapplicable desegregation cases, misstatements of admitted dicta, and other noncontrolling pronouncements, Justice Breyer's dissent candidly dismisses the significance of this Court's repeated *holdings* that all racial classifications must be reviewed under strict scrutiny, arguing that a different standard of review should be applied because the districts use race for beneficent rather than malicious purposes.

This Court has recently reiterated, however, that "'*all* racial classifications [imposed by government]... must be analyzed by a reviewing court under strict scrutiny.'" *Johnson*, 543 U.S., at 505 (quoting *Adarand*, 515 U.S., at 227; emphasis added by *Johnson* Court). See also *Grutter*. Justice Breyer nonetheless relies on the good intentions and motives of the school districts, stating that he has found "no case that... repudiated this constitutional asymmetry between that which seeks to *exclude* and that which seeks to *include* members of minority races." (emphasis in original). We have found many....

The reasons for rejecting a motives test for racial classifications are clear enough. "The Court's emphasis on 'benign racial classifications' suggests confidence in its ability to distinguish good from harmful governmental uses of racial criteria. History should teach greater humility.... 'Benign' carries with it no independent meaning, but reflects only acceptance of the current generation's conclusion that a politically acceptable burden, imposed on particular citizens on the basis of race, is reasonable."...

Justice Breyer speaks of bringing "the races" together (putting aside the purely black-and-white nature of the plans), as the justification for excluding individuals on the basis of their race. Again, this approach to racial classifications is fundamentally at odds with our precedent, which makes clear that the Equal Protection Clause "protects *persons*, not *groups*." This fundamental principle goes back, in this context, to *Brown* itself. See *Brown* v. *Board of Education*, 349 U.S. 294, 300 (1955) (*Brown II*) ("At stake is the *personal* interest of the plaintiffs in admission to public schools... on a nondiscriminatory basis" (emphasis added)). For the dissent, in contrast, "'individualized scrutiny' is simply beside the point."

...

Justice Breyer's dissent ends on an unjustified note of alarm....

[It] suggests that other means for achieving greater racial diversity in schools are necessarily unconstitutional if the racial classifications at issue in these cases cannot survive strict scrutiny. These other means — e.g., where to construct new schools, how to allocate resources among schools, and which academic offerings to provide to attract students to certain schools — implicate different considerations than the explicit racial classifications at issue in these cases, and we express no opinion on their validity — not even in dicta. Rather, we employ the familiar and well-established analytic approach of strict scrutiny to evaluate the plans at issue today, an approach that in no way warrants the dissent's cataclysmic concerns. Under that approach, the school districts have not carried their burden of showing that the ends they seek justify the particular extreme means they have chosen — classifying individual students on the basis of their race and discriminating among them on that basis.

***

If the need for the racial classifications embraced by the school districts is unclear, even on the districts' own terms, the costs are undeniable. "Distinctions between citizens solely because of their ancestry are by their very nature odious to a free people whose institutions are founded upon the doctrine of equality."....

All this is true enough in the contexts in which these statements [have repeatedly been] made [by this Court, — in] government contracting, voting districts, allocation of broadcast licenses, and electing state officers — but when it comes to using race to assign children to schools, history will be heard. In *Brown* v. *Board of Education*, 347 U.S. 483 (1954) (*Brown I*), we held that segregation deprived black children of equal educational opportunities regardless of whether school facilities and other tangible factors were equal, because government classification and separation on grounds of race themselves denoted inferiority. It was not the inequality of the facilities but the fact of legally separating children on the basis of race on which the Court relied to find a constitutional violation in 1954. The next Term, we accordingly stated that "full compliance" with *Brown I* required school districts "to achieve a system of determining admission to the public schools *on a nonracial basis*." *Brown II*, 349 U.S., at 300-301 (emphasis added).

The parties and their *amici* debate which side is more faithful to the heritage of *Brown*, but the position of the plaintiffs in *Brown* was spelled out in their brief and could not have been clearer: "The Fourteenth Amendment prevents states from according differential treatment to American children on the basis of their color or race." Brief for Appellants in Nos. 1, 2, and 4 and for Respondents in No. 10 on Reargument in *Brown I*, O. T. 1953, p. 15 (Summary of Argument). What do the racial classifications at issue here do, if not accord differential treatment on the basis of race? As counsel who appeared before this Court for the plaintiffs in *Brown* put it: "We have one fundamental contention which we will seek to develop in the course of this argument, and that contention is that no State has any authority under the equal-protection clause of the Fourteenth Amendment to use race as a factor in affording educational opportunities among its citizens." Tr. of Oral Arg. in *Brown I*, p. 7 (Robert L. Carter, Dec. 9, 1952). There is no ambiguity in that statement. And it was that position that prevailed in this Court, which emphasized in its remedial opinion that what was "at stake is the personal interest of the plaintiffs in admission to public schools as soon as practicable *on a nondiscriminatory basis*," and what was required was "determining admission to the public schools *on a nonracial basis.*" *Brown II, supra*, at 300-301 (emphasis added). What do the racial classifications do in these cases, if not determine admission to a public school on a racial basis?

...

JUSTICE THOMAS, concurring.

...

I

...

A

...

Racial imbalance is not segregation.[2] Although presently observed racial imbalance might result from past *de jure* segregation, racial imbalance can also result from any number of innocent private decisions, including voluntary housing choices.

Although there is arguably a danger of racial imbalance in schools in Seattle and Louisville, there is no danger of resegregation. No one contends that Seattle has established or that Louisville has reestablished a dual school system that separates students on the basis of race.

...

B

Just as the school districts lack an interest in preventing resegregation, they also have no present interest in remedying past segregation.

...

2

This Court has carved out a narrow exception to [the] general rule [forbidding government use of race] for cases in which a school district has a "history of maintaining two sets of schools in a single school system deliberately operated to carry out a governmental policy to separate pupils in schools solely on the basis of race." In such cases, race-based remedial measures are sometimes required...[6]

---

2. The dissent refers repeatedly and reverently to "integration." However, outside of the context of remediation for past *de jure* segregation, "integration" is simply racial balancing. Therefore, the school districts' attempts to further "integrate" are properly thought of as little more than attempts to achieve a particular racial balance.

6. As I have explained elsewhere, the remedies this Court authorized lower courts to compel in early desegregation cases like *Green* and *Swann* were exceptional. Sustained resistance to *Brown* prompted the Court to authorize extraordinary race-conscious remedial

Neither of the programs before us today is compelled as a remedial measure, and no one makes such a claim.

...

II

Lacking a cognizable interest in remediation, neither of these plans can survive strict scrutiny because neither plan serves a genuinely compelling state interest. The dissent avoids reaching that conclusion by unquestioningly accepting the assertions of selected social scientists while completely ignoring the fact that those assertions are the subject of fervent debate.

...

B

...

2

[T]he dissent argues that the interest in integration has an educational element. The dissent asserts that racially balanced schools improve educational outcomes for black children. In support, the dissent unquestioningly cites certain social science research to support propositions that are hotly disputed among social scientists. In reality, it is far from apparent that coerced racial mixing has any educational benefits, much less that integration is necessary to black achievement.

Scholars have differing opinions as to whether educational benefits arise from racial balancing. Some have concluded that black students receive genuine educational benefits... Others have been more circumspect... And some have concluded that there are no demonstrable educational benefits...

Add to the inconclusive social science the fact of black achievement in "racially isolated" environments. See T. Sowell, Education: Assumptions Versus History 7-38 (1986). Before *Brown*, the most prominent example of an exemplary black school was Dunbar High School. *Id.,* at 29 ("In the period 1918-1923, Dunbar graduates earned fifteen degrees from Ivy League colleges, and ten degrees from Amherst, Williams, and Wesleyan"). Dunbar is by no means an isolated example. See *id.,* at 10-32 (discussing other successful black schools)... Even after *Brown*, some schools with predominantly black enrollments have achieved outstanding educational results...

---

measures (like compelled racial mixing) to turn the Constitution's dictate to desegregate into reality. Even if these measures were appropriate as remedies in the face of widespread resistance to *Brown*'s mandate, they are not forever insulated from constitutional scrutiny....

The Seattle school board itself must believe that racial mixing is not necessary to black achievement. Seattle operates a K-8 "African-American Academy," which has a "nonwhite" enrollment of 99%. That school was founded in 1990 as part of the school board's effort to "increase academic achievement." This racially imbalanced environment has reportedly produced test scores "higher across all grade levels in reading, writing and math." Contrary to what the dissent would have predicted, the children in Seattle's African American Academy have shown gains when placed in a "highly segregated" environment.

Given this tenuous relationship between forced racial mixing and improved educational results for black children, the dissent cannot plausibly maintain that an educational element supports the integration interest, let alone makes it compelling...

Perhaps recognizing as much, the dissent argues that the social science evidence is "strong enough to permit a democratically elected school board reasonably to determine that this interest is a compelling one." This assertion is inexplicable. It is not up to the school boards — the very government entities whose race-based practices we must strictly scrutinize — to determine what interests qualify as compelling under the Fourteenth Amendment to the United States Constitution. Rather, this Court must assess independently the nature of the interest asserted and the evidence to support it in order to determine whether it qualifies as compelling under our precedents... To adopt the dissent's deferential approach would be to abdicate our constitutional responsibilities.[14]

3

Finally, the dissent asserts a "democratic element" to the integration interest. It defines the "democratic element" as "an interest in producing an educational environment that reflects the 'pluralistic society' in which our children will

---

14. The dissent accuses me of "feeling confident that, to end invidious discrimination, one must end *all* governmental use of race-conscious criteria" and chastises me for not deferring to democratically elected majorities. Regardless of what Justice Breyer's goals might be, this Court does not sit to "create a society that includes all Americans" or to solve the problems of "troubled inner city schooling." We are not social engineers. The United States Constitution dictates that local governments cannot make decisions on the basis of race. Consequently, regardless of the perceived negative effects of racial imbalance, I will not defer to legislative majorities where the Constitution forbids it.

It should escape no one that behind Justice Breyer's veil of judicial modesty hides an inflated role for the Federal Judiciary. The dissent's approach confers on judges the power to say what sorts of discrimination are benign and which are invidious. Having made that determination (based on no objective measure that I can detect), a judge following the dissent's approach will set the level of scrutiny to achieve the desired result. Only then must the judge defer to a democratic majority. In my view, to defer to one's preferred result is not to defer at all.

live." Environmental reflection, though, is just another way to say racial balancing.

...

III

Most of the dissent's criticisms of today's result can be traced to its rejection of the color-blind Constitution. The dissent attempts to marginalize the notion of a color-blind Constitution by consigning it to me and Members of today's plurality. But I am quite comfortable in the company I keep. My view of the Constitution is Justice Harlan's view in *Plessy:* "Our Constitution is color-blind, and neither knows nor tolerates classes among citizens." *Plessy* v. *Ferguson*, 163 U.S. 537, 559 (1896) (dissenting opinion). And my view was the rallying cry for the lawyers who litigated *Brown.* ...

The dissent appears to pin its interpretation of the Equal Protection Clause to current societal practice and expectations, deference to local officials, likely practical consequences, and reliance on previous statements from this and other courts. Such a view was ascendant in this Court's jurisprudence for several decades. It first appeared in *Plessy,* where the Court asked whether a state law providing for segregated railway cars was "a reasonable regulation." 163 U.S., at 550. The Court deferred to local authorities in making its determination, noting that in inquiring into reasonableness "there must necessarily be a large discretion on the part of the legislature." ...

The segregationists in *Brown* embraced the arguments the Court endorsed in *Plessy.* Though *Brown* decisively rejected those arguments, today's dissent replicates them to a distressing extent. Thus, the dissent argues that "each plan embodies the results of local experience and community consultation." Similarly, the segregationists made repeated appeals to societal practice and expectation. The dissent argues that "weight [must be given] to a local school board's knowledge, expertise, and concerns," and with equal vigor, the segregationists argued for deference to local authorities. The dissent argues that today's decision "threatens to substitute for present calm a disruptive round of race-related litigation," and claims that today's decision "risks serious harm to the law and for the Nation." The segregationists also relied upon the likely practical consequences of ending the state-imposed system of racial separation. And foreshadowing today's dissent, the segregationists most heavily relied upon judicial precedent.

The similarities between the dissent's arguments and the segregationists' arguments do not stop there. Like the dissent, the segregationists repeatedly cautioned the Court to consider practicalities and not to embrace too theoretical a view of the Fourteenth Amendment. And just as the dissent argues that the need for these programs will lessen over time, the segregationists claimed that reliance on segregation was lessening and might eventually end.

What was wrong in 1954 cannot be right today. Whatever else the Court's rejection of the segregationists' arguments in *Brown* might have established, it certainly made clear that state and local governments cannot take from the Constitution a right to make decisions on the basis of race by adverse possession. The fact that state and local governments had been discriminating on the basis of race for a long time was irrelevant to the *Brown* Court. The fact that racial discrimination was preferable to the relevant communities was irrelevant to the *Brown* Court. And the fact that the state and local governments had relied on statements in this Court's opinions was irrelevant to the *Brown* Court. The same principles guide today's decision....

In place of the color-blind Constitution, the dissent would permit measures to keep the races together and proscribe measures to keep the races apart. Although no such distinction is apparent in the Fourteenth Amendment, the dissent would constitutionalize today's faddish social theories that embrace that distinction. The Constitution is not that malleable. Even if current social theories favor classroom racial engineering as necessary to "solve the problems at hand," the Constitution enshrines principles independent of social theories. See *Plessy*, 163 U.S., at 559 (Harlan, J., dissenting) ("The white race deems itself to be the dominant race in this country. And so it is, in prestige, in achievements, in education, in wealth and in power. So, I doubt not, it will continue to be for all time.... But in view of the Constitution, in the eye of the law, there is in this country no superior, dominant, ruling class of citizens.... Our Constitution is color-blind, and neither knows nor tolerates classes among citizens"). Indeed, if our history has taught us anything, it has taught us to beware of elites bearing racial theories.[30]

...

JUSTICE KENNEDY, concurring in part and concurring in the judgment.

The Nation's schools strive to teach that our strength comes from people of different races, creeds, and cultures uniting in commitment to the freedom of all. In these cases two school districts in different parts of the country seek to teach that principle by having classrooms that reflect the racial makeup of the surrounding community. That the school districts consider these plans to be necessary should remind us our highest aspirations are yet unfulfilled. But the solutions mandated by these school districts must themselves be lawful. To make race matter now so that it might not matter later may entrench the very prejudices we seek to overcome. In my view the state-mandated racial classifications at issue,

---

30. Justice Breyer's good intentions, which I do not doubt, have the shelf life of Justice Breyer's tenure. Unlike the dissenters, I am unwilling to delegate my constitutional responsibilities to local school boards and allow them to experiment with race-based decisionmaking on the assumption that their intentions will forever remain as good as Justice Breyer's...

official labels proclaiming the race of all persons in a broad class of citizens — elementary school students in one case, high school students in another — are unconstitutional as the cases now come to us.

. . .

II

Our Nation from the inception has sought to preserve and expand the promise of liberty and equality on which it was founded. Today we enjoy a society that is remarkable in its openness and opportunity. Yet our tradition is to go beyond present achievements, however significant, and to recognize and confront the flaws and injustices that remain. This is especially true when we seek assurance that opportunity is not denied on account of race. The enduring hope is that race should not matter; the reality is that too often it does.

This is by way of preface to my respectful submission that parts of the opinion by The Chief Justice imply an all-too-unyielding insistence that race cannot be a factor in instances when, in my view, it may be taken into account. The plurality opinion is too dismissive of the legitimate interest government has in ensuring all people have equal opportunity regardless of their race. The plurality's postulate that "the way to stop discrimination on the basis of race is to stop discriminating on the basis of race," is not sufficient to decide these cases. Fifty years of experience since *Brown* v. *Board of Education,* 347 U.S. 483 (1954), should teach us that the problem before us defies so easy a solution. School districts can seek to reach *Brown*'s objective of equal educational opportunity. The plurality opinion is at least open to the interpretation that the Constitution requires school districts to ignore the problem of *de facto* resegregation in schooling. I cannot endorse that conclusion. To the extent the plurality opinion suggests the Constitution mandates that state and local school authorities must accept the status quo of racial isolation in schools, it is, in my view, profoundly mistaken.

The statement by Justice Harlan that "our Constitution is color-blind" was most certainly justified in the context of his dissent in *Plessy* v. *Ferguson,* 163 U.S. 537, 559 (1896). The Court's decision in that case was a grievous error it took far too long to overrule. . . . [A]s an aspiration, Justice Harlan's axiom must command our assent. In the real world, it is regrettable to say, it cannot be a universal constitutional principle.

In the administration of public schools by the state and local authorities it is permissible to consider the racial makeup of schools and to adopt general policies to encourage a diverse student body, one aspect of which is its racial composition. Cf. *Grutter* v. *Bollinger,* 539 U.S. 306 (2003). If school authorities are concerned that the student-body compositions of certain schools interfere with the objective of offering an equal educational opportunity to all of their students, they are free to devise race-conscious measures to address the problem in a general way and without treating each student in different fashion solely on the basis of a systematic, individual typing by race.

School boards may pursue the goal of bringing together students of diverse backgrounds and races through other means, including strategic site selection of new schools; drawing attendance zones with general recognition of the demographics of neighborhoods; allocating resources for special programs; recruiting students and faculty in a targeted fashion; and tracking enrollments, performance, and other statistics by race. These mechanisms are race conscious but do not lead to different treatment based on a classification that tells each student he or she is to be defined by race, so it is unlikely any of them would demand strict scrutiny to be found permissible. See *Bush* v. *Vera*, 517 U.S. 952, 958 (1996) (plurality opinion) ("Strict scrutiny does not apply merely because redistricting is performed with consciousness of race.... Electoral district lines are 'facially race neutral' so a more searching inquiry is necessary before strict scrutiny can be found applicable in redistricting cases than in cases of 'classifications based explicitly on race'" (quoting *Adarand*, 515 U.S., at 213)). Executive and legislative branches, which for generations now have considered these types of policies and procedures, should be permitted to employ them with candor and with confidence that a constitutional violation does not occur whenever a decisionmaker considers the impact a given approach might have on students of different races. Assigning to each student a personal designation according to a crude system of individual racial classifications is quite a different matter; and the legal analysis changes accordingly.

. . .

In the cases before us it is noteworthy that the number of students whose assignment depends on express racial classifications is limited. I join Part III-C of the Court's opinion because I agree that in the context of these plans, the small number of assignments affected suggests that the schools could have achieved their stated ends through different means. These include the facially race-neutral means set forth above or, if necessary, a more nuanced, individual evaluation of school needs and student characteristics that might include race as a component. The latter approach would be informed by *Grutter*, though of course the criteria relevant to student placement would differ based on the age of the students, the needs of the parents, and the role of the schools.

III

. . .

A

[The dissent's reliance on *Grutter*] is, with all respect, simply baffling.

. . .

136

There the Court sustained a system that, it found, was flexible enough to take into account "all pertinent elements of diversity," and considered race as only one factor among many. Seattle's plan, by contrast, relies upon a mechanical formula that has denied hundreds of students their preferred schools on the basis of three rigid criteria: placement of siblings, distance from schools, and race. If those students were considered for a whole range of their talents and school needs with race as just one consideration, *Grutter* would have some application. That, though, is not the case. . . .

B

To uphold these programs the Court is asked to brush aside two concepts of central importance for determining the validity of laws and decrees designed to alleviate the hurt and adverse consequences resulting from race discrimination. The first is the difference between *de jure* and *de facto* segregation; the second, the presumptive invalidity of a State's use of racial classifications to differentiate its treatment of individuals.

In the immediate aftermath of *Brown* the Court addressed other instances where laws and practices enforced *de jure* segregation. But with reference to schools, the effect of the legal wrong proved most difficult to correct. To remedy the wrong, school districts that had been segregated by law had no choice, whether under court supervision or pursuant to voluntary desegregation efforts, but to resort to extraordinary measures including individual student and teacher assignment to schools based on race. So it was, as the dissent observes, that Louisville classified children by race in its school assignment and busing plan in the 1970's.

Our cases recognized a fundamental difference between those school districts that had engaged in *de jure* segregation and those whose segregation was the result of other factors. School districts that had engaged in *de jure* segregation had an affirmative constitutional duty to desegregate; those that were *de facto* segregated did not. The distinctions between *de jure* and *de facto* segregation extended to the remedies available to governmental units in addition to the courts. For example, in *Wygant* v. *Jackson Bd. of Ed.*, 476 U.S. 267, 274 (1986), the plurality noted: "This Court never has held that societal discrimination alone is sufficient to justify a racial classification. Rather, the Court has insisted upon some showing of prior discrimination by the governmental unit involved before allowing limited use of racial classifications in order to remedy such discrimination." . . .

From the standpoint of the victim, it is true, an injury stemming from racial prejudice can hurt as much when the demeaning treatment based on race identity stems from bias masked deep within the social order as when it is imposed by law. The distinction between government and private action, furthermore, can be amorphous both as a historical matter and as a matter of present-day finding of fact. Laws arise from a culture and vice versa. Neither can assign to the other all responsibility for persisting injustices.

Yet, like so many other legal categories that can overlap in some instances, the constitutional distinction between *de jure* and *de facto* segregation has been thought to be an important one. It must be conceded its primary function in school cases was to delimit the powers of the Judiciary in the fashioning of remedies. The distinction ought not to be altogether disregarded, however, when we come to that most sensitive of all racial issues, an attempt by the government to treat whole classes of persons differently based on the government's systematic classification of each individual by race. There, too, the distinction serves as a limit on the exercise of a power that reaches to the very verge of constitutional authority. Reduction of an individual to an assigned racial identity for differential treatment is among the most pernicious actions our government can undertake....

The cases here were argued upon the assumption, and come to us on the premise, that the discrimination in question did not result from *de jure* actions. And when *de facto* discrimination is at issue our tradition has been that the remedial rules are different. The State must seek alternatives to the classification and differential treatment of individuals by race, at least absent some extraordinary showing not present here.

C

... If it is legitimate for school authorities to work to avoid racial isolation in their schools, must they do so only by indirection and general policies? Does the Constitution mandate this inefficient result? Why may the authorities not recognize the problem in candid fashion and solve it altogether through resort to direct assignments based on student racial classifications? So, the argument proceeds, if race is the problem, then perhaps race is the solution.

The argument ignores the dangers presented by individual classifications, dangers that are not as pressing when the same ends are achieved by more indirect means. When the government classifies an individual by race, it must first define what it means to be of a race. Who exactly is white and who is nonwhite? To be forced to live under a state-mandated racial label is inconsistent with the dignity of individuals in our society. And it is a label that an individual is powerless to change.... On the other hand race-conscious measures that do not rely on differential treatment based on individual classifications present these problems to a lesser degree....

***

This Nation has a moral and ethical obligation to fulfill its historic commitment to creating an integrated society that ensures equal opportunity for all of its children. A compelling interest exists in avoiding racial isolation, an interest that a school district, in its discretion and expertise, may choose to pursue. Likewise, a district may consider it a compelling interest to achieve a diverse student population. Race may be one component of that diversity, but other demographic factors, plus special talents and needs, should also be considered. What the government is not permitted to do, absent a showing of necessity not made here, is to classify every student on the basis of race and to assign each of them to schools based on that classification. Crude measures of this sort threaten to reduce children to racial chits valued and traded according to one school's supply and another's demand.

. . .

The decision today should not prevent school districts from continuing the important work of bringing together students of different racial, ethnic, and economic backgrounds. Due to a variety of factors — some influenced by government, some not — neighborhoods in our communities do not reflect the diversity of our Nation as a whole. Those entrusted with directing our public schools can bring to bear the creativity of experts, parents, administrators, and other concerned citizens to find a way to achieve the compelling interests they face without resorting to widespread governmental allocation of benefits and burdens on the basis of racial classifications.

With this explanation I concur in the judgment of the Court.

JUSTICE STEVENS, dissenting.

. . .

There is a cruel irony in The Chief Justice's reliance on our decision in *Brown* v. *Board of Education,* 349 U.S. 294 (1955). The first sentence in the concluding paragraph of his opinion states: "Before *Brown,* schoolchildren were told where they could and could not go to school based on the color of their skin." This sentence reminds me of Anatole France's observation: "The majestic equality of the law, forbids rich and poor alike to sleep under bridges, to beg in the streets, and to steal their bread." The Chief Justice fails to note that it was only black schoolchildren who were so ordered; indeed, the history books do not tell stories of white children struggling to attend black schools. In this and other ways, The Chief Justice rewrites the history of one of this Court's most important decisions.

. . .

If we look at cases decided during the interim between *Brown* and *Adarand,* we can see how a rigid adherence to tiers of scrutiny obscures *Brown*'s clear message. Perhaps the best example is provided by our approval of the decision of the Supreme Judicial Court of Massachusetts in 1967 upholding a state statute mandating racial integration in that State's school system. See *School Comm. of Boston* v. *Board of Education,* 352 Mass. 693, 227 N.E.2d 729. Rejecting arguments comparable to those that the plurality accepts today, that court noted: "It would be the height of irony if the racial imbalance act, enacted as it was with the laudable purpose of achieving equal educational opportunities, should, by prescribing school pupil allocations based on race, founder on unsuspected shoals in the Fourteenth Amendment."

Invoking our mandatory appellate jurisdiction, the Boston plaintiffs prosecuted an appeal in this Court. Our ruling on the merits simply stated that the appeal was "dismissed for want of a substantial federal question." *School Comm. of Boston* v. *Board of Education*, 389 U.S. 572 (1968) *(per curiam)*. That decision not only expressed our appraisal of the merits of the appeal, but it constitutes a precedent that the Court overrules today. The subsequent statements by the unanimous Court in *Swann* v. *Charlotte-Mecklenburg Bd. of Ed.*, 402 U.S. 1, 16 (1971)... and by the host of state court decisions cited by Justice Breyer, were fully consistent with that disposition. Unlike today's decision, they were also entirely loyal to *Brown*.

The Court has changed significantly since it decided *School Comm. of Boston* in 1968. It was then more faithful to *Brown* and more respectful of our precedent than it is today. It is my firm conviction that no Member of the Court that I joined in 1975 would have agreed with today's decision.

JUSTICE BREYER, with whom JUSTICE STEVENS, JUSTICE SOUTER, and JUSTICE GINSBURG join, dissenting.

These cases consider the longstanding efforts of two local school boards to integrate their public schools. The school board plans before us resemble many others adopted in the last 50 years by primary and secondary schools throughout the Nation. All of those plans represent local efforts to bring about the kind of racially integrated education that *Brown* v. *Board of Education*, 347 U.S. 483 (1954), long ago promised — efforts that this Court has repeatedly required, permitted, and encouraged local authorities to undertake....

I

Facts

...

Between 1968 and 1980, the number of black children attending a school where minority children constituted more than half of the school fell from 77% to 63% in the Nation (from 81% to 57% in the South) but then reversed direction by the year 2000, rising from 63% to 72% in the Nation (from 57% to 69% in the South). Similarly, between 1968 and 1980, the number of black children attending schools that were more than 90% minority fell from 64% to 33% in the Nation (from 78% to 23% in the South), but that too reversed direction, rising by the year 2000 from 33% to 37% in the Nation (from 23% to 31% in the South). As of 2002, almost 2.4 million students, or over 5% of all public school enrollment, attended schools with a white population of less than

1%.... Today, more than one in six black children attend a school that is 99-100% minority. In light of the evident risk of a return to school systems that are in fact (though not in law) resegregated, many school districts have felt a need to maintain or to extend their integration efforts.

The upshot is that myriad school districts operating in myriad circumstances have devised myriad plans, often with race-conscious elements, all for the sake of eradicating earlier school segregation, bringing about integration, or preventing retrogression. Seattle and Louisville are two such districts, and the histories of their present plans set forth typical school integration stories.

. . .

In both Seattle and Louisville, the local school districts began with schools that were highly segregated in fact. In both cities plaintiffs filed lawsuits claiming unconstitutional segregation. In Louisville, a federal district court found that school segregation reflected pre-*Brown* state laws separating the races. In Seattle, the plaintiffs alleged that school segregation unconstitutionally reflected not only generalized societal discrimination and residential housing patterns, but also *school board policies and actions* that had helped to create, maintain, and aggravate racial segregation. In Louisville, a federal court entered a remedial decree. In Seattle, the parties settled after the school district pledged to undertake a desegregation plan. In both cities, the school boards adopted plans designed to achieve integration by bringing about more racially diverse schools. In each city the school board modified its plan several times in light of, for example, hostility to busing, the threat of resegregation, and the desirability of introducing greater student choice. And in each city, the school boards' plans have evolved over time in ways that progressively *diminish* the plans' use of explicit race-conscious criteria.

. . .

C

In both cases the efforts [to create more integrated schools] were in part remedial. Louisville began its integration efforts in earnest when a federal court in 1975 entered a school desegregation order. Seattle undertook its integration efforts in response to the filing of a federal lawsuit and as a result of its settlement of a segregation complaint filed with the federal [Office of Civil Rights, now in the Department of Education.]

The plans in both Louisville and Seattle grow out of these earlier remedial efforts. Both districts faced problems that reflected initial periods of severe racial segregation, followed by such remedial efforts as busing, followed by evidence of resegregation, followed by a need to end busing and encourage the return of, *e.g.*, suburban students through increased student choice. When formulating the plans under review, both districts drew upon their considerable experience with earlier plans, having revised their policies periodically in light of that experience. Both districts rethought their methods over time and explored a wide range of other means, including non-race-conscious policies. Both districts also considered elaborate studies and consulted widely within their communities.

Both districts sought greater racial integration for educational and democratic, as well as for remedial, reasons. Both sought to achieve these objectives while preserving their commitment to other educational goals, *e.g.*, districtwide commitment to high quality public schools, increased pupil assignment to neighborhood schools, diminished use of busing, greater student choice, reduced risk of white flight, and so forth. Consequently, the present plans expand student choice; they limit the burdens (including busing) that earlier plans had imposed upon students and their families; and they use race-conscious criteria in limited and gradually diminishing ways. In particular, they use race-conscious criteria only to mark the outer bounds of broad population-related ranges.

The histories also make clear the futility of looking simply to whether earlier school segregation was *de jure* or *de facto* in order to draw firm lines separating the constitutionally permissible from the constitutionally forbidden use of "race-conscious" criteria....

No one here disputes that Louisville's segregation was *de jure*. But what about Seattle's? Was it *de facto? De jure?* A mixture? Opinions differed. Or is it that a prior federal court had not adjudicated the matter? Does that make a difference?...

A court finding of *de jure* segregation cannot be the crucial variable. After all, a number of school districts in the South that the Government or private plaintiffs challenged as segregated *by law* voluntarily desegregated their schools *without a court order*—just as Seattle did.

Moreover, Louisville's history makes clear that a community under a court order to desegregate might submit a race-conscious remedial plan *before* the court dissolved the order, but with every intention of following that plan even *after* dissolution. How could such a plan be lawful the day before dissolution but then become unlawful the very next day? On what legal ground can the majority rest its contrary view?...

The histories also indicate the complexity of the tasks and the practical difficulties that local school boards face when they seek to achieve greater racial integration. The boards work in communities where demographic patterns change, where they must meet traditional learning goals, where they must attract and retain effective teachers, where they should (and will) take account of parents' views and maintain *their* commitment to public school education, where they must adapt to court intervention, where they must encourage voluntary student and parent action—where they will find that their own good faith, their knowledge, and their understanding of local circumstances are always necessary but often insufficient to solve the problems at hand.

...

142

II

The Legal Standard

A longstanding and unbroken line of legal authority tells us that the Equal Protection Clause permits local school boards to use race-conscious criteria to achieve positive race-related goals, even when the Constitution does not compel it. Because of its importance, I shall repeat what this Court said about the matter in *Swann*. Chief Justice Burger, on behalf of a unanimous Court in a case of exceptional importance, wrote:

> "School authorities are traditionally charged with broad power to formulate and implement educational policy and might well conclude, for example, that in order to prepare students to live in a pluralistic society each school should have a prescribed ratio of Negro to white students reflecting the proportion for the district as a whole. To do this as an educational policy is within the broad discretionary powers of school authorities."

The statement was not a technical holding in the case. But the Court set forth in *Swann* a basic principle of constitutional law — a principle of law that has found "wide acceptance in the legal culture."

. . .

If there were doubts before *Swann* was decided, they did not survive this Court's decision. Numerous state and federal courts explicitly relied upon *Swann*'s guidance for decades to follow. . . .

Courts are not alone in accepting as constitutionally valid the legal principle that *Swann* enunciated — *i.e.*, that the government may voluntarily adopt race-conscious measures to improve conditions of race even when it is not under a constitutional obligation to do so. That principle has been accepted by every branch of government and is rooted in the history of the Equal Protection Clause itself. Thus, Congress has enacted numerous race-conscious statutes that illustrate that principle or rely upon its validity. In fact, without being exhaustive, I have counted 51 federal statutes that use racial classifications. I have counted well over 100 state statutes that similarly employ racial classifications. Presidential administrations for the past half-century have used and supported various race-conscious measures. And during the same time, hundreds of local school districts have adopted student assignment plans that use race-conscious criteria.

That *Swann*'s legal statement should find such broad acceptance is not surprising. For *Swann* is predicated upon a well-established legal view of the Fourteenth Amendment. That view understands the basic objective of those who wrote the Equal Protection Clause as forbidding practices that lead to racial exclusion. The Amendment sought to bring into American society as full members those whom the Nation had previously held in slavery. See *Slaughter-House Cases*, 83 U.S. 36, 16 Wall. 36, 71 (1872) ("No one can fail to be impressed with the one pervading purpose found in [all the Reconstruction amendments]... we mean the freedom of the slave race"); *Strauder* v. *West Virginia*, 100 U.S. 303, 306 (1879) ("[The Fourteenth Amendment] is one of a series of constitutional provisions having a common purpose; namely, securing to a race recently emancipated... all the civil rights that the superior race enjoy").

There is reason to believe that those who drafted an Amendment with this basic purpose in mind would have understood the legal and practical difference between the use of race-conscious criteria in defiance of that purpose, namely to keep the races apart, and the use of race-conscious criteria to further that purpose, namely to bring the races together....

Sometimes Members of this Court have disagreed about the degree of leniency that the Clause affords to programs designed to include. But I can find no case in which this Court has followed Justice Thomas' "colorblind" approach. And I have found no case that otherwise repudiated this constitutional asymmetry between that which seeks to *exclude* and that which seeks to *include* members of minority races.

...

[The plurality claims] that later cases — in particular *Johnson, Adarand*, and *Grutter* — supplanted *Swann*. The plurality says that cases such as *Swann* and the others I have described all "were decided before this Court definitively determined that 'all racial classifications... must be analyzed by a reviewing court under strict scrutiny.'"

...

First, no case — not *Adarand, Gratz, Grutter*, or any other — has ever held that the test of "strict scrutiny" means that all racial classifications — no matter whether they seek to include or exclude — must in practice be treated the same. The Court did not say in *Adarand* or in *Johnson* or in *Grutter* that it was overturning *Swann* or its central constitutional principle.

[In *Adarand*,] the Court... sought to "*dispel the notion* that strict scrutiny" is as likely to condemn *inclusive* uses of "race-conscious" criteria as it is to invalidate *exclusionary* uses. That is, it is *not* in all circumstances "'strict in theory, but fatal in fact.'"

The Court in *Grutter* elaborated:

"Strict scrutiny is not 'strict in theory, but fatal in fact.'... Although all governmental uses of race are subject to strict scrutiny, not all are invalidated by it....

"Context matters when reviewing race-based governmental action under the Equal Protection Clause.... Not every decision influenced by race is equally objectionable, and strict scrutiny is designed to provide a framework for carefully examining the importance and the sincerity of the reasons advanced by the governmental decisionmaker for the use of race in that particular context.

The Court's holding in *Grutter* demonstrates that the Court meant what it said, for the Court upheld an elite law school's race-conscious admissions program.

. . .

Here, the context is one in which school districts seek to advance or to maintain racial integration in primary and secondary schools. It is a context, as *Swann* makes clear, where history has required special administrative remedies. And it is a context in which the school boards' plans simply set race-conscious limits at the outer boundaries of a broad range.

This context is *not* a context that involves the use of race to decide who will receive goods or services that are normally distributed on the basis of merit and which are in short supply. It is not one in which race-conscious limits stigmatize or exclude; the limits at issue do not pit the races against each other or otherwise significantly exacerbate racial tensions. They do not impose burdens unfairly upon members of one race alone but instead seek benefits for members of all races alike. The context here is one of racial limits that seek, not to keep the races apart, but to bring them together.

. . .

In my view, this contextual approach to scrutiny is altogether fitting. I believe that the law requires application here of a standard of review that is not "strict" in the traditional sense of that word. . . .

Nonetheless, in light of *Grutter* and other precedents, . . . I shall apply the version of strict scrutiny that those cases embody. I shall consequently ask whether the school boards in Seattle and Louisville adopted these plans to serve a "compelling governmental interest" and, if so, whether the plans are "narrowly tailored" to achieve that interest. If the plans survive this strict review, they would survive less exacting review *a fortiori*. . . .

III

Applying the Legal Standard

A

Compelling Interest

The principal interest advanced in these cases to justify the use of race-based criteria goes by various names. Sometimes a court refers to it as an interest in achieving racial "diversity." Other times a court, like the plurality here, refers to it as an interest in racial "balancing." I have used more general terms to signify that interest, describing it, for example, as an interest in promoting or preserving greater racial "integration" of public schools. By this term, I mean the school districts' interest in eliminating school-by-school racial isolation and increasing the degree to which racial mixture characterizes each of the district's schools and each individual student's public school experience.

Regardless of its name, however, the interest at stake possesses three essential elements. First, there is a historical and remedial element: an interest in setting right the consequences of prior conditions of segregation. This refers back to a time when public schools were highly segregated, often as a result of legal or administrative policies that facilitated racial segregation in public schools. It is an interest in continuing to combat the remnants of segregation caused in whole or in part by these school-related policies, which have often affected not only schools, but also housing patterns, employment practices, economic conditions, and social attitudes. It is an interest in maintaining hard-won gains. And it has its roots in preventing what gradually may become the *de facto* resegregation of America's public schools.

Second, there is an educational element: an interest in overcoming the adverse educational effects produced by and associated with highly segregated schools. Studies suggest that children taken from those schools and placed in integrated settings often show positive academic gains.

Other studies reach different conclusions. But the evidence supporting an educational interest in racially integrated schools is well established and strong enough to permit a democratically elected school board reasonably to determine that this interest is a compelling one.

. . .

Third, there is a democratic element: an interest in producing an educational environment that reflects the "pluralistic society" in which our children will live. It is an interest in helping our children learn to work and play together with children of different racial backgrounds. It is an interest in teaching children to engage in the kind of cooperation among Americans of all races that is necessary to make a land of three hundred million people one Nation.

Again, data support this insight. . . .

There are again studies that offer contrary conclusions. Again, however, the evidence supporting a democratic interest in racially integrated schools is firmly established and sufficiently strong to permit a school board to determine, as this Court has itself often found, that this interest is compelling.

. . .

For his part, Justice Thomas faults my citation of various studies supporting the view that school districts can find compelling educational and civic interests in integrating their public schools. He is entitled of course to his own opinion as to which studies he finds convincing.... If we are to insist upon unanimity in the social science literature before finding a compelling interest, we might never find one. I believe only that the Constitution allows democratically elected school boards to make up their own minds as to how best to include people of all races in one America.

B

Narrow Tailoring

. . .

First, the race-conscious criteria at issue only help set the outer bounds of *broad* ranges. They constitute but one part of plans that depend primarily upon other, nonracial elements. To use race in this way is not to set a forbidden "quota."

In fact, the defining feature of both plans is greater emphasis upon student choice. In Seattle, for example, in more than 80% of all cases, that choice alone determines which high schools Seattle's ninth graders will attend. After ninth grade, students can decide voluntarily to transfer to a preferred district high school (without any consideration of race-conscious criteria). *Choice*, therefore, is the "predominant factor" in these plans. *Race* is not.

Indeed, the race-conscious ranges at issue in these cases often have no effect, either because the particular school is not oversubscribed in the year in question, or because the racial makeup of the school falls within the broad range, or because the student is a transfer applicant or has a sibling at the school. In these respects, the broad ranges are less like a quota and more like the kinds of "useful starting points" that this Court has consistently found permissible, even when they set boundaries upon voluntary transfers, and even when they are based upon a community's general population.

Second, broad-range limits on voluntary school choice plans are less burdensome, and hence more narrowly tailored, than other race-conscious restrictions this Court has previously approved. Indeed, the plans before us are *more narrowly tailored* than the race-conscious admission plans that this Court approved in *Grutter*. Here, race becomes a factor only in a fraction of students' non-merit-based assignments — not in large numbers of students' merit-based applications. Moreover, the effect of applying race-conscious criteria here affects potentially disadvantaged students *less severely,* not more severely, than the criteria at issue in *Grutter*. Disappointed students are not rejected from a State's flagship graduate program; they simply attend a different one of the district's many public schools, which in aspiration and in fact are substantially equal....

Third, the manner in which the school boards developed these plans itself reflects "narrow tailoring." Each plan was devised to overcome a history of segregated public schools. Each plan embodies the results of local experience and community consultation. Each plan is the product of a process that has sought to enhance student choice, while diminishing the need for mandatory busing. And each plan's use of race-conscious elements is *diminished* compared to the use of race in preceding integration plans.

. . .

Moreover, giving some degree of weight to a local school board's knowledge, expertise, and concerns in these particular matters is not inconsistent with rigorous judicial scrutiny. It simply recognizes that judges are not well suited to act as school administrators. . . .

. . .

Nor could the school districts have accomplished their desired aims (*e.g.*, avoiding forced busing, countering white flight, maintaining racial diversity) by other means. . . .

[A]s to "strategic site selection," Seattle has built one new high school in the last 44 years (and that specialized school serves only 300 students). In fact, six of the Seattle high schools involved in this case were built by the 1920's; the other four were open by the early 1960's. As to "drawing" neighborhood "attendance zones" on a racial basis, Louisville tried it, and it worked only when forced busing was also part of the plan. As to "allocating resources for special programs," Seattle and Louisville have both experimented with this; indeed, these programs are often referred to as "magnet schools," but the limited desegregation effect of these efforts extends at most to those few schools to which additional resources are granted. In addition, there is no evidence from the experience of these school districts that it will make any meaningful impact. As to "recruiting faculty" on the basis of race, both cities have tried, but only as one part of a broader program. As to "tracking enrollments, performance and other statistics by race," tracking *reveals* the problem; it does not cure it.

. . .

V

Consequences

The Founders meant the Constitution as a practical document that would transmit its basic values to future generations through principles that remained workable over time. Hence it is important to consider the potential consequences of the plurality's approach, as measured against the Constitution's objectives. To do so provides further reason to believe that the plurality's approach is legally unsound.

For one thing, consider the effect of the plurality's views on the parties before us and on similar school districts throughout the Nation. . . .

The districts' past and current plans are not unique. They resemble other plans, promulgated by hundreds of local school boards, which have attempted a variety of desegregation methods that have evolved over time in light of experience.
. . .

At a minimum, the plurality's views would threaten a surge of race-based litigation. Hundreds of state and federal statutes and regulations use racial classifications for educational or other purposes. In many such instances, the contentious force of legal challenges to these classifications, meritorious or not, would displace earlier calm.

The wide variety of different integration plans that school districts use throughout the Nation suggests that the problem of racial segregation in schools, including *de facto* segregation, is difficult to solve. The fact that many such plans have used explicitly racial criteria suggests that such criteria have an important, sometimes necessary, role to play. The fact that the controlling opinion would make a school district's use of such criteria often unlawful (and the plurality's "colorblind" view would make such use always unlawful) suggests that today's opinion will require setting aside the laws of several States and many local communities.
. . .

The plurality, or at least those who follow Justice Thomas' "'color-blind'" approach, may feel confident that, to end invidious discrimination, one must end *all* governmental use of race-conscious criteria including those with inclusive objectives. By way of contrast, I do not claim to know how best to stop harmful discrimination; how best to create a society that includes all Americans; how best to overcome our serious problems of increasing *de facto* segregation, troubled inner city schooling, and poverty correlated with race. But, as a judge, I do know that the Constitution does not authorize judges to dictate solutions to these problems. Rather, the Constitution creates a democratic political system through which the people themselves must together find answers. And it is for them to debate how best to educate the Nation's children and how best to administer America's schools to achieve that aim. The Court should leave them to their work. And it is for them to decide, to quote the plurality's slogan, whether the best "way to stop discrimination on the basis of race is to stop discriminating on the basis of race."
. . .

***

Finally, what of the hope and promise of *Brown?* For much of this Nation's history, the races remained divided. It was not long ago that people of different races drank from separate fountains, rode on separate buses, and studied in separate schools. In this Court's finest hour, *Brown* v. *Board of Education*

149

challenged this history and helped to change it. For *Brown* held out a promise. It was a promise embodied in three Amendments designed to make citizens of slaves. It was the promise of true racial equality — not as a matter of fine words on paper, but as a matter of everyday life in the Nation's cities and schools. It was about the nature of a democracy that must work for all Americans. It sought one law, one Nation, one people, not simply as a matter of legal principle but in terms of how we actually live.

Not everyone welcomed this Court's decision in *Brown*. Three years after that decision was handed down, the Governor of Arkansas ordered state militia to block the doors of a white schoolhouse so that black children could not enter. The President of the United States dispatched the 101st Airborne Division to Little Rock, Arkansas, and federal troops were needed to enforce a desegregation decree. See *Cooper* v. *Aaron*, 358 U.S. 1, 78 S. Ct. 1401, 3 L. Ed. 2d 5 (1958). Today, almost 50 years later, attitudes toward race in this Nation have changed dramatically. Many parents, white and black alike, want their children to attend schools with children of different races. Indeed, the very school districts that once spurned integration now strive for it. The long history of their efforts reveals the complexities and difficulties they have faced. And in light of those challenges, they have asked us not to take from their hands the instruments they have used to rid their schools of racial segregation, instruments that they believe are needed to overcome the problems of cities divided by race and poverty. The plurality would decline their modest request.

The plurality is wrong to do so. The last half-century has witnessed great strides toward racial equality, but we have not yet realized the promise of *Brown*. To invalidate the plans under review is to threaten the promise of *Brown*. The plurality's position, I fear, would break that promise. This is a decision that the Court and the Nation will come to regret.

I must dissent.

Notes on Parents Involved

In *Parents Involved*, the Justices almost seem more focused on the meaning of *Brown* than on the meaning of the Fourteenth Amendment. Consider the following views.

> *Brown v. Board of Education* [is one] of the key lightning rods of modern constitutional law.... Thus, when the Court faces cases involving public school desegregation..., part of what the Court does is to invoke, once again, the mantle of [this] decisio[n]....
>
> The Court was quite conscious in *Parents Involved* that the Justices were involved in a struggle over the meaning of *Brown v. Board of Education*. Chief Justice Roberts's opinion for the Court sought to end the debate by

quoting what the counsel for the Brown plaintiffs said at oral argument: "'We have one fundamental contention which we will seek to develop in the course of this argument, and that contention is that no State has any authority under the equal-protection clause of the Fourteenth Amendment to use race as a factor in affording educational opportunities among its citizens.'" The Court saw "no ambiguity in that statement."....

The attorney who made that statement, Robert L. Carter, is now a distinguished federal district judge. Asked for his reaction to the Court's statement, [he responded].... "'All that race was used for at that point in time was to deny equal opportunity to black people,' Judge Carter said of the 1950s. "It's to stand that argument on its head to use race the way they use [it] now.'"

Karlan, The Law of Small Numbers: Gonzales v. Carhart, Parents Involved in Community Schools, and Some Themes from the First Full Term of the Roberts Court, 86 N.C.L. Rev. 1369, 1393, 1396 (2008).

Tellingly, the forty-one-page plurality opinion in *Seattle/Louisville* contains only one quotation from *Brown*: a paltry sentence fragment: "The impact [of segregation] is greater when it has the sanction of the law" — that omits the crucial adjacent words locating the illegality of segregation in its detrimental effects on black children. This inattention leads the plurality to identify the violation in 1954 as "differential treatment on the basis of race," again implying equal burdens on blacks and whites. But *Brown* did not speak of the violation that way. The Court nowhere used the term "colorblind" or availed itself of the familiar quotation from Harlan's dissent in *Plessy*. Instead, *Brown*'s most memorable utterance was its recognition that segregation harms black children by "generat[ing] a feeling of inferiority as to their status in the community that may affect their hearts and minds in a way unlikely ever to be undone."....

Liu, "History Will Be Heard": An Appraisal of the Seattle/Louisville Decision, 2 Harv. L. & Pol'y Rev. 53, 62 (2008).

The long and intricate opinions in *Parents Involved* reach a result that can be simply described: for Chief Justice Roberts and Justice Thomas, special attempts to aid minorities, looking at race as one salient factor, are no longer permitted. Three characteristics of the prevailing opinion are striking in the light of our legal history: the astonishing use of *Brown* in defense of an analysis that is utterly unlike *Brown* in spirit and result; the failure to confront with perception the history and current reality of racial segregation in the United States; and the obtuse formalism....

Both Chief Justice Roberts and Justice Thomas invoke *Brown* as if it stood for the proposition that race must never be taken into account in education, no matter whether the reason for doing so is to include or exclude.Of course *Brown* stood for no such thing.... Chief Justice Roberts appears to reduce the meaning of *Brown* to little more than what I have named lofty formalism: in reality, *Brown* was the unmasking of just such formalism, in the name of a practical concern for substantive equality....

[In *Parents Involved,*] the Court ignored the asymmetry between exclusion and inclusion, which is among the most striking features of the history of race relations in the United States. Neglecting this, Chief Justice Roberts's argument can be neither accurate nor fully fair....

The legacy of the civil rights movement consists, above all, in a certain quality of imagination, in which the experience of exclusion is understood, in which the measure of its pain and indignity is taken, and in which it is strongly distinguished from governmental approaches that seek to include and remedy. For the libertarian minimalist, the two actions of government look similar: both represent exactly the sort of governmental engineering that the libertarian dislikes.

In one sense, then, Chief Justice Roberts's opinion was libertarian: it instructed governments to stop discriminating. It is important to bear in mind, however, that in another way it was not in the least libertarian: the opinion argued that the strong power of the federal government should be used to stop local communities from making choices informed by their own sense of their history.

Nussbaum, Constitutions and Capabilities: "Perception" Against Lofty Formalism, 121 Harv. L. Rev. 4, 88-89, 91-92 (2007):

Justice Kennedy's concurrence plays a pivotal role in the case. In this regard, consider Gerken, Justice Kennedy and the Domains of Equal Protection, 121 Harv. L. Rev. 104, 108, 114-17 (2007):

Most of us think we already know the story of race. We tell the same story no matter what the domain. But every domain — schools, the marketplace, democracy — has an overarching narrative. What if we tried to fit race within that narrative rather than vice versa?....

The way Justice Kennedy frames his opinion provides some evidence that a domain-centered narrative is driving him.... Chief Justice Roberts, for instance, opens his analysis by invoking general equal protection principles and ends with the aphorism that "the way to stop discrimination on the basis of race is to stop discriminating on the basis of race." Justice Thomas begins his concurrence by characterizing the case as being about "state entities" rather than public schools, and he ends by invoking general language on race from *Dred Scott* and Justice Harlan's dissent in *Plessy*.

Justice Kennedy, in sharp contrast, anchors his concurrence in the domain of education. He opens his opinion by trumpeting the role that public schools play in teaching civic morality and explicitly linking that role to integration.... This opening certainly resonates with parts of *Brown*'s legacy. But its core narrative is less about equal educational opportunity, the dominant note in any equal protection story, than about the role schools play in teaching civic morality....

Public schools are, of course, a place where the state regulates pervasively, and at least on Kennedy's account, their job is to teach students to be citizens. This combination — pervasive regulation and an identifiable mission — makes it particularly hard to insist upon a race-neutral approach.... [E]ven a judge committed to the colorblind ideal might worry, as Kennedy seems to, that the value of colorblindness cannot be learned in a racially segregated school. The narrative of the educational domain, then, may be what focuses Justice Kennedy on the poor fit between his preference for a race-neutral state and his desire for a race-neutral society. Perhaps this is why the question for Kennedy seems to have changed in the domain of education. It is no longer whether the state can act race consciously, but how....

[P]erhaps Justice Kennedy sincerely believes what Scalia suggested only sarcastically in *Grutter*: that "cross-racial understanding" and "good citizenship" are lessons to be learned by "people three feet shorter and 20 years younger than the full-grown adults at the University of Michigan Law School, in... public-school kindergartens."

With respect to Justice Breyer's dissent, consider Wilkinson, The Seattle and Louisville School Cases: There Is No Other Way, 121 Harv. L. Rev. 158 , 176, 177-79 (2007):

[Justice Breyer's] dissent rests in part on a shrewd tactical maneuver. The Justice seeks to co-opt all the traditional conservative arguments against race-based decisionmaking and harness them to his own ends....

It has long been an article of faith among conservatives that the Constitution permits the use of race only for strictly remedial ends... Justice Breyer converts the term "remedial" to his own uses, declaring that school boards retain a continued "interest in setting right the consequences of prior conditions of segregation," whether or not imposed by law....

[I]t has long been critical to the conservative self-perception that opponents were "activist" and that conservatives were guardians of "restraint." It was, after all, the Warren Court that made activism "a dirty word," and

Roe v. Wade that exemplified intrusive jurisprudence at its worst. Conservatives saw themselves as protectors of restraint, stability, and the federal system with all its appreciation of democratic values and of the rights of states and localities to pursue their own distinctive policies.

In *Parents Involved*, Justice Breyer seeks to turn the tables. In some respects, the opinion is one long paean to the tradition of local control over local school systems.... "The Court should leave them to their work." This will bring calm, he says, as opposed to the disruption wrought by the activist solutions of activist judges.

And then there is the final competition over the concept of balkanization. To the conservative view that race preferment promotes a "politics of racial hostility" and constitutes "the most divisive of all policies," the Justice rejoins that it is inclusive efforts aimed at promoting integration that will produce, in his repeated words, "one Nation." That term, or "one America," appears four times in the Breyer opinion....

The Justice has left no stone unturned. It is his view, he says, that will foster the deference to democracy, the appreciation for local experimentation, the diminished litigation, the judicial restraint, and, above all, the binding ties to one nation that conservatives have wanted all along. The opinion consciously seeks to use the terminology of the other side and flip it. In one sense the dissent is unrelenting; in another it seeks to make a conciliatory case. The maneuver must be admired for its shrewdness and its attempt to appeal to opponents in a case made largely through their values and on their terms.

Why then does this best case fail ultimately to persuade? It fails because it recognizes few, if any, limits to the explicit use of race and ethnicity in public decisions. It fails because it risks abandoning America to a race-based course.... Without the prospect of strict judicial scrutiny of race-based classifications, it is anything but certain that racial proportionality would not become more prevalent as citizens and their representatives demand that public benefits be based on race, namely their own. At a minimum, supporters of racial allocation must offer analytical breaks on a practice that, once blessed, would start rolling downhill.

Earlier, in discussing Justice Kennedy's concurrence, Judge Wilkinson observed:

In permitting the use of just a little bit of race, courts cannot overlook the limited accountability of those making the racial judgment calls.... Most school boards and local governing bodies are elected to be sure, but the race-based decisions, like many others, somehow seem to end up in the bowels of the bureaucracy. The Fourteenth Amendment indicates, at a minimum, that these decisions are too important to leave there. One of the strongest points in Justice Kennedy's concurrence is that while race was concededly being used in Jefferson County school assignments, no one seemed to know exactly how. . . .

If the Justices could not entirely figure out when race was and was not used, heaven help the parents and students who tried to do so. Such lack of accountability, one fears, is not isolated but systemic. It demonstrates the dangers an absence of simple measures of accountability lends to even the limited use of race in student assignments and admissions.

Id. at 172-73.

Page 498.   Before the last paragraph of the Note, add the following:

But consider the following argument: those who believe that *Brown* failed are not considering it in context. School desegregation did not take place in a vacuum; it happened against a backdrop of segregation in neighborhoods, economic disparities, and deeply ingrained racial animus. Perhaps the most surprising result is that despite other societal forces, *Brown* accomplished as much as it did. See Wells et al., The Space Between School Desegregation Court Orders and Outcomes: The Struggle to Challenge White Privilege, 90 Va. L. Rev. 1721 (2004) (describing a study of six communities whose schools attempted racial integration, documenting replication of white privilege within these schools, and describing the circumstances under which courts can be an effective vehicle for social change).

Page 499.   After the citation to the Mickelson article in the first full paragraph, add the following:

See also Schofield & Hausmann, The Conundrum of School Desegregation: Positive Student Outcomes and Waning Support, 66 U. Pitt. L. Rev. 83 (2004) (summarizing 20 years of social science research that suggests early integration is beneficial to black and white students, particularly by long-range social and academic measures, and arguing that the paradoxical retreat from integration is due to latent racism, disproportionate distribution of the burdens of desegregation, and widespread attribution of the socioeconomic gap between blacks and whites to a dearth of ability endemic to blacks).

B. Equal Protection Methodology: Rational Basis Review

Page 506. At the end of section 2 of the Note, add the following:

Is leveling down incompatible with the norms of equality, even if it results in uniform treatment? See Brake, When Equality Leaves Everyone Worse Off: The Problem of Leveling Down in Equality Law, 46 Wm. & Mary L. Rev. 513 (2004). In what situations might leveling down produce a functionally unequal — though uniform — result?

Page 521. At the end of section 4 of the Note, add the following:

Are legislatures simply better equipped than courts to evaluate and weigh competing considerations? Consider the following view:

> A statute can provide a detailed set of regulations for one subject area and a different set for another, while leaving a third area largely untouched. [T]he flexibility inherent in legislative action allows Congress to more effectively detect and remedy the merely occasional equal protection violations that burden most groups in society.
> Judicial decisionmaking does not allow for this flexibility. A court considering a rational basis challenge to a government action tests the facts against the single, broad legal principle that government action may not be based on animus. [Thus,] a court's decision striking down a government action as lacking a rational basis is almost necessarily particularistic. [A court's application of rational review is akin to an] arbitrary lightning bolt that, when effective at all, completely wipes out one action but leaves similarly problematic conduct untouched.

Araiza, The Section 5 Power and the Rational Basis Standard for Equal Protection, 79 Tulane L. Rev. 519, 563-564 (2005).

Page 523.   At the end of section 6 of the Note, add the following:

In Enquist v. Oregon Dep't of Agriculture, 128 S. Ct. 2146 (2008), the Court considered the availability of "class of one" claims in the context of public employment. Enquist worked for a division of the Oregon Department of Agriculture. After her position was eliminated and she refused demotion to a lower-level position (and was thus effectively laid off), she brought suit claiming, among other things, that she had been fired for for "arbitrary, vindictive, and malicious reasons" in violation of the equal protection clause.

The Supreme Court, in an opinion by Chief Justice Roberts, held that the class-of-one theory does not apply to public employment. It saw a crucial difference between the government's exercise of its regulatory power with respect to individual citizens and its activities as an employer managing its internal operations. The Court pointed to a number of areas in which the government as employer is given more leeway with respect to constitutional constraints, such as under the First and Fourth Amendments. Employment, the Court declared, was a form of state action that by its nature "involve[s] discretionary decisionmaking based on a vast array of subjective, individualized assessments. In such cases the rule that people should be 'treated alike, under like circumstances and conditions' is not violated when one person is treated differently from others, because treating like individuals differently is an accepted consequence of the discretion granted. In such situations, allowing a challenge based on the arbitrary singling out of a particular person would undermine the very discretion that such state officials are entrusted to exercise." Recognizing class-of-one claims alleging that a public employer had treated an employee differently from others for a bad reason unconnected to a particular constitutional provision (such as discrimination on the basis of race or religion or gender) would undermine the concept of at-will employment, and the Court found that the "Constitution does not require repudiating that familiar doctrine." By contrast, the Court explained, in *Olech* and similar cases, there was "a clear standard against which departures, even for a single plaintiff, could be readily assessed."

Justice Stevens, joined by Justices Souter and Ginsburg, dissented. He saw no reason to treat property owners differently from employees and drew a distinction between discretionary decisionmaking and arbitrary decisionmaking. "A discretionary decision represents a choice of one among two or more rational alternatives. The choice may be mistaken or unwise without being irrational. If the arguments favoring each alternative are closely balanced, the need to make a choice may justify using a coin toss as a tie breaker. Moreover, the Equal Protection Clause proscribes arbitrary decisions — decisions unsupported by any rational basis — not unwise ones."

C. Equal Protection Methodology: Heightened Scrutiny and the Problem of Race

Page 567.   After the fourth paragraph of the Note, add the following:

In Johnson v. California, 545 U.S. 162 (2005), the Supreme Court, in an opinion by Justice Stevens, rejected a California requirement that defendants raising a *Batson* claim establish, as part of their prima facie case, that discriminatory intent was "more likely than not" the explanation for the prosecutor's strikes.

[I]n describing the burden-shifting framework, we assumed in *Batson* that the trial judge would have the benefit of all relevant circumstances, including the prosecutor's explanation, before deciding whether it was more likely than not that the challenge was improperly motivated. We did not intend the first step to be so onerous that a defendant would have to persuade the judge — on the basis of all the facts, some of which are impossible for the defendant to know with certainty — that the challenge was more likely than not the product of purposeful discrimination. Instead, a defendant satisfies the requirements of *Batson's* first step by producing evidence sufficient to permit the trial judge to draw an inference that discrimination has occurred....

Batson, of course, explicitly stated that the defendant ultimately carries the "burden of persuasion" to "prove the existence of purposeful discrimination." This burden of persuasion "rests with, and never shifts from, the opponent of the strike." Thus, even if the State produces only a frivolous or utterly nonsensical justification for its strike, the case does not end — it merely proceeds to step three. The first two *Batson* steps govern the production of evidence that allows the trial court to determine the persuasiveness of the defendant's constitutional claim. "It is not until the third step that the persuasiveness of the justification becomes relevant — the step in which the trial court determines whether the opponent of the strike has carried his burden of proving purposeful discrimination."

Page 569.   At the end of the Note, add the following:

Miller-El v. Dretke, 545 U.S. 231 (2005), provides an illustration of the difficulties of enforcing the *Batson* principle. In 1985, shortly before *Batson* was decided, Miller-El was tried for capital murder. Dallas County prosecutors used peremptory challenges to remove 10 of the 11 qualified black venire members. After *Batson* was decided, the trial court reviewed the record of the voir dire and, after hearing the prosecutor's explanations, decided that the jurors had not been struck because of their race. After more than a decade of litigation and two trips to the Supreme Court, the Court held, in an opinion by Justice Souter, that Miller-El was entitled to a new trial because prosecutors had used their peremptory challenges in a racially discriminatory fashion.

In a concurring opinion, Justice Breyer reiterated a point made by Justice Marshall in his concurring opinion in *Batson* that perhaps the "only way to 'end the racial discrimination that peremptories inject into the jury-selection process'" would be "to 'eliminate peremptory challenges entirely.'"

> [T]his case illustrates the practical problems of proof that Justice Marshall described. As the Court's opinion makes clear, Miller-El marshaled extensive evidence of racial bias. But despite the strength of his claim, Miller-El's challenge has resulted in 17 years of largely unsuccessful and protracted litigation — including 8 different judicial proceedings and 8 different judicial opinions, and involving 23 judges, of whom 6 found the *Batson* standard violated and 16 the contrary....
>
> *Batson* asks judges to engage in the awkward, sometime hopeless, task of second-guessing a prosecutor's instinctive judgment — the underlying basis for which may be invisible even to the prosecutor exercising the challenge....
>
> Given the inevitably clumsy fit between any objectively measurable standard and the subjective decisionmaking at issue, I am not surprised to find studies and anecdotal reports suggesting that, despite *Batson,* the discriminatory use of peremptory challenges remains a problem. See, e.g., Baldus, Woodworth, Zuckerman, Weiner, & Broffitt, The Use of Peremptory Challenges in Capital Murder Trials: A Legal and Empirical Analysis, 3 U. Pa. J. Const. L. 3, 52-53, 73, n. 197 (2001) (in 317 capital trials in Philadelphia between 1981 and 1997, prosecutors struck 51% of black jurors and 26% of nonblack jurors; defense counsel struck 26% of black jurors and 54% of nonblack jurors; and race-based uses of prosecutorial peremptories declined by only 2% after *Batson*); Rose, The Peremptory Challenge Accused of Race or Gender Discrimination? Some Data from One County, 23 Law and Human Behavior 695, 698-699 (1999) (in one North Carolina county, 71% of excused black jurors were removed by the prosecution; 81% of excused white jurors were removed by the defense); Tucker, In Moore's Trials, Excluded Jurors Fit Racial Pattern, Washington Post, Apr. 2, 2001, p. A1 (in D.C. murder case spanning four trials, prosecutors excused 41 blacks or other minorities and 6 whites; defense counsel struck 29 whites and 13 black venire members); Mize, A Legal Discrimina-

tion; Juries Are Not Supposed to be Picked on the Basis of Race and Sex, But It Happens All the Time, Washington Post, Oct. 8, 2000, p. B8 (authored by judge on the D.C. Superior Court); see also Melilli, *Batson in Practice: What We Have Learned About Batson and Peremptory Challenges*, 71 Notre Dame L. Rev. 447, 462-464 (1996) (finding *Batson* challenges' success rates lower where peremptories were used to strike black, rather than white, potential jurors); Brand, The Supreme Court, Equal Protection and Jury Selection: Denying That Race Still Matters, 1994 Wis. L. Rev. 511, 583-589 (examining judicial decisions and concluding that few *Batson* challenges succeed); Note, *Batson v. Kentucky* and *J. E. B. v. Alabama ex rel. T. B.*: Is the Peremptory Challenge Still Preeminent?, 36 Boston College L. Rev. 161, 189, and n. 303 (1994) (same); Montoya, The Future of the Post-*Batson* Peremptory Challenge: Voir Dire by Questionnaire and the "Blind" Peremptory Challenge, 29 U. Mich. J. L. Reform 981, 1006, nn. 126-127, 1035 (1996) (reporting attorneys' views on the difficulty of proving *Batson* claims).

Justice Breyer also suggested that "peremptory challenges seem increasingly anomalous in our judicial system. On the one hand, the Court has widened and deepened *Batson's* basic constitutional rule. [On] the other hand, the use of race-and gender-based stereotypes in the jury-selection process seems better organized and more systematized than ever before." After pointing to jury-selection guides, bar journal articles, and other training materials advising lawyers on how to take demographic factors, including race, into account, Justice Breyer noted:

[T]hese examples reflect a professional effort to fulfill the lawyer's obligation to help his or her client. Nevertheless, the outcome in terms of jury selection is the same as it would be were the motive less benign. And as long as that is so, the law's antidiscrimination command and a peremptory jury-selection system that permits or encourages the use of stereotypes work at cross-purposes.

Finally, a jury system without peremptories is no longer unthinkable. Members of the legal profession have begun serious consideration of that possibility. And England, a common-law jurisdiction that has eliminated peremptory challenges, continues to administer fair trials based largely on random jury selection....

I recognize that peremptory challenges have a long historical pedigree. They may help to reassure a party of the fairness of the jury. But long ago, Blackstone recognized the peremptory challenge as an "arbitrary and capricious species of [a] challenge." 4 W. Blackstone, Commentaries on the

Laws of England 346 (1769). If used to express stereotypical judgments about race, gender, religion, or national origin, peremptory challenges betray the jury's democratic origins and undermine its representative function. The "scientific" use of peremptory challenges may also contribute to public cynicism about the fairness of the jury system and its role in American government. And, of course, the right to a jury free of discriminatory taint is constitutionally protected — the right to use peremptory challenges is not.

Does the Supreme Court's repeated intervention in particular cases raising *Batson* challenges suggest the unworkability of the standard it announced, resistance by lower courts to full enforcement of the right, or some other problem? In this light, consider Snyder v. Louisiana, 128 S. Ct. 1203 (2008). The case involved a capital murder prosecution of a black defendant in Louisiana. After the court finished disqualifying jurors for cause, the prosecutor used five of his peremptory challenges to remove all the remaining black members of the venire. The defendant was convicted and sentenced to death. On appeal, the Louisiana Supreme Court rejected his *Batson* claim and the U.S. Supreme Court granted his petition for certiorari and vacated and remanded the case for further consideration in light of *Miller-El*. The Louisiana Supreme Court reaffirmed its original judgment. The United States Supreme Court then granted certiorari and found that a *Batson* violation had occurred. Justice Alito's opinion for the Court examined in great detail the reasons given for striking one of the black venire members and concluded that the race-neutral explanations were not persuasive.

Page 576. At the end of section 2 of the Note, add the following:

By contrast, Professor Harcourt argues that data upon which current research rests is of little empirical use; since most studies include only the number and proportion of searched drivers' races, and the success rate of searches, it is easy to draw disparate conclusions from identical data. Absent data regarding natural offending rates by racial group and the comparative elasticity of offending to policing, Harcourt suggests, it is difficult to articulate how racial profiling should be used in policing. Harcourt, Rethinking Racial Profiling: A Critique of the Economics, Civil Liberties, and Constitutional Literature, and of Criminal Profiling More Generally, 71 U. Chi. L. Rev. 1275 (2004). Assuming this data were attainable, what findings should be sufficient to overcome a claim of racial discrimination in policing?

Page 576.   At the end of section 3 of the Note, add the following:

For some observations regarding the possible effects of *judges'* race and sex on sentencing decisions, see Schanzenbach, Racial and Sex Disparities in Prison Sentences: The Effect of District-Level Judicial Demographics, 34 J. Legal Stud. 57 (2005).

Page 606.   Before the Note, add the following:

JOHNSON v. CALIFORNIA, 543 U.S. 499 (2005). The California Department of Corrections (CDC) had an unwritten policy of assigning inmates to cells on the basis of race for up to 60 days each time a prisoner entered a new correctional facility, based on its view that such segregation prevented violence caused by racial gangs. The court of appeals held that the policy's constitutionality should be reviewed under the deferential standard articulated in Turner v. Safley, 482 U.S. 78 (1987), which asks whether a regulation that burdens a prisoner's fundamental rights is "reasonably related" to "legitimate penological interests." Using that standard, the Ninth Circuit upheld California's policy.

Justice O'Connor delivered the opinion of the Court: "We have held that '*all* racial classifications [imposed by government]... must be analyzed by a reviewing court under strict scrutiny.' Adarand Constructors, Inc. v. Pena, 515 U.S. 200 (1995) (emphasis added). Under strict scrutiny, the government has the burden of proving that racial classifications 'are narrowly tailored measures that further compelling governmental interests.' We have insisted on strict scrutiny in every context, even for so-called 'benign' racial classifications, such as race-conscious university admissions policies, see Grutter v. Bollinger, 539 U.S. 306 (2003), [and] race-based districting intended to improve minority representation, see Shaw v. Reno, 509 U.S. 630 (1993)....

"The CDC claims that its policy should be exempt from our categorical rule because it is 'neutral' — that is, it 'neither benefits nor burdens one group or individual more than any other group or individual.' [The] CDC's argument ignores our repeated command that 'racial classifications receive close scrutiny even when they may be said to burden or benefit the races equally.' Indeed, we rejected the notion that separate can ever be equal — or 'neutral' — 50 years ago in Brown v. Board of Education, 347 U.S. 483 (1954), and we refuse to resurrect it today....

"We have previously applied a heightened standard of review in evaluating racial segregation in prisons. In Lee v. Washington, 390 U.S. 333 (1968) (per curiam), we upheld a three-judge court's decision striking down Alabama's policy of segregation in its prisons. Alabama had argued that desegregation would undermine prison security and discipline, but we rejected that contention. . . .

"The need for strict scrutiny is no less important here, where prison officials cite racial violence as the reason for their policy. As we have recognized in the past, racial classifications 'threaten to stigmatize individuals by reason of their membership in a racial group and to incite racial hostility.' Indeed, by insisting that inmates be housed only with other inmates of the same race, it is possible that prison officials will breed further hostility among prisoners and reinforce racial and ethnic divisions. By perpetuating the notion that race matters most, racial segregation of inmates 'may exacerbate the very patterns of [violence that it is] said to counteract.' Shaw, supra, at 648; see also Trulson & Marquart, The Caged Melting Pot: Toward an Understanding of the Consequences of Desegregation in Prisons, 36 Law & Soc. Rev. 743, 774 (2002) (in a study of prison desegregation, finding that "over [10 years] the rate of violence between inmates segregated by race in double cells surpassed the rate among those racially integrated"). . . .

"The CDC's policy is unwritten. [Virtually] all other States and the Federal Government manage their prison systems without reliance on racial segregation. [Indeed,] the United States argues, based on its experience with the [Federal Bureau of Prisons], that it is possible to address 'concerns of prison security through individualized consideration without the use of racial segregation, unless warranted as a necessary and temporary response to a race riot or other serious threat of race-related violence.' As to transferees, in particular, whom the CDC has already evaluated at least once, it is not clear why more individualized determinations are not possible. . . .

"The CDC invites us to make an exception to the rule that strict scrutiny applies to all racial classifications, and instead to apply the deferential standard of review articulated in Turner v. Safley, 482 U.S. 78 (1987), because its segregation policy applies only in the prison context. We decline the invitation. . . .

"We have never applied Turner to racial classifications. Turner itself did not involve any racial classification, and it cast no doubt on Lee. We think this unsurprising, as we have applied Turner's reasonable-relationship test only to rights that are 'inconsistent with proper incarceration.' Thus, for example, we have relied on Turner in addressing First Amendment challenges to prison regulations, including restrictions on freedom of association, limits on inmate correspondence, restrictions on inmates' access to courts, restrictions on receipt of subscription publications, and work rules limiting prisoners' attendance at

163

religious services. We have also applied *Turner* to some due process claims, such as involuntary medication of mentally ill prisoners, and restrictions on the right to marry.

"The right not to be discriminated against based on one's race is not susceptible to the logic of *Turner*. It is not a right that need necessarily be compromised for the sake of proper prison administration. On the contrary, compliance with the Fourteenth Amendment's ban on racial discrimination is not only consistent with proper prison administration, but also bolsters the legitimacy of the entire criminal justice system. [For] similar reasons, we have not used Turner to evaluate Eighth Amendment claims of cruel and unusual punishment in prison. [This] is because the integrity of the criminal justice system depends on full compliance with the Eighth Amendment. See Spain v. Procunier, 600 F.2d 189, 193-194 (CA9 1979) (Kennedy, J.) ('[T]he full protections of the eighth amendment most certainly remain in force [in prison]. The whole point of the amendment is to protect persons convicted of crimes. [Mechanical] deference to the findings of state prison officials in the context of the eighth amendment would reduce that provision to a nullity in precisely the context where it is most necessary' (internal quotation marks omitted))....

"The CDC argues that '[d]eference to the particular expertise of prison officials in the difficult task of managing daily prison operations' requires a more relaxed standard of review for its segregation policy. But we have refused to defer to state officials' judgments on race in other areas where those officials traditionally exercise substantial discretion. For example, we have held that, despite the broad discretion given to prosecutors when they use their peremptory challenges, using those challenges to strike jurors on the basis of their race is impermissible. Similarly, in the redistricting context, despite the traditional deference given to States when they design their electoral districts, we have subjected redistricting plans to strict scrutiny when States draw district lines based predominantly on race....

"[W]e explicitly reaffirm what we implicitly held in *Lee*: The 'necessities of prison security and discipline' are a compelling government interest justifying only those uses of race that are narrowly tailored to address those necessities....

"The CDC protests that strict scrutiny will handcuff prison administrators and render them unable to address legitimate problems of race-based violence in prisons. Not so. Strict scrutiny is not 'strict in theory, but fatal in fact.' Strict scrutiny does not preclude the ability of prison officials to address the compelling interest in prison safety. Prison administrators, however, will have to demonstrate that any race-based policies are narrowly tailored to that end....

"The fact that strict scrutiny applies 'says nothing about the ultimate validity of any particular law; that determination is the job of the court applying strict scrutiny.' *Adarand.* At this juncture, no such determination has been made. On remand, the CDC will have the burden of demonstrating that its policy is narrowly tailored with regard to new inmates as well as transferees. Prisons are dangerous places, and the special circumstances they present may justify racial classifications in some contexts. Such circumstances can be considered in applying strict scrutiny, which is designed to take relevant differences into account."

Justice Ginsburg, joined by Justices Souter and Breyer, concurred, reiterating her position in *Grutter* and *Gratz* that "the same standard of review ought not control judicial inspection of every official race classification." Because there was "no pretense here [that] the California Department of Corrections (CDC) installed its segregation policy to 'correct inequalities,'" she agreed that strict scrutiny was warranted.

Justice Stevens dissented. Although he agreed that strict scrutiny was required, he would have held that the CDC's policy violated the equal protection clause, rather than merely remanding the case for application of strict scrutiny.

Justice Thomas, joined by Justice Scalia, also dissented. He saw the case as lying at the intersection of "two conflicting lines of precedent": one requiring strict scrutiny of all racial classifications and the other holding that a "relaxed" standard of review "applies to all circumstances in which the needs of prison administration implicate constitutional rights."

"Emphasizing the former line of cases, the majority resolves the conflict in favor of strict scrutiny. I disagree. The Constitution has always demanded less within the prison walls. Time and again, even when faced with constitutional rights no less 'fundamental' than the right to be free from state-sponsored racial discrimination, we have deferred to the reasonable judgments of officials experienced in running this Nation's prisons. There is good reason for such deference in this case. [The] majority is concerned with sparing inmates the indignity and stigma of racial discrimination. California is concerned with their safety and saving their lives. . . .

"Traditionally, federal courts rarely involved themselves in the administration of state prisons, 'adopt[ing] a broad hands-off attitude toward problems of prison administration.' For most of this Nation's history, only law-abiding citizens could claim the cover of the Constitution: Upon conviction and incarceration, defendants forfeited their constitutional rights and possessed instead only those rights that the State chose to extend them. In recent decades, however, this Court has decided that incarceration does not divest prisoners of all constitutional protections.

"At the same time, this Court quickly recognized that the extension of the Constitution's demands behind prison walls had to accommodate the needs of prison administration. This Court reached that accommodation in Turner v. Safley, which 'adopted a unitary, deferential standard for reviewing prisoners' constitutional claims.' That standard should govern Johnson's claims, as it has governed a host of other claims challenging conditions of confinement, even when restricting the rights at issue would otherwise have occasioned strict scrutiny. Under the *Turner* standard, the CDC's policy passes constitutional muster, because it is reasonably related to legitimate penological interests.…

"[I]n light of the four factors enunciated in *Turner,* California's policy is constitutional: The CDC's policy is reasonably related to a legitimate penological interest; alternative means of exercising the restricted right remain open to inmates; racially integrating double cells might negatively impact prison inmates, staff, and administrators; and there are no obvious, easy alternatives to the CDC's policy.…

"The majority's test eviscerates *Turner.* Inquiring whether a given right is consistent with 'proper prison administration' calls for precisely the sort of judgments that *Turner* said courts were ill equipped to make.…

"The majority contends that the Court '[has] put the burden on state actors to demonstrate that their race-based policies are justified,' and '[has] refused to defer to state officials' judgments on race in other areas where those officials traditionally exercise substantial discretion.' Yet two Terms ago, in upholding the University of Michigan Law School's affirmative-action program, this Court deferred to the judgment by the law school's faculty and administrators on their need for diversity in the student body. Deference would seem all the more warranted in the prison context, for whatever the Court knows of administering educational institutions, it knows much less about administering penal ones. The potential consequences of second-guessing the judgments of prison administrators are also much more severe. See White v. Morris, 832 F. Supp. 1129, 1130 (SD Ohio 1993) (racially integrated double celling that resulted from federal consent decree was a factor in the worst prison riot in Ohio history)…

"Even under strict scrutiny analysis, 'it is possible, even likely, that prison officials could show that the current policy meets the test.'…

"Perhaps on remand the CDC's policy will survive strict scrutiny, but in the event that it does not, Johnson may well have won a Pyrrhic victory."

Page 607. At the end of section 1 of the Note, add the following:

Is *Grutter* a passive approach to the broad constitutional equality the Court had envisioned in *Brown*? Consider the following argument:

> The fact that the Court decided *Grutter* without a re-examination of equal protection speaks volumes about the Court's deep ambivalence concerning a transformative role of the Equal Protection Clause. Examined closely,

Grutter also reveals the Court's ambivalence over the project of constitutionally mandated equality. *Grutter* sanctions voluntary inclusion efforts but requires all such efforts to run the expensive gauntlet of strict scrutiny and its inevitable accompanying litigation. At the same time, no constitutionally mandated restructuring of opportunity is possible without an equally onerous burden of intentional discrimination.

Read narrowly, *Grutter* encourages, but does not require, minority inclusion in the nation's elite public universities. *Grutter* also does not require that law schools or other public universities eliminate the de facto segregation that may result from the usual and customary admissions criteria, nor does *Grutter* require that these institutions rethink their policies to provide greater opportunity to minorities. Moreover, *Grutter* does not condemn the narrow conceptions of merit that produce segregated educational institutions.

Greene, From *Brown* to *Grutter,* 36 Loy. U. Chi. L.J. 1, 17 (2004).

Consider the disagreement within the Court expressed in Parents Involved in Community Schools v. Seattle School District No. 1, 127 S. Ct. 2736 (2007), a case concerning race-conscious student assignment policies in public schools. (An extensive excerpt from the case appears earlier in this supplement with respect to page 497 of the principal text.)

In his opinion for the Court, Chief Justice Roberts wrote that public school assignment policies "are not governed by *Grutter*" because "[i]n upholding the admissions plan in *Grutter,*... this Court relied upon considerations unique to institutions of higher education, noting that in light of 'the expansive freedoms of speech and thought associated with the university environment, universities occupy a special niche in our constitutional tradition.'" By contrast, in dissent, Justice Breyer emphasized as part of his view that the school districts had a compelling interest in taking race into account that "there is a democratic element: an interest in producing an educational environment that reflects the 'pluralistic society' in which our children will live. It is an interest in helping our children learn to work and play together with children of different racial backgrounds. It is an interest in teaching children to engage in the kind of cooperation among Americans of all races that is necessary to make a land of three hundred million people one Nation."

Page 608.   Before section 3 of the Note, add the following:

2a. *The unitary nature of the strict scrutiny standard.* What are the implications of *Grutter* for strict scrutiny more generally? Does the case represent a straightforward application of strict scrutiny, or does it instead adopt a new form of scrutiny? Should the nature of the scrutiny vary depending on the nature of the institution at issue? See Ancheta, Contextual Strict Scrutiny and Race-Conscious Policy Making, 36 Loy. U. Chi. L.J. 21 (2004). Of racial preference cases thus far, which, if any, would have come out differently under a contextual scrutiny regime? Is Ancheta merely articulating explicitly what the Court already does implicitly? If so, what implications might such a change still have?

Page 608.   Before section 4 of the Note, add the following:

3a. *The efficacy of law school affirmative action.* In the wake of *Grutter,* Professor Sander offered a different critique of race-conscious affirmative action in law schools, claiming that black students admitted to law school through racial preferences are disadvantaged in the long term. As a result of affirmative action, Sander argues, black students are subject to an "academic mismatch": they have significantly lower credentials (LSAT scores and undergraduate grades) than students admitted without regard to race. Mismatched students, Sander argues, are less likely to perform well in law school (where instruction will be pitched toward students with better academic preparation), less likely to graduate, and less likely to pass the bar:

> [T]he absolute number of black law graduates passing the bar on their first attempt — an achievement important both for a lawyer's self-esteem and for success in the legal market — would be much larger under a race-blind regime than under the current system of preferences.... [T]he elimination of racial preferences would put blacks into schools where they were perfectly competitive with all other students — and that would lead to dramatically higher performance in law school and on the bar. Black students' grades, graduation rates, and bar passage rates would all converge toward white students' rates. The overall rate of blacks graduating from law school and passing the bar on their first attempt would rise from ... 45% ... to somewhere between 64% and 70%. Conversely, the black students excluded by a switch to a race-blind system have such weak academic credentials that they add only a comparative handful of attorneys to total national production.

Sander, A Systemic Analysis of Affirmative Action in American Law Schools, 57 Stan. L. Rev. 367, 474 (2004). Sander's empirical methods, as well as the conclusions he draws from his data sets, have been extensively criticized. One study found that students with the same LSAT score, undergraduate GPA, and gender performed similarly on the bar regardless of which law school they attended and concluded that "[w]hile it is true that similarly qualified black students get lower grades as a result of going to a higher-tier school, they perform equally well on the bar irrespective of law school tier." Ho, Why Affirmative Action Does Not Cause Black Students to Fail the Bar, 114 Yale L.J. 1997, 2004 (2005). Another study found a "reverse mismatch" effect: for both white and black students, attending a higher-tier school was positively correlated with ultimately becoming a lawyer:

> When students are overmatched by their classmates, they appear to be carried along to more success. The mismatch hypothesis is plausible, when it comes to law school grades — after all, if courses are graded on the curve, students with better entering credentials are more likely to get the limited supply of "A"s. But the mismatch theory is more ambiguous with regard to success after law school. Overmatched students in more selective academic settings may be mentored and inspired by their better-credentialed peers or teachers, or obtain the advantages of greater institutional commitment of resources to academics in more competitive schools. It is entirely sensible that students receive some marginal benefit from going to stronger schools, but what is striking about [the results we find] is how much better students do on the bar when they go to a school with better-credentialed peers and a better tradition of bar passage success. Even here, the mismatch hypothesis must at some point have traction — sending a second-grader to study corporate finance is surely folly. But it is not irrational for parents to want to get their kids into the best possible school (even if they are overmatched). When it comes to ultimate success, choosing the right peers might favor either the mismatch or the reverse mismatch.

Ayres & Brooks, Does Affirmative Action Reduce the Number of Black Lawyers?, 57 Stan. L. Rev. 1807, 1824-1825 (2005); see also Alon & Tienda, Assessing the "Mismatch" Hypothesis: Differential in College Graduation Rates by Institutional Selectivity 78 Soc. Educ. 295 (2005) (finding that the likelihood of minority students graduating from college increases as the selec-tivity of the institution attended rises). For other empirical critiques of Sander's work, see, e.g., Harris & Kidder, The Black Student Mismatch Myth in Legal Education: The Systemic Flaws in Richard Sander's Affirmative Action Study, J. Blacks Higher Educ. 103 (Winter 2005); Johnson & Onwuachi-Willig, Cry Me a River: The Limits of "A Systemic Analysis of Affirmative Action in American Law Schools," 7 Afr.-Am. L. & Poly. Rep. 1 (2005).

Consider two goals of affirmative action: promoting diversity and remedying past wrongs. To what extent is Sander's argument useful in addressing these goals? In this regard, consider Wilkins, A Systematic Response to Systemic Disadvantage: A Response to Sander, 57 Stan. L. Rev. 1915, 1938 (2005):

> Sander treats the success of the black graduates from elite law schools as if this were solely a benefit to the individuals involved. This seriously underestimates the importance of developing a viable black elite. Blacks who have achieved positions of power and influence in the legal profession, most of whom, as we have seen, are graduates of elite law schools, have played a critical role in opening the doors of opportunity for other black lawyers. Black partners routinely serve on hiring committees, form organizations dedicated to improving the hiring and retention of minority lawyers, and devote countless hours to mentoring black associates and law students. As many blacks have left law firms for in-house counsel positions, these newly minted purchasing agents have sought to use their new positions of authority to distribute work to minority lawyers and to press firms to report their progress on diversity and improve upon it.
>
> These efforts have improved the job prospects of every black law student. Predictably, recent black graduates from elite schools have benefited the most from these efforts by their alumni predecessors. This, of course, is simply a reflection of the many benefits of joining the elite networks to which such graduates automatically belong. But black lawyers from lower-ranked schools are also better off as a result of the doors that have been opened by elite black lawyers. Black partners have been at the forefront of pushing law firms and other employers to look beyond the graduates of top law schools when recruiting black students. Employing a variation of Willie Sutton's famous quip about the reason why he robbed banks — "it's where the money is!" — black partners and general counsel have vigorously pressed firms to recruit at historically black law schools and to attend minority job fairs in order to increase the number of black applicants that they see. At the same time, black general counsel have worked to ensure that minority law firms gain access to at least some corporate business and that blacks in small-and medium-sized firms are included as well. These efforts have been critical in producing the improvement in the earnings prospects of black graduates from lower-ranked schools. . . .

Additionally, Sander recommends that schools make their admissions policies "transparent," so students can consider the grades and scores of students in their demographic group and make informed decisions about their chances of success at a particular law school. Do you agree? Would making this information more available serve the goals of affirmative action? Compare Ayres & Brooks, *supra*, at 1851 (suggesting better disclosure might be beneficial), with Wilkins, *supra*, at 1955-1959 (suggesting greater disclosure might under-mine the goals of affirmative action).

Page 621.   At the end of section 4a of the Note, add the following:

In League of United Latin American Citizens v. Perry, 548 U.S. 399 (2006), the Supreme Court addressed wide-ranging challenge to Texas's mid-decade redistricting of its congressional seats. Ultimately, the Court rejected all of the claims except a Voting Rights Act-related challenge to the redrawing of a majority-Latino district in West Texas. (The Court's opinion is addressed in more detail in Chapter 6 of the Supplement.) Along the way, six Justices expressed the view that compliance with section 5 of the Voting Rights Act, which forbids specified jurisdictions from making changes to their election laws that diminish the voting strength of racial minority groups, constitutes a com-pelling state interest that can justify using race in drawing district lines. Justice Scalia's opinion, concurring in the judgment in part (to the extent it rejected the challengers' claims) and dissenting in part (with respect to the one district struck down as a violation of section 2 of the Voting Rights Act), joined by the Chief Justice and Justices Thomas and Alito in relevant part, stated:

We have in the past left undecided whether compliance with federal antidiscrimination laws can be a compelling state interest. I would hold that compliance with §5 of the Voting Rights Act can be such an interest. We long ago upheld the constitutionality of §5 as a proper exercise of Congress's authority under §2 of the Fifteenth Amendment to enforce that Amendment's prohibition on the denial or abridgment of the right to vote. If compliance with §5 were not a compelling state interest, then a State could be placed in the impossible position of having to choose between compliance with §5 and compliance with the Equal Protection Clause. Moreover, the compelling nature of the State's interest in §5 compliance is supported by our recognition in previous cases that race may be used where necessary to remedy identified past discrimination. Congress enacted §5 for just that purpose, and that provision applies only to jurisdictions with a history of official discrimination. In the proper case, therefore, a covered jurisdiction may have a compelling interest in complying with §5.

In his opinion concurring in part and dissenting in part, Justice Stevens, joined by Justice Breyer, simply noted his agreement with Justice Scalia that compliance with section 5 constitutes a compelling state interest. The other three Justices did not address the issue.

D. *Equal Protection Methodology: Heightened Scrutiny and the Problem of Gender*

Page 648. At the end of section 1 of the Note, add the following:

Assuming that sex-segregated schools would pose disadvantages to women analogous to those addressed in *Brown*, would these disappear if women, but not men, were given the option of single-sex public education? Consider the following argument:

> Single-sex middle or high schools for girls with no male counterpart are considerably more defensible than the nursing school in *Hogan*. Such a middle or high school can be explained in terms that do not so obviously incorporate harmful gender stereotypes — that is, as an attempt to respond to special problems widely experienced by adolescent girls and as providing an environment in which teaching methods can most easily be tailored to ways of learning that girls generally seem to find most congenial. These explanations, however, are not unambiguously affirming of girls' abilities and potential, and altogether it is difficult to deny that there is some risk that the creation of the girls school sends a message to both girls and boys that girls are in some sense inferior to boys — whether that means more needy, less adaptable, more fragile, or some other disempowering comparative generalization.

Simson, Separate But Equal and Single-Sex Schools, 90 Cornell L. Rev. 443, 456 (2005).

Page 656. Before section 2 of the Note, add the following:

1a. *The role of gender in law school and other facially neutral institutions.* Marjorie Kornhauser found significant gender segregation within law school faculties, finding that nearly 80 percent of courses had "a disproportionate number of men or women teaching the subject as compared to the gender composition of all law school professors" and that this disparity had increased over time:

> Courses with a female disparity — such as Juvenile Law, Poverty Law, and Legal Writing and Research — generally fit within a typical gender schema of "feminine." These courses are less central to the core of law and law school, less prestigious, and often associated with traditionally female traits such as care and relationships. Similarly, men are over-concentrated in the most traditional, and hence most "masculine," courses such as Constitutional Law, Evidence, Corporations, and Government Contracts. Men are also over-concentrated in "hot" or prestigious courses such as Law and Economics and Constitutional Law.

Kornhauser, Rooms of Their Own: An Empirical Study of Occupational Segregation by Gender Among Law Professors, 73 UMKC L. Rev. 293, 324 (2004). Does it matter whether women and men voluntarily choose different teaching packages? Kornhauser notes that the question of prestige is complex. Does this complicate determining in which direction causation runs — that is, whether fields become less prestigious because they attract disproportionate numbers of female teachers or whether women are assigned to fields because they are less prestigious?

Is law school itself "gendered"? Empirical research suggests women are less comfortable than men participating in certain aspects of law school, such as volunteering answers and approaching professors outside of class. For an overview of research on race and gender in law school, see L. Guinier et al., Becoming Gentlemen: Women, Law School, and Institutional Change (1997); Cassman & Pruitt, A Kinder, Gentler Law School? Race, Ethnicity, Gender, and Legal Education at King Hall, 38 U.C. Davis L. Rev. 1209 (2005).

Page 658. At the end of section 3 of the Note, add the following:

What about policies that permit or favor a personal or physical characteristic in one sex and prohibit or disfavor it in another — such as forbidding long hair on men or privileging passive women? Yuracko, in Trait Discrimination as Sex Discrimination: An Argument Against Neutrality, 83 Tex. L. Rev. 167 (2004), calls such policies "trait discrimination." She advocates a "power-access" approach in determining which instances of trait discrimination are permissible:

The reason an employer allows women but not men to wear dresses is because women who wear dresses are social conformists while men who wear dresses are not. The power-access approach demands an examination of the gender norms driving the trait discrimination in each case and recognizes that not all gender norms are created equal. Some are far more dangerous to sex equality than others. Moreover, it also recognizes the significant costs to employers and employees that are likely to flow from an enforced blindness to all gender norms. The power-access approach calls, therefore, for a necessarily context-specific process of social transformation whereby nondiscrimination is equated not with formal neutrality but with the elimination of only particularly harmful or limiting gender norms.

Id. at 225-226.

E. Equal Protection Methodology: The Problem of Sexual Orientation

Page 667. At the end of section 1 of the Note, add the following:

Consider the following argument: Discussions about sexual orientation tend to assign people to categories — gay or lesbian, straight, and bisexual — perhaps because such delineations are useful in issues of race and gender equality. But neither the "acts" nor the "desires" categorization is entirely helpful to understanding the nature of the class at issue. Nor is sexual orientation — whether genetically influenced or not — necessarily fixed. This may be one reason the class at issue is less readily definable than in race discrimination, and that categorizing people as "gay" or "straight" does not fully clarify the rights at issue.

Page 685. Before the second full paragraph, add the following:

With respect to the question of civil unions, see Samar, Privacy and the Debate over Same-Sex Marriage Versus Unions, 54 DePaul L. Rev. 783 (2005) (arguing that a separate system of marriage would never be equal because marriage has autonomous social meaning in American culture and creating separate institutions would overlook ways that culture affects individuals).

Is the rationality of states' restrictions of marriage to opposite-sex couples amenable to empirical debate? In this light, consider the following argument:

Consider one [often discussed issue]: whether legal recognition of same-sex marriage would benefit or harm children. Proponents, opponents, and those skeptical of same-sex marriage all cite studies in support of their positions. But what if we could get beyond methodological sparring? Would most of the [participants in the debate] really change their minds, or would their hearts leave them unmoved by contrary evidence? ...

Suppose ... that there were reliable evidence that children raised by same-sex couples were, by their own account, less happy as adults than their counterparts raised by opposite-sex couples; suppose further that there were evidence that recognizing same-sex marriages increased the number of gay couples who choose to have children or otherwise increased the number of parents who enter into same-sex relationships. ... [Would supporters of same-sex marriage] respond, as one of the Justices did at the argument in *Loving*, that we "don't know what is cause, and what is effect"? It may well be that any unhappiness or difference in outcomes is a product of continuing societal discrimination against gay men and lesbians. ...

Or suppose it were shown that children raised by same-sex parents reported the same levels of subjective happiness and performed as well along whatever objective dimensions we might care about as their counterparts raised by opposite-sex parents. ... [F]aced with the fact that large numbers of children already live in households headed by same-sex couples, would [opponents of same-sex marriage] respond to claims that the lives of these children would be improved by allowing their parents to marry by arguing that changing the definition of marriage poses dangers to the welfare of other children because their parents' commitment to the institution may be undermined by laws that reject "the moral and religious considerations ordinary people rely upon to strengthen their marriages"?

Karlan, Same-Sex Marriage as a Moving Story, 16 Stan. L. & Poly. Rev. 1, 3-5 (2005). For general discussion of the issue, see Symposium, Same-Sex Couples: Defining Marriage in the Twenty-First Century, 16 Stan. L. & Poly. Rev. 1 (2005).

To what extent does litigation surrounding same-sex relationships mirror the post-*Plessy* equality suits on which the NAACP focused before *Brown?* How far could equal protection, as discussed by Justice O'Connor in *Lawrence*, advance the rights of adults in same-sex sexual relationships? For a discussion of litigation strategies in sexual orientation discrimination suits, see Reinhardt,

Legal and Political Perspectives on the Battle over Same-Sex Marriage, 16 Stan. L. & Poly. Rev. 11 (2005).

Page 685. After the citation to Kramer, add the following:

For an opposing view, see Borchers, The Essential Irrelevance of the Full Faith and Credit Clause to the Same-Sex Marriage Debate, 38 Creighton L. Rev. 353 (2005) (arguing that the Full Faith and Credit Clause is not "an all-encompassing rule of the transportability of such relationships across state lines" and cannot meaningfully restrict states from resting their decisions on choices of state law).

Page 688. Before the first full paragraph, add the following:

Consider Yuracko's "trait discrimination" discussed in the previous section of this chapter. Even if Koppelman's argument proved false, to what extent might prohibitions on same-sex sexual activity stem from cultural constructs of masculinity and femininity? For extended discussion of the relation between equal rights in sex and sexual orientation, see Appleton, Missing in Action? Searching for Gender Talk in the Same-Sex Marriage Debate, 16 Stan. L. & Poly. Rev. 97 (2005).

6
IMPLIED FUNDAMENTAL RIGHTS

A. Introduction

Page 720. At the end of section 5 of the Note, add the following:

In Colby, The Federal Marriage Amendment and the False Promise of Originalism, 108 Colum. L. Rev. 529 (2008), the author uses debate about a contemporary constitutional amendment proposal to explore the problems with originalist methodology. He examines the Federal Marriage Amendment, which, if enacted, would provide that "Marriage in the United States shall consist only of a union of a man and a woman." He concludes that the framers of the amendment are in disagreement as to the amendment's effect on civil unions and that, therefore, the amendment has no "public meaning." In this instance and in others, he claims, because it is not possible to find and apply a meaning that does not exist, "the central premise of originalism — that it can effectively eliminate judicial subjectivity — is a false one."

C. The Incorporation Controversy

Page 741. Before section 3 of the Note, add the following:

For an argument that constitutional rights should be "tailored" depending upon the level of government to which they apply, see Rosen, The Surprisingly Strong Case for Tailoring Constitutional Principles, 153 U. Pa. L. Rev. 1513 (2005). Rosen identifies five respects in which different levels of government might be sufficiently different to justify a different interpretation of constitutional rights:

> First, each level is susceptible to distinctive political malfunctions. Second, as a result of each level's particular geographic scope, identical restrictions may have systematically different consequences across the different levels of government. Third, because there are divergent exit costs across the different levels of government, there might be systematic variations with regard to whether and to what extent competition among polities can generate efficient and diverse public goods. Fourth, identical restrictions can have very different consequences vis-à-vis democracy since each level of government requires a different number of people to garner a majority and thereby translate its preferences into law. Fifth, and finally, each level of government may have certain distinctive responsibilities.

Id. at 1522.

E. Fundamental Interests and the Equal Protection Clause

Page 781. After section 6 of the Note, add the following:

7. *Voter identification.* In Crawford v. Marion County Election Bd., 128 S. Ct. 1610 (2008), the Court rejected a facial challenge to an Indiana statute that required citizens to present a government-issued photo identification before voting. The state offered free photo identification to qualified voters who could establish their residence and identity. An indigent voter, or one who had a religious objection to being photographed, could cast a provisional ballot that would be counted only if she executed an appropriate affidavit with a circuit county clerk within ten days following the election. Voters who had photo identification but were unable to present the identification on election day could also file provisional ballots that would be counted if they brought photo identification to the clerk's office within the ten-day period.

Writing for himself, Chief Justice Roberts, and Justice Kennedy, Justice Stevens stated that the strict scrutiny applied in *Harper* was inapplicable because this was not a case where the restriction was an invidious limitation unrelated to voter qualifications. Instead, he applied the "general rule" that required the court to "identify and evaluate the interests put forward by the

State as justifications for the burden imposed by its rule, and then make the 'hard judgment' that our adversary system demands."

In support of the rule, Justice Stevens emphasized the need to prevent voter fraud. Although noting that "[the] record contains no evidence of any such [in-person] fraud actually occurring in Indiana at any time in its history," the Court observed that there had been "flagrant examples of such fraud in other parts of the country" and that "[there] is no question about the legitimacy or importance of the State's interest in counting only the votes of eligible voters." In Justice Stevens's view, this interest counterbalanced the burden placed upon voters who lacked, or failed to produce, photo identification.

> [On] the basis of the record that has been made in this litigation, we cannot conclude that the statute imposes excessively burdensome requirements' on any class of voters. A facial challenge must fail where the statute has a "'plainly legitimate sweep.'" When we consider only the statute's broad application to all Indiana voters we conclude that it "imposes only a limited burden on voters' rights."

Justice Scalia, joined by Justices Thomas and Alito, concurred in the judgment. Although agreeing with Justice Stevens's conclusion, Justice Scalia would have applied "deferential" scrutiny on the ground that strict scrutiny was appropriate only for laws that "severely restrict the right to vote."

Justice Souter filed a dissenting opinion in which Justice Ginsburg joined. Justice Breyer also filed a dissenting opinion.

Page 797. Before section 5 of the Note, add the following:

4a. *"Fair representation" and "one person, one vote." City of Mobile* holds that a "fair representation" system is not constitutionally mandatory, but it does not address the constitutional permissibility of such a system. For the Court's struggle with that question, see pages 615-622 of the main volume. Does adherence to the "one person, one vote" standard make sense in a context in which the government is attempting to protect a minority from vote dilution? Consider Hayden, Resolving the Dilemma of Minority Representation, 92 Cal. L. Rev. 1589, 1592 (2004):

> [Requiring] districts to be equally populous makes the creation of majority-minority districts a zero-sum game. Concentrating minority voters automatically draws them away from surrounding districts, which may, in the long run, dilute their overall influence on the political process. This, along with

the geographically and constitutionally limited number of places to draw such districts, has effectively put a lid on minority political participation...

[Strict] adherence to the one person, one vote standard, especially in the context of minority-vote-dilution claims, is nonsensical. [It] is time for the Supreme Court to back away from strict adherence [to this standard] in minority-vote-dilution cases, eliminating the dilemma of minority representation and removing the ceiling on minority political participation.

Page 802.   Before section c, add the following:

The Court reconsidered the problem of partisan gerrymandering in Vieth v. Jubelirer, 541 U.S. 267 (2004). (The case is excerpted at greater length on page 137 of the main volume). Writing for four justices, Justice Scalia rejected a variety of proposed standards for judging the constitutionality of partisan gerrymandering and would have held that all such challenges were barred by the political question doctrine. Justice Kennedy concurred in the judgment, but would not have "[foreclosed] all possibility of judicial relief if some limited and precise rationale were found to correct an established violation of the Constitution in some redistricting cases." Justices Stevens, Souter (joined by Justice Ginsburg), and Breyer filed separate dissents. Consider the views of Justice Breyer:

"[One] should begin by asking why [the] Constitution does not insist that the membership of legislatures better reflect different political views held by different groups of voters. [The] answer [lies] in the fact that a single-member-district system helps to ensure certain democratic objectives better than many 'more representative' (*i.e.*, proportional) electoral systems. [Single-member] districts [diminish] the need for coalition governments. And that fact makes it easier for voters to identify which party is responsible for government decision-making (and which rascals to throw out) while simultaneously providing greater legislative stability. ...

"If single-member districts are the norm, however, then political considerations will likely play an important, and proper, role in the drawing of district boundaries. [Given] a fairly large state population with a fairly large congressional delegation, districts assigned so as to be perfectly random in respect to politics would translate a small shift in political sentiment, say a shift from 51% Republican to 49% Republican, into a seismic shift in the makeup of the legislative delegation, say from 100% Republican to 100% Democratic. [Any] such exaggeration of tiny electoral changes — virtually wiping out legislative representation of the minority party — would itself seem highly undemocratic.

"Given the resulting need for single-member districts with nonrandom boundaries, it is not surprising that 'traditional' districting principles have rarely, if ever, been politically neutral. . . .

"At the same time, these considerations can help identify at least one circumstance where use of purely political boundary-drawing factors can amount to a serious, and remediable, abuse, namely the *unjustified* use of political factors to entrench a minority in power. By entrenchment I mean a situation in which a party that enjoys only minority support among the populace has nonetheless contrived to take, and hold, legislative power. By *unjustified* entrenchment, I mean that the minority's hold on power is purely the result of partisan manipulation and not other factors. . . .

"Courts need not intervene often to prevent the kind of abuse I have described, because those harmed constitute a political majority, and a majority normally can work its political will. . . .

"But we cannot always count on a severely gerrymandered legislature itself to find and implement a remedy. . . .

"When it is necessary, a court should prove capable of finding an appropriate remedy. . . .

"[Courts] can identify a number of strong indicia of abuse. The presence of actual entrenchment, while not always unjustified (being perhaps a chance occurrence) is such a sign, particularly when accompanied by the use of partisan boundary drawing criteria [*i.e.*], a use that both departs from traditional criteria and cannot be explained other than by efforts to achieve partisan advantage. [The] scenarios fall along a continuum: The more permanently entrenched the minority's hold on power becomes, the less evidence courts will need that the minority engaged in gerrymandering to achieve the desired result."

Compare Justice Scalia's response:

"The criterion Justice Breyer proposes is nothing more precise than 'the *unjustified* use of political factors to entrench a minority in power.' While he invokes in passing the Equal Protection Clause, it should be clear to any reader that what constitutes *unjustified* entrenchment depends on his own theory of 'effective government.' While one must agree with Justice BREYER's incredibly abstract starting point that our Constitution sought to create a 'basically democratic' form of government, that is a long and impassable distance away from the conclusion that the Judiciary may assess whether a group (somehow defined) has achieved a level of political power (somehow defined) commensurate with that to which they would be entitled absent *unjustified* political machinations (whatever that means)."

Given the fact that no opinion in *Vieth* attracted the votes of a majority of the justices, how should lower court judges dispose of partisan gerrymandering claims? As we have seen, the Court has held that race based districting is subject to strict scrutiny when "race [is] the predominant factor motivating the legislature's decision to place a significant number of voters within or without a particular district. To make this showing, a plaintiff must prove that the legislature subordinated traditional race-neutral districting principles, including but not limited to compactness, contiguity, respect for political subdivisions or communities defined by actual shared interests, to racial considerations." Miller v. Johnson, page 618 of the main volume. Are there good reasons why it is more difficult to develop judicially manageable standards for partisan districting than for racial districting? Are partisan districting standards more elusive than standards for, say, complex free speech or dormant commerce clause cases? If not, is there some other reason why judicial control of partisan districting is especially problematic?

LEAGUE OF UNITED LATIN AMERICAN CITIZENS v. PERRY, 548 U.S. 399 (2006). This case arose out of controversial efforts by Texas Republicans to redraw congressional district lines in 2003 after Republicans had gained control of the State House of Representatives and, hence, both Houses of the legislature in 2002.

After the 1990 census, Democrats, then in control of the state legislature and governorship, redrew district lines in a fashion that led to only 13 Republican seats out of 30 despite Republicans carrying 59% of the state-wide vote. After the 2000 census, the legislature, then divided between a Republican Senate and a Democratic House, could not agree on a districting plan. As a result, a federal district court imposed a new plan that, to the extent possible, tracked the 1990 plan. The Court-imposed plan gave the Republicans an advantage in 20 of the 32 congressional seats, but in the actual election (held in 2002), Republicans were unable to fully capitalize on this advantage and won only 15 of the 32 seats.

When the Republicans gained control of the State House of Representatives, the Republican Governor called a special session of the legislature in order to replace the court-imposed plan. The result was a dramatic standoff, with the legislature temporarily unable to act because Democratic Senators left the state so as to deprive the Senate of a quorum. Eventually, a plan was enacted which, the district court found, had the "single-minded purpose of [gaining] partisan advantage." In elections held under the new plan in 2004, Republicans gained 6 congressional seats over their 2002 total.

In a portion of his opinion announcing the judgment in which he wrote only for himself, Justice Kennedy rejected the argument that mid-decennial redistricting, when solely motivated by partisan objectives, is unconstitutional:

"To begin with, the state appellees dispute the assertion that partisan gain was the 'sole' motivation for the decision to replace [the court ordered plan]. There is some merit to that criticism, for the pejorative label overlooks indications that partisan motives did not dictate the plan in its entirety. The legislature does seem to have decided to redistrict with the sole purpose of achieving a Republican congressional majority, but partisan aims did not guide every line it drew. . . .

"We are skeptical [of] a claim that seeks to invalidate a statute based on a legislature's unlawful motive but does so without reference to the content of the legislation enacted.

"Even setting this skepticism aside, a successful claim attempting to identify unconstitutional acts of partisan gerrymandering must do what appellants' sole-motivation theory explicitly disavows: show a burden, as measured by a reliable standard, on the complainants' representational rights. . . .

"The sole-intent standard offered here is no more compelling when it is linked to the circumstance that [the new plan] is mid-decennial legislation. The text and structure of the Constitution and our case law indicate there is nothing inherently suspect about a legislature's decision to replace mid-decade a court-ordered plan with one of its own. And even if there were, the fact of mid-decade redistricting alone is no sure indication of unlawful political gerrymanders. Under appellants' theory, a highly effective partisan gerrymander that coincided with decennial redistricting would receive less scrutiny than a bumbling, yet solely partisan, mid-decade redistricting. . . .

"[The new plan] can be seen as making the party balance more congruent to statewide party power. To be sure, there is no constitutional requirement of proportional representation, and equating a party's statewide share of the vote with its portion of the congressional delegation is a rough measure at best. Nevertheless, a congressional plan that more closely reflects the distribution of state party power seems a less likely vehicle for partisan discrimination than one that entrenches an electoral minority. By this standard [the new plan] can be seen as fairer than the plan that survived in *Vieth* and the two previous Texas [plans]."

Justice Kennedy rejected a "symmetry" test for partisan bias. Under this test, an electoral system must treat similarly-situated parties equally, so that each receives the same fraction of legislative seats for a particular vote percentage as the other party would receive if it had received the same vote percentage. According to Justice Kennedy, "[the] existence or degree of asymmetry may in large part depend on conjecture about where possible vote-switchers will reside. Even assuming a court could choose reliably among different models of shifting voter preferences, we are wary of adopting a constitutional standard that invalidates a map based on unfair results that would occur in a hypothetical state of affairs. [More] fundamentally, a counterfactual plaintiff would face the same problem as the present, actual appellants: providing a standard for decid-ing how much partisan dominance is too much."

In a portion of his opinion joined by Justices Souter, Ginsburg, and Stevens, Justice Kennedy also rejected appellants' claim that mid-decade redistricting for exclusively partisan purposes violated the one-person one-vote requirement.

Appellants argued that because the population of Texas had shifted since the 2000 census, the 2003 redistricting, which relied on that census, created unlawful interdistrict population variations. Justice Kennedy responded as follows: "Appellants do not contend that a decennial redistricting plan would violate equal representation three or five years into the decade if the State's population had shifted substantially. As they must, they concede that States operate under the legal fiction that their plans are constitutionally apportioned throughout the decade, a presumption that is necessary to avoid constant redistricting with accompanying costs and instability. ...

"In appellants' view, however, this fiction should not provide a safe harbor for a legislature that enacts a voluntary, mid-decade plan overriding a legal court-drawn [plan]. This is particularly so [when] a legislature acts because of an exclusively partisan motivation. ...

"[This] is a test that turns not on whether a redistricting furthers equal-population principles but rather on the justification for redrawing a plan in the first place. In that respect appellants' approach merely restates the question whether it was permissible for the Texas Legislature to redraw the districting map. Appellants' answer, which mirrors their attack on mid-decennial redistricting solely motivated by partisan considerations, is unsatisfactory for reasons we have already discussed."

Writing for himself and Justice Breyer, Justice Stevens dissented from the portion of the Court's judgment upholding mid-decennial partisan districting:

"Unlike *Vieth*, the narrow question presented by the statewide challenge in this litigation is whether the State's decision to draw the map in the first place, when it was under no legal obligation to do so, was permissible. It is undeniable that identifying the motive for making that basic decision is a readily manageable judicial task. [Although] the Constitution places no *per se* ban on midcycle redistricting, a legislature's decision to redistrict in the middle of the census cycle, when the legislature is under no legal obligation to do so, makes the judicial task of identifying the legislature's motive simpler than it would otherwise be. ...

"By taking an action for the sole purpose of advantaging Republicans and disadvantaging Democrats, the State of Texas violated its constitutional obligation to govern impartially.

"Justice Kennedy maintains that even if legislation is enacted based solely on a desire to harm a politically unpopular minority, this fact is insufficient to establish unconstitutional partisan gerrymandering absent proof that the legislation did in fact burden 'the complainants' representative rights.' This conclusion — which clearly goes to the merits, rather than the manageability, of a partisan gerrymandring claim — is not only inconsistent with the constitutional requirement that state action must be supported by a legitimate interest, but also provides an insufficient response to appellants' claim on the merits. ...

"[Justice] Kennedy's additional requirement that there be proof that the gerrymander did in fact burden the complainants' representative rights is clearly satisfied by the record in this ligitation. . . .

"That [the new plan] produced a 'roughly proportional' congressional delegation in 2004 does not [answer] the question whether the plan has a discriminatory effect against Democrats. [Whether] a districting map is biased against a political party depends upon the bias in the map itself — in other words, it depends upon the opportunities that the map offers each party regardless of how candidates perform in a given year. And, as the State's expert found in this litigation, [the new plan] clearly has a discriminatory effect in terms of the opportunities it offers the two principal political parties in Texas. Indeed, that discriminatory effect is severe.

"At the very least, once plaintiffs have established that the legislature's sole purpose in adopting a plan was partisan — as plaintiffs have established in this action, [a] severe discriminatory effect should be sufficient to meet any additional burden they have to demonstrate that the redistrticting may accomplishes its discriminatory purpose. [It] would, of course, be an eminently manageable standard for the Court to conclude that deviations of over 10% from symmetry create a prima facie case of an unconstitutional gerrymander, just as population deviations among districts of more than 10% create such a prima facie case. Or, the Court could conclude that a significant departure from symmetry is one relevant factor in analyzing whether, under the totality of circumstances, a districiting plan is an unconstitutional partisan gerrymander. At any rate, proponents of the symmetry standard have provided a helpful (though certainly not talismanic) tool in this type of litigation."

Writing for himself and Justice Ginsburg, Justice Souter stated that he saw "nothing to be gained by working through these cases on the standard I would have applied in *Vieth* because here as in *Vieth* we have no majority for any single criterion of impermissible gerrymander. [I] therefore treat the broad issue of gerrymander much as the subject of an improvident grant of certiorari." He added that he did not "share Justice Kennedy's seemingly flat rejection of any test of gerrymander turning on the process followed in redistricting" and did not "rule out the utility of a criterion of symmetry as a test."

Writing for himself and Justice Alito, Chief Justice Roberts agreed with the determination that appellants have not provided "a reliable standard for identifying unconstitutional political gerrymanders." And he stated that "[t]he question whether any such standard exists — that is, whether a challenge to a political gerrymander presents a justiciable case or controversy — has not been argued in these cases. I therefore take no position on that question, which has divided the Court."

Justice Scalia, joined by Justice Thomas, wrote an opinion concurring in the judgment in part and dissenting in part:

"Justice Kennedy's discussion of appellants' political-gerrymandering claims ably demonstrates that, yet again, no party or judge has put forth a judicially discernable standard by which to evaluate them. Unfortunately, the opinion then concludes that appellants have failed to state a claim as to political gerrymandering, without ever articulating what the elements of such a claim consist of. That is not an available disposition of this appeal. We must either conclude that the claim is nonjusticiable and dismiss it, or else set forth a standard and measure appellant's claim against it. Instead, we again dispose of this claim in a way that provides no guidance to lower-court judges and perpetuates a cause of action with no discernible content. We should simply dismiss appellants' claims as nonjusticiable."

Page 842. Correction.

The paragraph beginning "[A] legislative classification that threatens the creation of an underclass. . . . " should appear as part of the concurring opinion by Justice Powell, rather than as part of the dissenting opinion of Chief Justice Burger.

F. *Modern Substantive Due Process: Privacy, Personhood, and Family*

Page 854. At the end of subsection c of the Note, add the following:

Compare Bedi, Repudiating Morals Legislation: Rendering the Constitutional Right to Privacy Obsolete, 53 Clev. St. L. Rev. 447, 448, 451 (2005-06):

[No] one ever says to the straight married couple about to engage in procreative, non-kinky sex, "what you do in your bedroom is your business!" . . .

By invoking the right to privacy to protect certain behavior, [we] have ipso facto deemed it abnormal. . . .

Since straight sex does not require the protection of the right to privacy, the state ends up implicitly compelling us to engage in certain sexual acts and not others. The normalization that Rubenfeld so decries occurs not only through laws prohibiting certain acts, but also by the social stigma that attaches to sexual acts that, although legally permitted, require the suspect appeal to privacy and its theory of tolerance. Thus, [Rubenfeld's] reason for the right to privacy [pushes] against its very adoption.

Page 864. At the end of section 3b of the Note, add the following:

Does the abortion right imply a right not to be a genetic, as opposed to a gestational, parent? Suppose, for example, that a married couple uses in vitro fertilization and freezes some of the resulting preembryos. If the parties then divorce, is it constitutional for the state to permit the wife to implant these preembryos if the husband objects? For an argument that there is no right not to be a genetic parent when genetic parenthood is divorced from gestatational and legal parenthood, see Cohen, The Constitution and the Rights Not To Procreate, 60 Stan. L. Rev. 1135 (2008).

Page 869. At the end of section 8 of the Note, add the following:

Might the Court have avoided this attack by crafting a different sort of opinion? Consider Eskridge, Pluralism and Distrust: How Courts Can Support Democracy by Lowering the Stakes of Politics, 114 Yale L. J. 1279, 1312-13 (2005):

> [A] more appropriate resolution [of *Roe*] would have been one that reversed the burden of legislative inertia. The year before *Roe*, Judges Lumbard and Newman ruled Connecticut's 1860 abortion law invalid on due process obsolescence grounds. [In] *Roe* itself, Justice Blackmun's original draft opinion would have invalidated the aged Texas law on vagueness grounds. . . .
> [Either] approach would have had the pluralism-facilitating advantage of sweeping off the statute books a woman-burdening law enacted before women could vote, without the disadvantage of raising the stakes of politics as much as the privacy opinion in *Roe* did. Pro-life forces could have returned to the Texas legislature and procured new legislation. [But any new legislation] would [have] been accompanied by a more complete examination of exactly what neutral state interests are advanced by prohibiting or regulating the right to choose abortions.

Page 916.   After the end of Justice Thomas's dissent and before Section 3, add the following:

Note: Stenberg *and the Health Exception*

1. *The necessity of a health exception.* Would *Stenberg* have come out the other way if the statute had contained a "health exception," permitting the otherwise prohibited partial birth abortion method when necessary to protect the mother's health? For an affirmative answer, see WMPC v. Taft, 353 F.3d 436 (6th Cir. 2003).

2. *Reading a health exception into an otherwise constitutionally problematic statute.* If a health exception was sufficient to save the *Stenberg* statute, should the Court have read the exception into the statute? The Court addressed this problem in Ayotte v. Planned Parenthood of Northern New England, 546 U.S. 320 (2006). A New Hampshire statute prohibited physicians from performing abortions on pregnant minors until 48 hours after written notice of the pending abortion was delivered to a parent or guardian. The provision had a judicial bypass exception and another exception for circumstances where an immediate abortion was necessary to prevent the minor's death. However, no provision allowed for abortions in medical emergencies where the procedure was necessary to protect the minor's health.

The court of appeals held that the absence of a health exception was unconstitutional and affirmed an injunction prohibiting enforcement of the entire statute. When the case reached the Supreme Court, the state conceded that the statute was constitutionally flawed, but argued that the lower court erred by enjoining its enforcement even in cases where there was no health risk. The Supreme Court, in a unanimous opinion written by Justice O'Connor, agreed that "the lower courts need not have invalidated the law wholesale" and remanded the case for further consideration.

According to the Court, it was "understandable" that the lower court had invalidated the entire statute, since in *Stenberg* "we, too [invalidated] an abortion statute in its entirety because of the same constitutional flaw. But the parties in *Stenberg* did not ask for, and we did not contemplate, relief more finely drawn." On the facts before the Court in *Ayotte*, "only a few applications of New Hampshire's parental notification statute would present a constitutional problem. So long as they are faithful to legislative intent, then, in this case the lower courts can issue a declaratory judgment and an injunction prohibiting [only] the statute's unconstitutional application." The Court remanded the case so that the lower courts could determine whether the legislature intended the statute to be subject to this remedy, or whether it would have preferred invalidation of the entire statute to the imposition of a health exception.

Page 916.   Before Section 3, add the following:

GONZALES v. CARHART
127 S. Ct. 1610 (2007)

JUSTICE KENNEDY delivered the opinion of the Court.

These cases require us to consider the validity of the Partial-Birth Abortion Ban Act of 2003 (Act), a federal statute regulating abortion procedures. In recitations preceding its operative provisions, the Act refers to the Court's opinion in Stenberg v. Carhart, which also addressed the subject of abortion procedures used in the later stages of pregnancy. Compared to the state statute at issue in *Stenberg,* the Act is more specific concerning the instances to which it applies and, in this respect, more precise in its coverage. We conclude the Act should be sustained against the objections lodged by the broad, facial attack brought against it.

. . .

I

A

The Act proscribes a particular manner of ending fetal life, so it is necessary here, as it was in *Stenberg,* to discuss abortion procedures in some detail. Three United States District Courts heard extensive evidence describing the procedures. . . .

[Between] 85 and 90 percent of the approximately 1.3 million abortions performed each year in the United States take place in the first three months of pregnancy, which is to say in the first trimester. The most common first-trimester abortion method is vacuum aspiration (otherwise known as suction curettage) in which the physician vacuums out the embryonic tissue. Early in this trimester an alternative is to use medication, such as mifepristone (commonly known as RU-486), to terminate the pregnancy. The Act does not regulate these procedures.

Of the remaining abortions that take place each year, most occur in the second trimester. The surgical procedure referred to as "dilation and evacuation" or "D & E" is the usual abortion method in this trimester. Although individual techniques for performing D & E differ, the general steps are the same.

A doctor must first dilate the cervix at least to the extent needed to insert surgical instruments into the uterus and to maneuver them to evacuate the fetus. . . .

After sufficient dilation the surgical operation can commence. The woman is placed under general anesthesia or conscious sedation. The doctor, often guided by ultrasound, inserts grasping forceps through the woman's cervix and into the uterus to grab the fetus. The doctor grips a fetal part with the forceps and pulls it back through the cervix and vagina, continuing to pull even after meeting resistance from the cervix. The friction causes the fetus to tear apart. For example, a leg might be ripped off the fetus as it is pulled through the cervix and out of the woman. The process of evacuating the fetus piece by piece continues until it has been completely removed. A doctor may make 10 to 15 passes with the forceps to evacuate the fetus in its entirety, though sometimes removal is completed with fewer passes. Once the fetus has been evacuated, the placenta and any remaining fetal material are suctioned or scraped out of the uterus. The doctor examines the different parts to ensure the entire fetal body has been removed.

Some doctors, especially later in the second trimester, may kill the fetus a day or two before performing the surgical evacuation. [Fetal] demise may cause contractions and make greater dilation possible. Once dead, moreover, the fetus' body will soften, and its removal will be easier. Other doctors refrain from injecting chemical agents, believing it adds risk with little or no medical benefit.

The abortion procedure that was the impetus for the numerous bans on "partial-birth abortion," including the Act, is a variation of this standard D & E. [For] discussion purposes this D & E variation will be referred to as intact D & E. The main difference between the two procedures is that in intact D & E, a doctor extracts the fetus intact or largely intact with only a few passes. There are no comprehensive statistics indicating what percentage of all D & Es are performed in this manner. ...

In an intact D & E procedure, the doctor extracts the fetus in a way conducive to pulling out its entire body, instead of ripping it apart. One doctor, for example, testified:

> "If I know I have good dilation and I reach in and the fetus starts to come out and I think I can accomplish it, the abortion with an intact delivery, then I use my forceps a little bit differently. I don't close them quite so much, and I just gently draw the tissue out attempting to have an intact delivery, if possible."

Rotating the fetus as it is being pulled decreases the odds of dismemberment. A doctor also "may use forceps to grasp a fetal part, pull it down, and re-grasp the fetus at a higher level — 'sometimes using both his hand and a forceps' — to exert traction to retrieve the fetus intact until the head is lodged in the [cervix]."

Intact D & E gained public notoriety when, in 1992, Dr. Martin Haskell gave a presentation describing his method of performing the operation. In the usual intact D & E the fetus' head lodges in the cervix, and dilation is insufficient to allow it to pass. Haskell explained the next step as follows:

> "'At this point, the right-handed surgeon slides the fingers of the left [hand] along the back of the fetus and hooks the shoulders of the fetus with the index and ring fingers (palm down).
>
> "'While maintaining this tension, lifting the cervix and applying traction to the shoulders with the fingers of the left hand, the surgeon takes a pair of blunt curved Metzenbaum scissors in the right hand. He carefully advances the tip, curved down, along the spine and under his middle finger until he feels it contact the base of the skull under the tip of his middle finger.
>
> "'[T]he surgeon then forces the scissors into the base of the skull or into the foramen magnum. Having safely entered the skull, he spreads the scissors to enlarge the opening.
>
> "'The surgeon removes the scissors and introduces a suction catheter into this hole and evacuates the skull contents. With the catheter still in place, he applies traction to the fetus, removing it completely from the patient.'"

This is an abortion doctor's clinical description. Here is another description from a nurse who witnessed the same method performed on a 26 1/2-week fetus and testified before the Senate Judiciary Committee:

> "'Dr. Haskell went in with forceps and grabbed the baby's legs and pulled them down into the birth canal. Then he delivered the baby's body and the arms — everything but the head. The doctor kept the head right inside the uterus. . . .
>
> "'The baby's little fingers were clasping and unclasping, and his little feet were kicking. Then the doctor stuck the scissors in the back of his head, and the baby's arms jerked out, like a startle reaction, like a flinch, like a baby does when he thinks he is going to fall.
>
> "'The doctor opened up the scissors, stuck a high-powered suction tube into the opening, and sucked the baby's brains out. Now the baby went completely limp. . . .
>
> "'He cut the umbilical cord and delivered the placenta. He threw the baby in a pan, along with the placenta and the instruments he had just used.'"

Dr. Haskell's approach is not the only method of killing the fetus once its head lodges in the cervix, and "the process has evolved" since his presentation. Another doctor, for example, squeezes the skull after it has been pierced "so that enough brain tissue exudes to allow the head to pass through." Still other physicians reach into the cervix with their forceps and crush the fetus' skull. Others continue to pull the fetus out of the woman until it disarticulates at the neck, in effect decapitating it. These doctors then grasp the head with forceps, crush it, and remove it.

Some doctors performing an intact D & E attempt to remove the fetus without collapsing the skull. Yet one doctor would not allow delivery of a live fetus younger than 24 weeks because "the objective of [his] procedure is to perform an abortion," not a birth. The doctor thus answered in the affirmative when asked whether he would "hold the fetus' head on the internal side of the [cervix] in order to collapse the skull" and kill the fetus before it is born. Another doctor testified he crushes a fetus' skull not only to reduce its size but also to ensure the fetus is dead before it is removed. For the staff to have to deal with a fetus that has "some viability to it, some movement of limbs," according to this doctor, "[is] always a difficult situation."

D & E and intact D & E are not the only second-trimester abortion methods. Doctors also may abort a fetus through medical induction. The doctor medicates the woman to induce labor, and contractions occur to deliver the fetus. Induction can last as little as 6 hours but can take longer than 48. It accounts for about five percent of second-trimester abortions before 20 weeks of gestation and 15 percent of those after 20 weeks....

B

In 2003, after this Court's decision in *Stenberg,* Congress passed the Act at issue here....

The Act responded to *Stenberg* in two ways. First, Congress made factual findings. Congress determined that this Court in *Stenberg* "was required to accept the very questionable findings issued by the district court judge," but that Congress was "not bound to accept the same factual findings." Congress found, among other things, that "[a] moral, medical, and ethical consensus exists that the practice of performing a partial-birth abortion ... is a gruesome and inhumane procedure that is never medically necessary and should be prohibited."

Second, and more relevant here, the Act's language differs from that of the Nebraska statute struck down in *Stenberg.* The operative provisions of the Act provide in relevant part:

> "(a) Any physician who, in or affecting interstate or foreign commerce, knowingly performs a partial-birth abortion and thereby kills a human fetus shall be fined under this title or imprisoned not more than 2 years, or both. This subsection does not apply to a partial-birth abortion that is necessary to save the life of a mother whose life is endangered by a physical disorder, physical illness, or physical injury, including a life-endangering physical

condition caused by or arising from the pregnancy itself. This subsection takes effect 1 day after the enactment.

"(b) As used in this section —

(1) the term "partial-birth abortion" means an abortion in which the person performing the abortion —

"(A) deliberately and intentionally vaginally delivers a living fetus until, in the case of a head-first presentation, the entire fetal head is outside the body of the mother, or, in the case of breech presentation, any part of the fetal trunk past the navel is outside the body of the mother, for the purpose of performing an overt act that the person knows will kill the partially delivered living fetus; and

"(B) performs the overt act, other than completion of delivery, that kills the partially delivered living fetus; and

"(2) the term "physician" means a doctor of medicine or osteopathy legally authorized to practice medicine and surgery by the State in which the doctor performs such activity, or any other individual legally authorized by the State to perform abortions: *Provided, however,* That any individual who is not a physician or not otherwise legally authorized by the State to perform abortions, but who nevertheless directly performs a partial-birth abortion, shall be subject to the provisions of this section.

. . .

"(d)(1) A defendant accused of an offense under this section may seek a hearing before the State Medical Board on whether the physician's conduct was necessary to save the life of the mother whose life was endangered by a physical disorder, physical illness, or physical injury, including a life-endangering physical condition caused by or arising from the pregnancy itself.

"(2) The findings on that issue are admissible on that issue at the trial of the defendant. Upon a motion of the defendant, the court shall delay the beginning of the trial for not more than 30 days to permit such a hearing to take place.

"(e) A woman upon whom a partial-birth abortion is performed may not be prosecuted under this section, for a conspiracy to violate this section, or for an offense under section 2, 3, or 4 of this title based on a violation of this section."

. . .

II

The principles set forth in the joint opinion in *Planned Parenthood of Southeastern Pa. v. Casey* did not find support from all those who join the instant opinion. Whatever one's views concerning the *Casey* joint opinion, it is evident a premise central to its conclusion — that the government has a legitimate and substantial interest in preserving and promoting fetal life — would be repudiated were the Court now to affirm the judgments of the Courts of Appeals [which had invalidated the Act]. ...

We assume the following principles for the purposes of this opinion. Before viability, a State "may not prohibit any woman from making the ultimate decision to terminate her pregnancy." [*Casey,* plurality opinion] It also may not impose upon this right an undue burden, which exists if a regulation's "purpose or effect is to place a substantial obstacle in the path of a woman seeking an abortion before the fetus attains viability." On the other hand, "[r]egulations which do no more than create a structural mechanism by which the State, or the parent or guardian of a minor, may express profound respect for the life of the unborn are permitted, if they are not a substantial obstacle to the woman's exercise of the right to choose." *Casey,* in short, struck a balance. The balance was central to its holding. We now apply its standard to the cases at bar.

III

A straightforward reading of the Act's text demonstrates its purpose and the scope of its provisions: It regulates and proscribes, with exceptions or qualifications to be discussed, performing the intact D & E procedure.

Respondents agree the Act encompasses intact D & E, but they contend its additional reach is both unclear and excessive. Respondents assert that, at the least, the Act is void for vagueness because its scope is indefinite. In the alternative, respondents argue that the Act's text proscribes all D & Es. Because D & E is the most common second-trimester abortion method, respondents suggest the Act imposes an undue burden. In this litigation the Attorney General does not dispute that the Act would impose an undue burden if it covered standard D & E.

We conclude that the Act is not void for vagueness, does not impose an undue burden from any overbreadth, and is not invalid on its face.

A

The Act punishes "knowingly perform[ing]" a "partial-birth abortion." ... First, the person performing the abortion must "vaginally delive[r] a living fetus." The Act does not restrict an abortion procedure involving the delivery of an expired fetus. The Act, furthermore, is inapplicable to abortions that do not involve vaginal delivery (for instance, hysterotomy or hysterectomy). The Act does apply both previability and postviability because, by common understanding and scientific terminology, a fetus is a living organism while within the womb, whether or not it is viable outside the womb. ...

194

Second, the Act's definition of partial-birth abortion requires the fetus to be delivered "until, in the case of a head-first presentation, the entire fetal head is outside the body of the mother, or, in the case of breech presentation, any part of the fetal trunk past the navel is outside the body of the mother." The Attorney General concedes, and we agree, that if an abortion procedure does not involve the delivery of a living fetus to one of these "anatomical 'landmarks' " — where, depending on the presentation, either the fetal head or the fetal trunk past the navel is outside the body of the mother — the prohibitions of the Act do not apply.

Third, to fall within the Act, a doctor must perform an "overt act, other than completion of delivery, that kills the partially delivered living fetus." For purposes of criminal liability, the overt act causing the fetus' death must be separate from delivery, and the overt act must occur after the delivery to an anatomical landmark. This is because the Act proscribes killing "the partially delivered" fetus, which, when read in context, refers to a fetus that has been delivered to an anatomical landmark.

Fourth, the Act contains scienter requirements concerning all the actions involved in the prohibited abortion. To begin with, the physician must have "deliberately and intentionally" delivered the fetus to one of the Act's anatomical landmarks. If a living fetus is delivered past the critical point by accident or inadvertence, the Act is inapplicable. In addition, the fetus must have been delivered "for the purpose of performing an overt act that the [doctor] knows will kill [it]." If either intent is absent, no crime has occurred. This follows from the general principle that where scienter is required no crime is committed absent the requisite state of mind.

B

. . .

[U]nlike the statutory language in *Stenberg* that prohibited the delivery of a " 'substantial portion' " of the fetus — where a doctor might question how much of the fetus is a substantial portion — the Act defines the line between potentially criminal conduct on the one hand and lawful abortion on the other. Doctors performing D & E will know that if they do not deliver a living fetus to an anatomical landmark they will not face criminal liability.

This conclusion is buttressed by the intent that must be proved to impose liability. . . . Just as the Act's anatomical landmarks provide doctors with objective standards, they also "establish minimal guidelines to govern law enforcement." The scienter requirements narrow the scope of the Act's prohibition and limit prosecutorial discretion. . . .

C

We next determine whether the Act imposes an undue burden, as a facial matter, because its restrictions on second-trimester abortions are too broad. A review of the statutory text discloses the limits of its reach. The Act prohibits intact D & E; and, notwithstanding respondents' arguments, it does not prohibit the D & E procedure in which the fetus is removed in parts.

1

The Act prohibits a doctor from intentionally performing an intact D & E. The dual prohibitions of the Act, both of which are necessary for criminal liability, correspond with the steps generally undertaken during this type of procedure. First, a doctor delivers the fetus until its head lodges in the cervix, which is usually past the anatomical landmark for a breech presentation. Second, the doctor proceeds to pierce the fetal skull with scissors or crush it with forceps. This step satisfies the overt-act requirement because it kills the fetus and is distinct from delivery. The Act's intent requirements, however, limit its reach to those physicians who carry out the intact D & E after intending to undertake both steps at the outset.

The Act excludes most D & Es in which the fetus is removed in pieces, not intact. If the doctor intends to remove the fetus in parts from the outset, the doctor will not have the requisite intent to incur criminal liability....

The statute in *Stenberg* prohibited "'deliberately and intentionally delivering into the vagina a living unborn child, or a substantial portion thereof, for the purpose of performing a procedure that the person performing such procedure knows will kill the unborn child and does kill the unborn child.'" The Court concluded that this statute encompassed D & E because "D & E will often involve a physician pulling a 'substantial portion' of a still living fetus, say, an arm or leg, into the vagina prior to the death of the fetus." ...

Congress, it is apparent, responded to these concerns because the Act departs in material ways from the statute in *Stenberg*. It adopts the phrase "delivers a living fetus," instead of "'delivering ... a living unborn child, or a substantial portion thereof.'" The Act's language, unlike the statute in *Stenberg*, expresses the usual meaning of "deliver" when used in connection with "fetus," namely, extraction of an entire fetus rather than removal of fetal pieces.... The Act thus displaces the interpretation of "delivering" dictated by the Nebraska statute's reference to a "substantial portion" of the fetus....

The identification of specific anatomical landmarks to which the fetus must be partially delivered also differentiates the Act from the statute at issue in *Stenberg*. The Court in *Stenberg* interpreted "'substantial portion'" of the fetus to include an arm or a leg. The Act's anatomical landmarks, by contrast, clarify that the removal of a small portion of the fetus is not prohibited. The landmarks also require the fetus to be delivered so that it is partially "outside the body of the mother." To come within the ambit of the Nebraska statute, on the other hand, a substantial portion of the fetus only had to be delivered into the vagina; no part of the fetus had to be outside the body of the mother before a doctor could face criminal sanctions.

By adding an overt-act requirement Congress sought further to meet the Court's objections to the state statute considered in *Stenberg*. ... The fatal overt act must occur after delivery to an anatomical landmark, and it must be something "other than [the] completion of delivery." This distinction matters because, unlike intact D & E, standard D & E does not involve a delivery followed by a fatal act.

The canon of constitutional avoidance, finally, extinguishes any lingering doubt as to whether the Act covers the prototypical D & E procedure ...

2

Contrary arguments by the respondents are unavailing. Respondents look to situations that might arise during D & E, situations not examined in *Stenberg*. They contend — relying on the testimony of numerous abortion doctors — that D & E may result in the delivery of a living fetus beyond the Act's anatomical landmarks in a significant fraction of cases. This is so, respondents say, because doctors cannot predict the amount the cervix will dilate before the abortion procedure. The cervix might dilate to a degree that the fetus will be removed largely intact. To complete the abortion, doctors will commit an overt act that kills the partially delivered fetus. Respondents thus posit that any D & E has the potential to violate the Act, and that a physician will not know beforehand whether the abortion will proceed in a prohibited manner.

This reasoning, however, does not take account of the Act's intent requirements, which preclude liability from attaching to an accidental intact D & E. ... The evidence also supports a legislative determination that an intact delivery is almost always a conscious choice rather than a happenstance. ... This evidence belies any claim that a standard D & E cannot be performed without intending or foreseeing an intact D & E.

...

IV

Under the principles accepted as controlling here, the Act, as we have interpreted it, would be unconstitutional "if its purpose or effect is to place a substantial obstacle in the path of a woman seeking an abortion before the fetus attains viability." *Casey,* 505 U. S., at 878 (plurality opinion). The abortions affected by the Act's regulations take place both previability and postviability; so the quoted language and the undue burden analysis it relies upon are applicable. The question is whether the Act, measured by its text in this facial attack, imposes a substantial obstacle to late-term, but previability, abortions. The Act does not on its face impose a substantial obstacle, and we reject this further facial challenge to its validity.

A

The Act's purposes are set forth in recitals preceding its operative provisions. A description of the prohibited abortion procedure demonstrates the rationale for the congressional enactment. The Act proscribes a method of abortion in which a fetus is killed just inches before completion of the birth process. ... The Act expresses respect for the dignity of human life.

Congress was concerned, furthermore, with the effects on the medical community and on its reputation caused by the practice of partial-birth abortion. The findings in the Act explain:

> "Partial-birth abortion ... confuses the medical, legal, and ethical duties of physicians to preserve and promote life, as the physician acts directly against the physical life of a child, whom he or she had just delivered, all but the head, out of the womb, in order to end that life." ...

Casey reaffirmed these governmental objectives. The government may use its voice and its regulatory authority to show its profound respect for the life within the woman. ... Where it has a rational basis to act, and it does not impose an undue burden, the State may use its regulatory power to bar certain procedures and substitute others, all in furtherance of its legitimate interests in regulating the medical profession in order to promote respect for life, including life of the unborn.

The Act's ban on abortions that involve partial delivery of a living fetus furthers the Government's objectives. No one would dispute that, for many, D & E is a procedure itself laden with the power to devalue human life. ...

Respect for human life finds an ultimate expression in the bond of love the mother has for her child. The Act recognizes this reality as well. Whether to have an abortion requires a difficult and painful moral decision. While we find no reliable data to measure the phenomenon, it seems unexceptionable to conclude some women come to regret their choice to abort the infant life they once created and sustained. See Brief for Sandra Cano et al. as *Amici Curiae* in No. 05-380, pp. 22-24. Severe depression and loss of esteem can follow. See *ibid.*

In a decision so fraught with emotional consequence some doctors may prefer not to disclose precise details of the means that will be used, confining themselves to the required statement of risks the procedure entails. From one standpoint this ought not to be surprising. Any number of patients facing imminent surgical procedures would prefer not to hear all details, lest the usual anxiety preceding invasive medical procedures become the more intense. This is likely the case with the abortion procedures here in issue.

It is, however, precisely this lack of information concerning the way in which the fetus will be killed that is of legitimate concern to the State. The State has an interest in ensuring so grave a choice is well informed. It is self-evident that a mother who comes to regret her choice to abort must struggle with grief more anguished and sorrow more profound when she learns, only after the event, what she once did not know: that she allowed a doctor to pierce the skull and vacuum the fast-developing brain of her unborn child, a child assuming the human form.

It is a reasonable inference that a necessary effect of the regulation and the knowledge it conveys will be to encourage some women to carry the infant to full term, thus reducing the absolute number of late-term abortions. The medical profession, furthermore, may find different and less shocking methods to abort the fetus in the second trimester, thereby accommodating legislative demand. The State's interest in respect for life is advanced by the dialogue that better informs the political and legal systems, the medical profession, expectant mothers, and society as a whole of the consequences that follow from a decision to elect a late-term abortion.

It is objected that the standard D & E is in some respects as brutal, if not more, than the intact D & E, so that the legislation accomplishes little. What we have already said, however, shows ample justification for the regulation. Partial-birth abortion, as defined by the Act, differs from a standard D & E because the former occurs when the fetus is partially outside the mother to the point of one of the Act's anatomical landmarks. It was reasonable for Congress to think that partial-birth abortion, more than standard D & E, "undermines the public's perception of the appropriate role of a physician during the delivery process, and perverts a process during which life is brought into the world." There would be a flaw in this Court's logic, and an irony in its jurisprudence, were we first to conclude a ban on both D & E and intact D & E was overbroad and then to say it is irrational to ban only intact D & E because that does not proscribe both procedures. ...

B

The Act's furtherance of legitimate government interests bears upon, but does not resolve, the next question: whether the Act has the effect of imposing an unconstitutional burden on the abortion right because it does not allow use of the barred procedure where "necessary, in appropriate medical judgment, for [the] preservation of the ... health of the mother." The prohibition in the Act would be unconstitutional, under precedents we here assume to be controlling, if it "subject[ed] [women] to significant health risks." In *Ayotte* [*v. Planned Parenthood of Northern New England,* 546 U.S. 320 (2006),] the parties agreed a health exception to the challenged parental-involvement statute was necessary "to avert serious and often irreversible damage to [a pregnant minor's] health."

Here, by contrast, whether the Act creates significant health risks for women has been a contested factual question. The evidence presented in the trial courts and before Congress demonstrates both sides have medical support for their position.

Respondents presented evidence that intact D & E may be the safest method of abortion, for reasons similar to those adduced in *Stenberg*. Abortion doctors testified, for example, that intact D & E decreases the risk of cervical laceration or uterine perforation because it requires fewer passes into the uterus with surgical instruments and does not require the removal of bony fragments of the dismembered fetus, fragments that may be sharp. Respondents also presented evidence that intact D & E was safer both because it reduces the risks that fetal parts will remain in the uterus and because it takes less time to complete. Respondents, in addition, proffered evidence that intact D & E was safer for women with certain medical conditions or women with fetuses that had certain anomalies.

These contentions were contradicted by other doctors who testified in the District Courts and before Congress. They concluded that the alleged health advantages were based on speculation without scientific studies to support them. They considered D & E always to be a safe alternative.

There is documented medical disagreement whether the Act's prohibition would ever impose significant health risks on women. ...

The question becomes whether the Act can stand when this medical uncertainty persists. The Court's precedents instruct that the Act can survive this facial attack. The Court has given state and federal legislatures wide discretion to pass legislation in areas where there is medical and scientific uncertainty.

This traditional rule is consistent with *Casey,* which confirms the State's interest in promoting respect for human life at all stages in the pregnancy. Physicians are not entitled to ignore regulations that direct them to use reasonable alternative procedures. The law need not give abortion doctors unfettered choice in the course of their medical practice, nor should it elevate their status above other physicians in the medical community. ...

Medical uncertainty does not foreclose the exercise of legislative power in the abortion context any more than it does in other contexts. The medical uncertainty over whether the Act's prohibition creates significant health risks provides a sufficient basis to conclude in this facial attack that the Act does not impose an undue burden. ...

In reaching the conclusion that the Act does not require a health exception, we reject certain arguments made by the parties on both sides of these cases. On the one hand, the Attorney General urges us to uphold the Act on the basis of the congressional findings alone. Although we review congressional fact-finding under a deferential standard, we do not in the circumstances here place dispositive weight on Congress' findings. The Court retains an independent constitutional duty to review factual findings where constitutional rights are at stake. . . .

On the other hand, relying on the Court's opinion in *Stenberg,* respondents contend that an abortion regulation must contain a health exception "if 'substantial medical authority supports the proposition that banning a particular procedure could endanger women's health.'" As illustrated by respondents' arguments and the decisions of the Courts of Appeals, *Stenberg* has been interpreted to leave no margin of error for legislatures to act in the face of medical uncertainty.

A zero tolerance policy would strike down legitimate abortion regulations, like the present one, if some part of the medical community were disinclined to follow the proscription. This is too exacting a standard to impose on the legislative power, exercised in this instance under the Commerce Clause, to regulate the medical profession. Considerations of marginal safety, including the balance of risks, are within the legislative competence when the regulation is rational and in pursuit of legitimate ends. When standard medical options are available, mere convenience does not suffice to displace them; and if some procedures have different risks than others, it does not follow that the State is altogether barred from imposing reasonable regulations. The Act is not invalid on its face where there is uncertainty over whether the barred procedure is ever necessary to preserve a woman's health, given the availability of other abortion procedures that are considered to be safe alternatives.

V

The considerations we have discussed support our further determination that these facial attacks should not have been entertained in the first instance. In these circumstances the proper means to consider exceptions is by as-applied challenge. . . . This is the proper manner to protect the health of the woman if it can be shown that in discrete and well-defined instances a particular condition has occurred or is likely to occur in which the procedure prohibited by the Act must be used. In an as-applied challenge the nature of the medical risk can be better quantified and balanced than in a facial attack.

. . .

***

Respondents have not demonstrated that the Act, as a facial matter, is void for vagueness, or that it imposes an undue burden on a woman's right to abortion based on its overbreadth or lack of a health exception. For these reasons the judgments of the Courts of Appeals for the Eighth and Ninth Circuits are reversed.

It is so ordered.

JUSTICE THOMAS, with whom JUSTICE SCALIA joins, concurring.

I join the Court's opinion because it accurately applies current jurisprudence. I write separately to reiterate my view that the Court's abortion jurisprudence has no basis in the Constitution. I also note that whether the Act constitutes a permissible exercise of Congress' power under the Commerce Clause is not before the Court. The parties did not raise or brief that issue; it is outside the question presented; and the lower courts did not address it.

Justice Ginsburg, with whom Justice Stevens, Justice Souter, and Justice Breyer join, dissenting.

In *Planned Parenthood of Southeastern Pa. v. Casey,* the Court declared that "[l]iberty finds no refuge in a jurisprudence of doubt." There was, the Court said, an "imperative" need to dispel doubt as to "the meaning and reach" of the Court's 7 to 2 judgment, rendered nearly two decades earlier in *Roe v. Wade. . . .*

Taking care to speak plainly, the *Casey* Court restated and reaffirmed *Roe's* essential holding. . . .

[O]f signal importance here, the *Casey* Court stated with unmistakable clarity that state regulation of access to abortion procedures, even after viability, must protect "the health of the woman."

Seven years ago, in *Stenberg v. Carhart,* the Court invalidated a Nebraska statute criminalizing the performance of a medical procedure that, in the political arena, has been dubbed "partial birth abortion." With fidelity to the *Roe Casey* line of precedent, the Court held the Nebraska statute unconstitutional in part because it lacked the requisite protection for the preservation of a woman's health.

Today's decision is alarming. It refuses to take *Casey* and *Stenberg* seriously. It tolerates, indeed applauds, federal intervention to ban nationwide a procedure found necessary and proper in certain cases by the American College of Obstetricians and Gynecologists (ACOG). It blurs the line, firmly drawn in *Casey,* between previability and postviability abortions. And, for the first time since *Roe,* the Court blesses a prohibition with no exception safeguarding a woman's health.

I dissent from the Court's disposition. Retreating from prior rulings that abortion restrictions cannot be imposed absent an exception safeguarding a woman's health, the Court upholds an Act that surely would not survive under the close scrutiny that previously attended state-decreed limitations on a woman's reproductive choices.

I

A

As *Casey* comprehended, at stake in cases challenging abortion restrictions is a woman's "control over her [own] destiny." "There was a time, not so long ago," when women were "regarded as the center of home and family life, with attendant special responsibilities that precluded full and independent legal status under the Constitution." Women, it is now acknowledged, have the talent, capacity, and right "to participate equally in the economic and social life of the Nation." Their ability to realize their full potential, the Court recognized, is intimately connected to "their ability to control their reproductive lives." Thus, legal challenges to undue restrictions on abortion procedures do not seek to vindicate some generalized notion of privacy; rather, they center on a woman's autonomy to determine her life's course, and thus to enjoy equal citizenship stature.

In keeping with this comprehension of the right to reproductive choice, the Court has consistently required that laws regulating abortion, at any stage of pregnancy and in all cases, safeguard a woman's health.
...

In *Stenberg,* we expressly held that a statute banning intact D & E was unconstitutional in part because it lacked a health exception We noted that there existed a "division of medical opinion" about the relative safety of intact D & E, but we made clear that as long as "substantial medical authority supports the proposition that banning a particular abortion procedure could endanger women's health," a health exception is required.
...

B

[T]he congressional findings on which the Partial-Birth Abortion Ban Act rests do not withstand inspection, as the lower courts have determined and this Court is obliged to concede. ...

Congress claimed there was a medical consensus that the banned procedure is never necessary. But the evidence "very clearly demonstrate[d] the opposite." ...

Similarly, Congress found that "[t]here is no credible medical evidence that partial-birth abortions are safe or are safer than other abortion procedures." But the congressional record includes letters from numerous individual physicians stating that pregnant women's health would be jeopardized under the Act, as well as statements from nine professional associations, including ACOG, the American Public Health Association, and the California Medical Association, attesting that intact D & E carries meaningful safety advantages over other methods. ...

C

In contrast to Congress, the District Courts made findings after full trials at which all parties had the opportunity to present their best evidence. ...

During the District Court trials, "numerous" "extraordinarily accomplished" and "very experienced" medical experts explained that, in certain circumstances and for certain women, intact D & E is safer than alternative procedures and necessary to protect women's health. ...

According to the expert testimony plaintiffs introduced, the safety advantages of intact D & E are marked for women with certain medical conditions, for example, uterine scarring, bleeding disorders, heart disease, or compromised immune systems. Further, plaintiffs' experts testified that intact D & E is significantly safer for women with certain pregnancy-related conditions, such as placenta previa and accreta, and for women carrying fetuses with certain abnormalities, such as severe hydrocephalus. ...

Based on thoroughgoing review of the trial evidence and the congressional record, each of the District Courts to consider the issue rejected Congress' findings as unreasonable and not supported by the evidence. ...

The Court acknowledges some of this evidence, but insists that, because some witnesses disagreed with the ACOG and other experts' assessment of risk, the Act can stand. In this insistence, the Court brushes under the rug the District Courts' well-supported findings that the physicians who testified that intact D & E is never necessary to preserve the health of a woman had slim authority for their opinions. They had no training for, or personal experience with, the intact D & E procedure, and many performed abortions only on rare occasions. ...

II

A

The Court offers flimsy and transparent justifications for upholding a nation-wide ban on intact D & E *sans* any exception to safeguard a women's health. Today's ruling, the Court declares, advances "a premise central to [*Casey's*] conclusion" — *i.e.*, the Government's "legitimate and substantial interest in preserving and promoting fetal life." But the Act scarcely furthers that interest: The law saves not a single fetus from destruction, for it targets only a *method* of performing abortion. ...

As another reason for upholding the ban, the Court emphasizes that the Act does not proscribe the nonintact D & E procedure. But why not, one might ask. Nonintact D & E could equally be characterized as "brutal," involving as it does "tear[ing] [a fetus] apart" and "ripp[ing] off" its limbs. ...

Delivery of an intact, albeit nonviable, fetus warrants special condemnation, the Court maintains, because a fetus that is not dismembered resembles an infant. But so, too, does a fetus delivered intact after it is terminated by injection a day or two before the surgical evacuation, or a fetus delivered through medical induction or cesarean. ...

Ultimately, the Court admits that "moral concerns" are at work, concerns that could yield prohibitions on any abortion. ... By allowing such concerns to carry the day and case, overriding fundamental rights, the Court dishonors our precedent. See, *e.g.*, *Casey*, 505 U. S., at 850 ("Some of us as individuals find abortion offensive to our most basic principles of morality, but that cannot control our decision. Our obligation is to define the liberty of all, not to mandate our own moral code."); Lawrence v. Texas, 539 U. S. 558, 571 (2003) (Though "[f]or many persons [objections to homosexual conduct] are not trivial concerns but profound and deep convictions accepted as ethical and moral principles," the power of the State may not be used "to enforce these views on the whole society through operation of the criminal law."

Revealing in this regard, the Court invokes an antiabortion shibboleth for which it concededly has no reliable evidence: Women who have abortions come to regret their choices, and consequently suffer from "[s]evere depression and loss of esteem."[1] Because of women's fragile emotional state and because of the "bond of love the mother has for her child," the Court worries, doctors may withhold information about the nature of the intact D & E procedure. The solution the Court approves, then, is *not* to require doctors to inform women, accurately and adequately, of the different procedures and their attendant risks. Instead, the Court deprives women of the right to make an autonomous choice, even at the expense of their safety.

This way of thinking reflects ancient notions about women's place in the family and under the Constitution — ideas that have long since been discredited.

Though today's majority may regard women's feelings on the matter as "self-evident," this Court has repeatedly confirmed that "[t]he destiny of the woman must be shaped ... on her own conception of her spiritual imperatives and her place in society."

B

In cases on a "woman's liberty to determine whether to [continue] her pregnancy," this Court has identified viability as a critical consideration. "[T]here is no line [more workable] than viability," the Court explained in *Casey*, for viability is "the time at which there is a realistic possibility of maintaining and nourishing a life outside the womb, so that the independent existence of the second life can in reason and all fairness be the object of state protection that now overrides the rights of the woman. ... In some broad sense it

---

1. The Court is surely correct that, for most women, abortion is a painfully difficult decision. But "neither the weight of the scientific evidence to date nor the observable reality of 33 years of legal abortion in the United States comports with the idea that having an abortion is any more dangerous to a woman's long-term mental health than delivering and parenting a child that she did not intend to have. ..." Cohen, Abortion and Mental Health: Myths and Realities, 9 Guttmacher Policy Rev. 8 (2006). [The dissent then cites a number of studies regarding the effects of abortions on women who have had them.]

might be said that a woman who fails to act before viability has consented to the State's intervention on behalf of the developing child."

Today, the Court blurs that line, maintaining that "[t]he Act [legitimately] appl[ies] both previability and postviability because. . . . a fetus is a living organism while within the womb, whether or not it is viable outside the womb." Instead of drawing the line at viability, the Court refers to Congress' purpose to differentiate "abortion and infanticide" based not on whether a fetus can survive outside the womb, but on where a fetus is anatomically located when a particular medical procedure is performed. . . .

III

A

The Court further confuses our jurisprudence when it declares that "facial attacks" are not permissible in "these circumstances," *i.e.,* where medical uncertainty exists. ("In an as-applied challenge the nature of the medical risk can be better quantified and balanced than in a facial attack."). This holding is perplexing given that, in materially identical circumstances we held that a statute lacking a health exception was unconstitutional on its face. . . .

Without attempting to distinguish *Stenberg* and earlier decisions, the majority asserts that the Act survives review because respondents have not shown that the ban on intact D & E would be unconstitutional "in a large fraction of relevant cases." But *Casey* makes clear that, in determining whether any restriction poses an undue burden on a "large fraction" of women, the relevant class is *not* "all women," nor "all pregnant women," nor even all women "seeking abortions." Rather, a provision restricting access to abortion "must be judged by reference to those [women] for whom it is an actual rather than an irrelevant restriction," *ibid.* Thus the absence of a health exception burdens *all* women for whom it is relevant — women who, in the judgment of their doctors, require an intact D & E because other procedures would place their health at risk. . . .

B

If there is anything at all redemptive to be said of today's opinion, it is that the Court is not willing to foreclose entirely a constitutional challenge to the Act. . . . But the Court offers no clue on what a "proper" lawsuit might look like. Nor does the Court explain why the injunctions ordered by the District Courts should not remain in place, trimmed only to exclude instances in which another procedure would safeguard a woman's health at least equally well. . . .

The Court envisions that in an as-applied challenge, "the nature of the medical risk can be better quantified and balanced." But it should not escape notice that the record already includes hundreds and hundreds of pages of testimony identifying "discrete and well-defined instances" in which recourse to an intact D & E would better protect the health of women with particular conditions. Record evidence also documents that medical exigencies, unpredictable in advance, may indicate to a well-trained doctor that intact D & E is the safest procedure. . . .

IV

Though today's opinion does not go so far as to discard *Roe* or *Casey,* the Court, differently composed than it was when we last considered a restrictive abortion regulation, is hardly faithful to our earlier invocations of "the rule of law" and the "principles of *stare decisis.*" . . .

In sum, the notion that the Partial-Birth Abortion Ban Act furthers any legitimate governmental interest is, quite simply, irrational. The Court's defense of the statute provides no saving explanation. In candor, the Act, and the Court's defense of it, cannot be understood as anything other than an effort to chip away at a right declared again and again by this Court — and with increasing comprehension of its centrality to women's lives. . . .

Note: The Future of Abortion Rights

1. *The government interest in regulation.* What legitimate government interest is advanced by the Partial Birth Abortion Ban Act? Consider the following possibilities:

a. "The Act expresses respect for the dignity of human life." Note that the statute regulates the method by which abortions are performed, not whether they are performed. In what sense, then, does the statute protect the dignity of human life? Given the Court's description of the two procedures, might not one argue that the substitution of the regular D & E method for the intact D&E method actually denigrates the dignity of human life?

b. "Under our precedents it is clear the State has a significant role to play in regulating the medical profession." Is this interest, standing alone, sufficient if no other legitimate government interest is served by the regulation? Does an unadorned concern for the ethics or reputation of the medical profession provide a sufficient justification for regulation in the absence of some other argument demonstrating that the regulated practices are in fact unethical or harmful?

c. The state has an interest in "draw[ing] a bright line that clearly distinguishes abortion and infanticide." Does the statute accomplish this objective? Is there really a "bright line" between the destruction of a fetus that remains wholly within the uterus at the moment of destruction and one that is partially removed at that moment? If a bright line is required, why shouldn't the line be drawn at the complete removal of the fetus from the body of the woman?

d. "The State has an interest in ensuring so grave a choice is well informed." How does this interest differentiate intact D & E procedures from other abortion procedures? How does banning a procedure altogether serve to ensure that patients are "well informed" about it?

e. "It is a reasonable inference that a necessary effect of the regulation and the knowledge it conveys will be to encourage some women to carry the infant to full term, thus reducing the absolute number of late term abortions." How does the banning of a procedure convey knowledge about it? Why does the knowledge gained about a banned procedure result in women choosing to carry an "infant" to full term rather than choosing to use a permitted procedure to abort it?

f. "While we find no reliable data to measure the phenomenon, it seems unexceptionable to conclude some women come to regret their choice to abort the infant life they once created and sustained." Consider the possibility that the pursuit of this governmental purpose is, itself, unconstitutional, and that, to the extent that this purpose motivated the statute, it makes the case for the statute's constitutionality weaker rather than stronger. *See* Siegel, The New Politics of Abortion: An Equality Analysis of Woman-Protective Abortion Restrictions, 2007 U. Ill. L. Rev. 991: "Under the equal protection cases, the government cannot require a woman seeking an abortion to become a mother for the reason that the state knows a pregnant woman's desires and needs better than the pregnant woman herself. [The] Constitution forbids paternalism of this kind because of the mistaken and harmful judgments about women it engenders. Lawmakers reasoning from traditional forms of gender paternalism may not recognize that women who have abortions are competent decision makers grappling with complex practical and relational considerations."

2. *Undue burden?* Does the Partial Birth Abortion Ban Act "unduly burden" the right to an abortion? Given the Court's limiting construction of the Act, does it remain plausible that doctors will be deterred from using standard abortion techniques because of the vagueness of the statute's command? In her dissenting opinion, Justice Ginsburg claims that "[the] law saves not a single fetus from destruction." If she is correct, how can it be that the statute unduly burdens the abortion right? Is the problem that even though the statute does prevent some abortions, it does so by an illegitimate means? May the state discourage an activity — even one that it could properly ban — by deliberately making the activity less safe?

3. *Facial versus as-applied challenge.* Notice that the Court leaves open the possibility that individual women can challenge the statute as applied to them

on the ground that a standard D & E would risk their health. Is this holding meaningfully different from reading a health exception into the statute? If the statute had had such an exception, would there be any question as to its constitutionality? How can an as-applied challenge be mounted? Do individual women have to go to court in order to obtain last-minute adjudications as to the health risks of various procedures? Suppose that as-applied challenges are mounted on behalf of particular classes of women, but courts make contra-dictory factual findings about health risks with regard to those classes. Would inconsistent trial outcomes make the procedure constitutional in some parts of the country but unconstitutional elsewhere?

4. *The law and politics of abortion.* Who are the long-term winners and losers in Gonzales v. Carhart? Consider the following possibilities:

a. The decision marks the beginning of the long-term unraveling of Roe v. Wade. It emboldens *Roe*'s opponents by providing them with a strong victory that has obvious implications for other sorts of restrictions. More-over, the decision vindicates the strategy of attacking *Roe* piecemeal in a way that will undermine it in the long term, just as the NAACP succeeded in gradually undermining the separate-but-equal doctrine until it was suffi-ciently weakened to allow for its total repudiation.

b. Despite outward appearances, the decision aids the defenders of *Roe*. The decision itself has very little impact on the availability of abortions. It does, however, change the political dynamics of the abortion debate. On the one hand, it eliminates the most emotionally charged and problematic form of abortion, the existence of which was used effectively to mobilize "pro-life" forces. On the other hand, the decision produces anxiety among "pro-choice" forces that the basic abortion right is at risk, thereby promoting political mobilization on their side.

c. The decision is all about symbolism and will have very little impact of any kind. The long-term future of the abortion right will be determined by cultural, social, economic, and technological forces rather than by consti-tutional doctrine.

Page 948. At the end of subsection a of the Note, add the following:

On the record before the Court, there was no indication that Lawrence was engaged in a long term, intimate relationship with his partner. The Court none-theless characterizes the case as involving "intimate conduct with another person [that] can be but one element in a personal bond that is more enduring."

Consider in this regard Hutchinson, The Majoritarian Difficulty: Affirmative Action, Sodomy, and Supreme Court Politics, 23 Law & Ineq. 1, 49 (2005):

> By framing the liberty interest around relationships rather than sexual conduct, which the statute regulates, the Court constructs a narrative of gay respectability: while "promiscuous" gay men cause unease in a heternormative society, partnered, monogamous gay sex receives greater tolerance in the dominant culture.

Hutchinson finds this focus disturbing:

> As lesbian and gay, feminist, critical race, and poverty theorists have demonstrated, pro-marriage discourse, same-sex or otherwise, often stigmatizes poor single mothers, marginalizes the familial arrangements of communities of color, taints gay male sexual practice, overstates the economic value of marriage to poor persons of color, and uncritically accepts the legitimacy of an institution that has historically supported the domination of women.

Professor Hutchinson and Justice Scalia strongly disagree about the appropriate role of the judiciary in reforming laws that disadvantage gay men and lesbians. Notice, though that both worry that despite the Court's disclaimer about gay marriage, parts of the *Lawrence* opinion seem to endorse legal recognition of committed gay relationships. Is the worry justified?

Consider Klarman, Brown and Lawrence (and Goodridge), 104 Mich. L. Rev. 431, 450 (2005):

> That [Justices] Kennedy and O'Connor would go to such lengths to deny that *Lawrence* has implications for same-sex marriage is not surprising. Just as at the time of Brown [v. Board of Education], a majority of Americans opposed public school segregation but overwhelmingly supported antimiscegenation laws, so at the time of *Lawrence* public opinion opposed criminal prosecution of private gay sex but supported by a two-to-one margin laws restricting marriage to unions between men and women. . . .
>
> Yet just as *Brown* led inexorably, albeit gradually, to a presumptive judicial ban on all racial classifications, so is *Lawrence* likely to lead eventually to a presumptive judicial ban on all classifications based on sexual orientation. [*Lawrence*] denies that "moral disapproval" of homosexuality is a legitimate state interest. It is difficult, however, to identify a state interest other than moral disapproval that would convincingly justify banning same-sex marriage.

For a book-length defense of gay marriage, see W. Eskridge, Jr., The Case for Same-Sex Marriage: From Sexual Liberty to Civilized Commitment (1994).

In response to *Lawrence,* as well as to state statutes and court decisions mandating gay marriage or "civil unions," Congress has considered a constitutional amendment dealing with the subject. The amendment provides:

> Marriage in the United States shall consist only of the union of a man and a woman. Neither this Constitution, nor the constitution of any State, shall be construed to require that marriage or the legal incidents thereof be conferred upon any union other than the union of a man and a woman.

If adopted, what effect would the amendment have? Would it prohibit state legislatures from granting to gay men and lesbians certain incidents of marriage, such as joint parental rights or rights to intestate succession? Suppose a state statute granted to gay men and lesbians *all* incidents of marriage, but called the relationship a "civil union"? If the clear language of a state constitution granted some legal incidents of marriage to gay couples, would the language have to be "construed"? How clear does the language have to be to avoid "construction"?

Consider Testimony of Louis Michael Seidman, Before the United States Senate Judiciary Committee, Subcommittee on the Constitution, Civil Rights, and Property Rights "An Examination of the Constitutional Amendment on Marriage" (Oct. 20, 2005):

> [The amendment] does nothing to change the Supreme Court's decision in Lawrence v. Texas, which invalidated sodomy statutes as applied to gay men and lesbians. Strikingly, that decision creates a constitutional right to engage in even casual sex with total strangers. When *Lawrence* is read together with this amendment, the upshot is a fundamental constitutional right to casual sex, but an absolute constitutional prohibition on long-term, committed gay relationships. The amendment, in effect, constitutionalizes the one night stand.

In a test vote on June 6, 2006, the amendment failed to achieve the necessary two-thirds majority in the Senate, with 49 senators voting in favor of the amendment and 48 against.

Page 967.   Before Section G, add the following:

In Philip Morris v. Williams, 549 U.S. 346 (2007), the Court, in a five-to-four decision written by Justice Breyer, held that "the Constitution's Due Process Clause forbids a State to use a punitive damages award to punish a defendant for injury that it inflicts upon nonparties or those whom they directly represent, *i.e.,* injury that it inflicts upon those who are, essentially, strangers to the litigation." The Court went on to note, however, that a plaintiff could show harm to others "in order to demonstrate reprehensibility. [Evidence] of actual harm to nonparties can help to show that the conduct that harmed the plaintiff also posed a substantial risk of harm to the general public, and so was particularly reprehensible, although counsel may argue in a particular case that conduct resulting in no harm to others nonetheless posed a grave risk to the public, or the converse." Justices Stevens and Thomas filed dissenting opinions. Justice Ginsburg also filed a dissenting opinion that was joined by Justices Thomas and Scalia.

G. Procedural Due Process

Page 972. Before the Note, add the following:

TOWN OF CASTLE ROCK, COLORADO V. GONZALES
545 U.S. 748 (2005)

JUSTICE SCALIA delivered the opinion of the Court.

We decide in this case whether an individual who has obtained a state-law restraining order has a constitutionally protected property interest in having the police enforce the restraining order when they have probable cause to believe it has been violated...

I

[Several weeks before the incident in question, a Colorado court issued a restraining order directed against Ms. Gonzales's husband in conjunction with a divorce action. The order directed the husband to stay away from Gonzales and her children. Preprinted text on the back of the order stated the following:

> YOU SHALL USE EVERY REASONABLE MEANS TO ENFORCE THIS RESTRAINING ORDER. YOU SHALL ARREST, OR, IF AN ARREST WOULD BE IMPRACTICAL UNDER THE CIRCUMSTANCES, SEEK A WARRANT FOR THE ARREST OF THE RESTRAINED PERSON WHEN YOU HAVE INFORMATION AMOUNTING TO PROBABLE CAUSE THAT THE RESTRAINED PERSON HAS VIOLATED OR ATTEMPTED TO VIOLATE ANY PROVISION OF THIS

ORDER AND THE RESTRAINED PERSON HAS BEEN PROPERLY
SERVED WITH A COPY OF THIS ORDER OR HAS RECEIVED
ACTUAL NOTICE OF THE EXISTENCE OF THIS ORDER.

This notice implemented a provision of Colorado law that provided the
following:

(a) Whenever a restraining order is issued, the protected person shall be
provided with a copy of such order. A peace officer shall use every reasonable means to enforce a restraining order.

(b) A peace officer shall arrest, or, if an arrest would be impractical under
the circumstances, seek a warrant for the arrest of a restrained person when
the peace officer has information amounting to probable cause that:

(I) The restrained person has violated or attempted to violate any provision of a restraining order; and

(II) The restrained person has been properly served with a copy of the
restraining order or the restrained person has received actual notice
of the existence and substance of such order.

(c) In making the probable cause determination described in paragraph (b)
of this subsection (3), a peace officer shall assume that the information
received from the registry is accurate. A peace officer shall enforce a
valid restraining order whether or not there is a record of the restraining
order in the registry.

Gonzales alleged that some two-and-one-half weeks after the order was entered,
at about 5 or 5:30 P.M., her husband took her three daughters in violation of the
order while they were playing outside the family house. At about 7:30 P.M., she
called the Castle Rock Police Department, which dispatched two officers. When
shown the restraining order, the officers said that there was nothing that they
could do about it and suggested that Gonzales call the police department again
if the children did not return by 10:00 P.M.

At about 8:30 P.M., Gonzales's husband telephoned her and told her that he
had the children at an amusement park in Denver. She called the police again
and asked them to "have someone check for" her husband at the amusement
park, but the officer refused to do so. At about 10:10 P.M. Gonzales called the
police and reported that her children were still missing, but she was now told to
wait until midnight. She called again at midnight to report that the children were
still missing and then went to her husband's apartment. Finding no one there,
she called the police yet again and was told to wait until an officer arrived.
When none came, she went to the police station at 12:50 A.M. and submitted an

incident report. Rather than make an effort to locate the children, the officer went to dinner.

At 3:20 A.M., Gonzales's husband arrived at the police station and opened fire with a semiautomatic handgun. Police shot back, killing him. Inside the cab of his pickup truck, they found the bodies of the three daughters, whom he had already murdered.

II

Respondent claims the benefit of [the fourteenth amendment's due process clause] on the ground that she had a property interest in police enforcement of the restraining order against her husband; and that the town deprived her of this property without due process by having a policy that tolerated non-enforcement of restraining orders.

[We] left a similar question unanswered in DeShaney v. Winnebago County Dept. of Social Servs., 489 U.S. 189, (1989), another case with "undeniably tragic" facts: Local child-protection officials had failed to protect a young boy from beatings by his father that left him severely brain damaged. We held that the so-called "substantive" component of the Due Process Clause does not "requir[e] the State to protect the life, liberty, and property of its citizens against invasion by private actors." We noted, however, that the petitioner had not properly preserved the argument that — and we thus "decline[d] to consider" whether — state "child protection statutes gave [him] an 'entitlement' to receive protective services in accordance with the terms of the statute, an entitlement which would enjoy due process protection." [The *DeShaney* case is excerpted and discussed on pages 1589-1591 and 1596-1601 of the main volume]. . . .

B

The Court of Appeals concluded that [the] statutory provision [quoted above] — especially taken in conjunction with a statement from its legislative history,[6] and with another statute restricting criminal and civil liability for

---

6. The Court of Appeals quoted one lawmaker's description of how the bill "'would really attack the domestic violence problems'":

[T]he entire criminal justice system must act in a consistent manner, which does not now occur. The police must make probable cause arrests. The prosecutors must prosecute every case. Judges must apply appropriate sentences, and probation officers must monitor their probationers closely. And the offender needs to be sentenced to offender-specific therapy.

[T]he entire system must send the same message . . . [that] violence is criminal. And so we hope that House Bill 1253 starts us down this road.

officers making arrests[7] — established the Colorado Legislature's clear intent "to alter the fact that the police were not enforcing domestic abuse retraining orders," and thus its intent "that the recipient of a domestic abuse restraining order have an entitlement to its enforcement." Any other result, it said, "would render domestic abuse restraining orders utterly valueless."

This last statement is sheer hyperbole. Whether or not respondent had a right to enforce the restraining order, it rendered certain otherwise lawful conduct by her husband both criminal and in contempt of court. The creation of grounds on which he could be arrested, criminally prosecuted, and held in contempt was hardly "valueless" — even if the prospect of those sanctions ultimately failed to prevent him from committing three murders and a suicide.

We do not believe that these provisions of Colorado law truly made enforcement of restraining orders *mandatory*. A well established tradition of police discretion has long coexisted with apparently mandatory arrest statutes...

Against that backdrop, a true mandate of police action would require some stronger indication from the Colorado Legislature than "shall use every reasonable means to enforce a restraining order" (or even "shall arrest ... or ... seek a warrant"). That language is not perceptibly more mandatory than the Colorado statute which has long told municipal chiefs of police that they "shall pursue and arrest any person fleeing from justice in any part of the state" and that they "shall apprehend any person in the act of committing any offense ... and, forthwith and without any warrant, bring such person before a ... competent authority for examination and trial." It is hard to imagine that a Colorado peace officer would not have some discretion to determine that — despite probable cause to believe a restraining order has been violated — the circumstances of the violation or the competing duties of that officer or his agency counsel decisively against enforcement in a particular instance ...

[Respondent] does not specify the precise means of enforcement that the Colorado restraining-order statute assertedly mandated — whether her interest lay in having police arrest her husband, having them seek a warrant for his arrest, or having them "use every reasonable means, up to and including arrest, to enforce the order's terms." Such indeterminacy is not the hallmark of a duty that is mandatory. Nor can someone be safely deemed "entitled" to something when the identity of the alleged entitlement is vague ...

Even if the statute could be said to have made enforcement of restraining orders "mandatory" because of the domestic-violence context of the underlying

---

7. Under Colo. Rev. Stat. § 18-6-803.5(5), "[a] peace officer arresting a person for violating a restraining order or otherwise enforcing a restraining order" was not to be held civilly or criminally liable unless he acted "in bad faith and with malice" or violated "rules adopted by the Colorado supreme court."

statute, that would not necessarily mean that state law gave *respondent* an entitlement to *enforcement* of the mandate. Making the actions of government employees obligatory can serve various legitimate ends other than the conferral of a benefit on a specific class of people. ...

C

Even if we were to think otherwise concerning the creation of an entitlement by Colorado, it is by no means clear that an individual entitlement to enforcement of a restraining order could constitute a "property" interest for purposes of the Due Process Clause. Such a right would not, of course, resemble any traditional conception of property. Although that alone does not disqualify it from due process protection, as *Roth* and its progeny show, the right to have a restraining order enforced does not "have some ascertainable monetary value," as even our "*Roth*-type property-as-entitlement" cases have implicitly required. Perhaps most radically, the alleged property interest here arises *incidentally*, not out of some new species of government benefit or service, but out of a function that government actors have always performed — to wit, arresting people who they have probable cause to believe have committed a criminal offense...

III

In light of today's decision and that in *DeShaney,* the benefit that a third party may receive from having someone else arrested for a crime generally does not trigger protections under the Due Process Clause, neither in its procedural nor in its "substantive" manifestations. This result reflects our continuing reluctance to treat the Fourteenth Amendment as "'a fount of tort law,'" but it does not mean States are powerless to provide victims with personally enforceable remedies. Although the framers of the Fourteenth Amendment and the Civil Rights Act of 1871 did not create a system by which police departments are generally held financially accountable for crimes that better policing might have prevented, the people of Colorado are free to craft such a system under state law.

The judgment of the Court of Appeals is reversed.

[A concurring opinion by Justice Souter, in which Justice Breyer joined, is omitted.]

JUSTICE STEVENS, with whom JUSTICE GINSBURG joins, dissenting.

The issue presented to us is much narrower than is suggested by the far-ranging arguments of the parties and their *amici*. Neither the tragic facts of the case, nor the importance of according proper deference to law enforcement professionals, should divert our attention from that issue. That issue is whether the restraining order entered by the Colorado trial court on June 4, 1999, created a "property" interest that is protected from arbitrary deprivation by the Due Process Clause of the Fourteenth Amendment.

It is perfectly clear, on the one hand, that neither the Federal Constitution itself, nor any federal statute, granted respondent or her children any individual entitlement to police protection. Nor, I assume, does any Colorado statute create any such entitlement for the ordinary citizen. On the other hand, it is equally clear that federal law imposes no impediment to the creation of such an entitlement by Colorado law. Respondent certainly could have entered into a contract with a private security firm, obligating the firm to provide protection to respondent's family; respondent's interest in such a contract would unquestionably constitute "property" within the meaning of the Due Process Clause. If a Colorado statute enacted for her benefit, or a valid order entered by a Colorado judge, created the functional equivalent of such a private contract by granting respondent an entitlement to mandatory individual protection by the local police force, that state-created right would also qualify as "property" entitled to constitutional protection.

I do not understand the majority to rule out the foregoing propositions, although it does express doubts. The central question in this case is therefore whether, as a matter of Colorado law, respondent had a right to police assistance comparable to the right she would have possessed to any other service the government or a private firm might have undertaken to provide. . . .

III

[The] Court places undue weight on the various statutes throughout the country that seemingly mandate police enforcement but are generally understood to preserve police discretion. As a result, the Court gives short shrift to the unique case of "mandatory arrest" statutes in the domestic violence context; states passed a wave of these statutes in the 1980's and 1990's with the unmistakable goal of eliminating police discretion in this area. [The] Court's formalistic analysis fails to take seriously the fact that the Colorado statute at issue in this case was enacted for the benefit of the narrow class of persons who are beneficiaries of domestic restraining orders, and that the order at issue in this case was specifically intended to provide protection to respondent and her children. [The] Court is simply wrong to assert that a citizen's interest in the government's commitment to provide police enforcement in certain defined circumstances does not resemble any "traditional conception of property"; in fact, a citizen's property interest in such a commitment is just as concrete and worthy of protection as her interest in any other important service the government or a private firm has undertaken to provide . . .

Accordingly, I respectfully dissent.

Page 976.   Before section 3 of the Note, add the following:

In Wilkinson v. Austin, 544 U.S. 209 (2005), the Court distinguished *Meachum* and *Sandin* and held that a prison inmate had a constitutionally protected liberty interest in avoiding transfer to a "Supermax" facility. Prisoners confined to this facility are held in cells measuring 7 by 14 feet for 23 hours per day for an indefinite period limited only by the length of the inmate's sentence. A light remains on in the cell at all times, although it is sometimes dimmed. The cells have solid metal doors with metal strips along the sides and bottoms designed to prevent any conversation or communication with other inmates. All meals are taken within the cells rather than in a common eating area.

Speaking for a unanimous court, Justice Kennedy noted that although the Constitution itself does not create a liberty interest in avoiding transfer to more adverse conditions of confinement, such an interest may arise from state policies and regulations. According to the Court, "the touchstone of the inquiry into the existence of [such] a protected, state-created liberty interest [is] not the language of regulations regarding those conditions but the nature of the conditions themselves 'in relation to ordinary incidents of prison life' " [quoting from *Sandin*]. The Court noted the difficulty under this test in "locating the appropriate baseline" against which to measure atypical hardships, but held that it "need not resolve the issue here, [for] we are satisfied that assignment to [the "Supermax" facility] imposes an atypical and significant hardship under any plausible baseline."

Page 984.   Before section 4 of the Note, add the following:

Compare Wilkinson v. Austin, 544 U.S. 209 (2005), where the Court upheld procedures under which, prior to transfer to a "Supermax" facility, inmates were provided with a written notice of reasons and a hearing at which they could offer explanations or objections but could not call witnesses. (For a description of the "Supermax" facility, see the supplement to page 976 in this volume.) The district court had held that these procedures were constitutionally inadequate and that, prior to the hearing, inmates had to be provided with a summary of all evidence upon which the transfer might be based. At the hearing itself, the district court held, inmates were constitutionally entitled to present documentary evidence and to call witnesses, when doing so would not be unduly hazardous or burdensome. Writing for a unanimous Court, Justice Kennedy found that these additional safeguards were constitutionally unnecessary. In so concluding, the Court placed "dominant" weight on the third factor of the *Matthews* balancing test, emphasizing the state's interest in prison security and in the allocation of scarce resources.

H. The Contracts and Takings Clauses

Page 1007. At the end of the Note, add the following:

3. Kelo. The Court reaffirmed (and arguably extended) *Midkiff in* Kelo v. City of New London, 545 U.S. 469 (2005). Decades of decline in New London caused state and city officials to target the city for economic revitalization. In 1998, Pfizer Inc. announced that it would build a $300 million research facility in the city. In an effort to capitalize on the new Pfizer facility, the city council approved a redevelopment plan requiring the acquisition of a 90-acre area adjoining the facility. The plan called for the creation of a waterfront conference hotel, a marina, restaurants, retail stores, and offices. Petitioners, including Wilhelmina Dery, who had been born in her house in 1918 and lived there all her life, challenged the condemnation of their property pursuant to the plan on the ground that it violated the public use requirement.

In a five-to-four decision, the Court, per Justice Stevens, upheld the condemnation. He began his analysis by arguing that condemned land need not literally be open to public use so long as the land is seized for a "public purpose." Moreover, "[without] exception, our cases have defined that concept broadly, reflecting our longstanding policy of deference to legislative judgments in this field."

Applying this test, Justice Stevens noted:

> The City has carefully formulated an economic development plan that it believes will provide appreciable benefits to the community, including — but by no means limited to — new jobs and increased tax revenue. [Given] the comprehensive character of the plan, the thorough deliberation that preceded its adoption, and the limited scope of our review, it is appropriate for us [to] resolve the challenges of the individual owners, not on a piece-meal basis, but rather in light of the entire plan. Because that plan unquestionably serves a public purpose, the takings challenged here satisfy the public use [requirement].

According to the Court, the case before it did not require it to determine the constitutionality of a transfer of property from one citizen to another for the sole reason that the other citizen would make more productive use of the property and pay more taxes. "Such a one-to-one transfer of property, executed outside the confines of an integrated development plan, is not presented in this case. While such an unusual exercise of government power would certainly raise a suspicion that a private purpose was afoot, the hypothetical cases [can] be confronted if and when they arise."

Justice Kennedy filed a concurring opinion. While agreeing with the majority that a rational basis approach was the appropriate level of review in public use cases, he emphasized that deferential review "does not [alter] the fact that transfers intended to confer benefits on particular, favored private entities, and with only incidental or pretextual public benefits, are forbidden by the Public Use Clause." According to Justice Kennedy, "[a] court applying rational-basis review under the Public Use Clause should strike down a taking that, by a clear showing, is intended to favor a particular private party, with only incidental or pretextual public benefits, just as a court applying rational-basis review under the Equal Protection Clause must strike down a government classification that is clearly intended to injure a particular class of private parties, with only incidental or pretextual public justifications." In addition, Justice Kennedy observed that

a more stringent standard of review [might] be appropriate for a more narrowly drawn category of takings. There may be private transfers in which the risk of undetected impermissible favoritism of private parties is so acute that a presumption (rebuttable or otherwise) of invalidity is warranted under the Public Use Clause. This demanding level of scrutiny, however, is not required simply because the purpose of the taking is economic development.

Justice O'Connor dissented in an opinion joined by Chief Justice Rehnquist and Justices Scalia and Thomas:

Today, the Court abandons [a] long-held, basic limitation on government power. Under the banner of economic development, all private property is now vulnerable to being taken and transferred to another private owner, so long as it might be upgraded — i.e., given to an owner who will use it in a way that the legislature deems more beneficial to the public — in the process. To reason, as the Court does, that the incidental public benefits resulting from the subsequent ordinary use of private property render economic development takings "for public use" is to wash out any distinction between private and public use of property — and thereby effectively to delete the words "for public use" from the Takings Clause of the Fifth Amendment.

Justice O'Connor distinguished *Midkiff* and Parker v. Berman on the ground that these cases had involved condemnation of property that was imposing an "affirmative harm on society — in *Berman* through blight resulting from extreme poverty and in *Midkiff* through oligopoly resulting from extreme wealth."

> Here, in contrast, New London does not claim that [the] well-maintained homes are the source of any social harm. Indeed, it could not so claim without adopting the absurd argument that any single-family home that might be razed to make way for an apartment building, or any church that might be replaced with a retail store, or any small business that might be more lucrative if it were instead part of a national franchise, is inherently harmful to society and thus within the government's power to condemn.

Justice Thomas filed a separate dissent in which he argued that the public use clause, as originally understood, allowed to government to take property only if after the condemnation the government owned the property or the public had a legal right to use the property. Consider also the following observations at the end of Justice Thomas's opinion:

> Allowing the government to take property solely for public purposes is bad enough, but extending the concept of public purpose to encompass any economically beneficial goal guarantees that these losses will fall disproportionately on poor communities. Those communities are not only systematically less likely to put their lands to the highest and best social use, but are also the least politically powerful. If ever there were justification for intrusive judicial review of constitutional provisions that protect "discrete and insular minorities," surely that principle would apply with great force to the powerless groups and individuals the Public Use Clause protects ...
>
> [The] legacy of this Court's "public purpose" test [is] an unhappy one. In the 1950's, no doubt emboldened in part by the expansive understanding of "public use" this Court adopted in *Berman,* cities "rushed to draw plans" for downtown development. "Of all the families displaced by urban renewal from 1949 through 1963, 63 percent of those whose race was known were nonwhite, and of these families, 56 percent of nonwhites and 38 percent of whites had incomes low enough to qualify for public housing, which, however, was seldom available to them." Public works projects in the 1950's and 1960's destroyed predominantly minority communities in St. Paul, Minnesota, and Baltimore, Maryland. In 1981, urban planners in Detroit, Michigan, uprooted the largely "lower-income and elderly" Poletown

neighborhood for the benefit of the General Motors Corporation. Urban renewal projects have long been associated with the displacement of blacks; "[i]n cities across the country, urban renewal came to be known as 'Negro removal.'" Over 97 percent of the individuals forcibly removed from their homes by the "slum-clearance" project upheld by this Court in *Berman* were black. Regrettably, the predictable consequence of the Court's decision will be to exacerbate these effects.

Page 1019.   At the bottom of the page, add the following:

In Lingle v. Chevron U.S.A., Inc., 544 U.S. 528 (2005), the Court repudiated the language quoted on page 1017 of the main text that regulation can amount to a taking if it "does not substantially advance legitimate state interests." The court of appeals had struck down a Hawaii statute limiting the rent that oil companies could charge to dealers who leased service stations from the companies. The court of appeals reasoned that this measure did not "substantially advance" the state's interest in preventing concentration of the retail gasoline market and high prices for consumers, and that the statute therefore amounted to an uncompensated taking. The Supreme Court, in a unanimous decision written by Justice O'Connor, reversed. The Court held that, as an analytic matter, the "substantially advances" standard "prescribes an inquiry in the nature of a due process, not a takings, test, and that it has no proper place in our takings jurisprudence." The Court left open the possibility that a regulation that failed the "substantially advances" test might violate due process. It warned however:

> The [formula] can be read to demand heightened means-ends review of virtually any regulation of private property. If so interpreted, it would require courts to scrutinize the efficacy of a vast array of state and federal regulations — a task for which courts are not well suited. Moreover, it would empower — and might often require — courts to substitute their predictive judgments for those of elected legislatures and expert agencies ...
>
> We have long eschewed such heightened scrutiny when addressing substantive due process challenges to government regulation.

In a short concurring opinion, Justice Kennedy emphasized that the "decision does not foreclose the possibility that a regulation might be so arbitrary or irrational as to violate due process. The failure of a regulation to accomplish a stated or obvious objective would be relevant to that inquiry."

7
FREEDOM OF EXPRESSION

B. Content-Based Restrictions: Dangerous Ideas and Information

Page 1070. At the end of *Debs*, add the following:

In 1920, while in prison, Debs was the Socialist candidate for President. He again received almost a million votes. President Harding released him from prison in 1921.

Other representative prosecutions under the Espionage Act include the following:

(a) Rose Pastor Stokes was convicted for saying, "I am for the people and the government is for the profiteers," during an antiwar talk to the Women's Dining Club of Kansas City. Although there were no soldiers — indeed, no men — in her intended audience, the government successfully argued that she had violated the act because "our armies ... can operate and succeed only so far as they are supported and maintained by the folks at home," and Stokes's statement had the tendency to "chill enthusiasm, extinguish confidence, and retard cooperation" of mothers, sisters, and sweethearts. She was sentenced to ten years in prison.

(b) The Reverend Clarence H. Waldron was convicted for distributing a pamphlet stating that "if Christians [are] forbidden to fight to preserve the Person of their Lord and Master, they may not fight to preserve themselves, or any city they should happen to dwell in." The government charged that in distributing this pamphlet Waldron had obstructed the recruiting service. He was sentenced to fifteen years in prison.

(c) Robert Goldstein was convicted for producing and exhibiting a motion picture about the American Revolution. The Spirit of '76 depicted Paul Revere's ride, the signing of the Declaration of Independence, and Washington at Valley Forge. It also included a scene accurately portraying the Wyoming Valley Massacre, in which British soldiers bayoneted women and children. The government charged that this could promote insubordination because it negatively portrayed America's ally in the war against Germany. Goldstein was sentenced to ten years in prison. See G. Stone, Perilous Times: Free Speech in Wartime 170-173 (2004).

Page 1073.   At the end of section 1 of the Note, add the following:

One of Abrams's co-defendants, Mollie Steimer, arrived at Ellis Island in 1913 with her parents and her five brothers and sisters, part of the flood of immigrants fleeing poverty and anti-Semitism in czarist Russia. Two days after her arrival, the fifteen-year-old went to work in a grimy garment factory amid the crowded tenements of New York's Lower East Side. Faced with continuing hardship and bleak prospects for the future, she began to explore radical literature and soon became a committed anarchist.

At the time of her trial, she was twenty years old, but looked much younger. At four feet nine inches and less than ninety pounds she was tiny, but she was tough as nails. After her conviction, she was sentenced to fifteen years in prison. In 1922, she was ordered deported to the Soviet Union. When she was informed of this action, she refused to leave the federal penitentiary, because there was a threatened railroad strike and would not ride on a train run by strikebreakers. After the strike was resolved, she was shipped back to Russia.

Once there, she immediately began protesting the injustices of Soviet society. In 1923, the Soviets deported Mollie Steimer to Germany. Few other people have the distinction of having been deported by both the United States and the Soviet Union. In 1933, when Hitler came to power, Steimer fled to Paris. Her Jewish and anarchist identities caught up with her, however, and after the Nazis occupied France she escaped to Mexico. Through her life, she remained a dedicated anarchist. Mollie Steimer died in Cuernavaca in 1980 at the age of eighty-two. See G. Stone, Perilous Times: Free Speech in Wartime 138-40, 232-33 (2004).

Page 1078.   At the end of the Note, add the following:

Whereas Learned Hand viewed express advocacy of law violations as outside the protection of "the freedom of speech," Holmes clearly rejected such a principle. Consider Blasi, Holmes and the Marketplace of Ideas, 2004 Sup. Ct. Rev. 1, 39:

The difference between them, I believe, is that Holmes, the old soldier and proud Darwinist, thought that one of the valuable functions of dissenting speech, including speech that advocates violent revolution, is its capacity to generate some of the grievances, aspirations, and mobilizations that force political adaptation and transformation. Such energies are activated and sustained not only by respectful petition and rational persuasion, but also by incitement, recruitment, and organization for collective action. [That] no viable political community could possibly recognize a comparable freedom to act does not, in this view, render incoherent or dysfunctional a capacious freedom to disseminate heretical political ideas, including ideas about the appropriate means for bringing about change.

Page 1082.   At the end of section 1 of the Note, add the following:

For a historical analysis of *Whitney* and of the Brandeis concurrence, see Collins & Skover, Curious Concurrence: Justice Brandeis's Vote in *Whitney v. California*, 2005 Sup. Ct. Rev. 333.

Page 1090.   After section 2 of the Note, add the following:

2a. *Fear and loathing.* Consider Wells, Fear and Loathing in Constitutional Decision-Making, 2005 Wis. L. Rev. 115, 117-119:

The [argument] that courts ought to protect civil liberties in times of crisis is an attractive one. [But courts] remain subject to the same passions, fears, and prejudices that sweep the rest of the nation. [Nowhere] is this more evident than in [*Dennis*]. A "trial of ideas" from the very beginning, [the evidence against the defendants] was weak, as there was no proof that they agreed to overthrow or advocate overthrow of the government. ...

Conventional wisdom roundly condemns *Dennis,* attributing the result to a Cold War hysteria that gripped the country and infected the judges' reasoning. [Conventional] wisdom, however, provides few answers regarding how to guard against *Dennis's* failings in the future. We cannot simply assume that judges armed with an understanding of past errors will act courageously. [What] we need, then, is a doctrine that can counteract the effects of fear and prejudice that lead to such action. ...

Page 1096.   After the end of section 2 of the Note, add the following:

Consider Stone, Free Speech in the Twenty-First Century: Ten Lessons from the Twentieth Century, ___ Pepperdine L. Rev. ___ (2008):

As a result of its experience in the *Schenck-Brandenburg* line of decisions, the Court learned three very practical lessons about the workings of "the system of free expression" — lessons that have come to play a critical role in shaping contemporary First Amendment jurisprudence.

First, the Court learned about the *chilling effect*. That is, the Court learned that people are easily deterred from exercising their freedom of speech. This is so because individual speakers usually gain very little personally from signing a petition, marching in a demonstration, handing out leaflets, or posting on a blog. [Thus], if they know they might go to jail for speaking, they will often forego their right to speak. This makes perfect sense for each individual. But if many individuals make this same decision, the net effect may be to mutilate the thought process of the community. The Court's gradual recognition of this "chilling effect," and of the consequent power of government to use intimidation to silence its critics, was a critical insight in shaping twentieth-century free speech doctrine.

Second, the Court learned about the *pretext effect*. That is, the Court learned that government officials will often defend their restrictions of speech on grounds quite different from their real motivations for the suppression, which will often be [to] silence their critics, [insulate] themselves from criticism, and preserve their own authority. ...

Third, the Court learned about the *crisis effect*. That is, the Court learned that in times of crisis, real or imagined, citizens and public officials tend to panic [and] to rush headlong to suppress speech that they demonize as dangerous, subversive, disloyal, or treasonable. Painful experience with this "crisis effect," especially during World War I and the Cold War, led the Court to embrace what Professor Vincent Blasi has termed a "pathological perspective" in crafting First Amendment doctrine. That is, the Court attempts to structure First Amendment doctrine to anticipate and to guard against the worst of times.

Consider also Masur, Probability Thresholds, 92 Iowa L. Rev. 1293, 1296-1298 (2007):

> Cost-benefit analysis demands that the judge simply and straightforwardly balance the cost of the dangerous speech — the harm that the expression is likely to cause if it is allowed — against the benefit (a better-informed public, for instance) one might expect the speech to produce. [Consider], for instance, the publication of the sailing date of a troop transport. [If] the government asserts that a newspaper publication of this date would create a five-percent probability that a submarine will sink the transport, and if the transport carried one hundred people, then the likely outcome of allowing publication of its sailing date will be five deaths. Only if the speech is worth more than five lives will the Constitution protect it.
>
> [In general,] cost-benefit analysis is ascendant within both the lower courts and the legal academy, and courts now decide cases that arise at the intersection of individual liberty and national security almost exclusively with reference to such a weighing of interests. [Yet] somehow the First Amendment has tread a different [path]. First Amendment doctrine [insists upon] a "probability threshold": a lower boundary on how likely a potential harm must be in order for that harm to register in the constitutional calculus, regardless of the harm's magnitude. ...
>
> [This approach is justified in the First Amendment context because three] mutually reinforcing factors conspire to exaggerate the importance of low-probability, high-magnitude threats. First, the government [will] tend to inflate the risks [posed] by the speech it attempts to stifle. [Second], individuals — both judges and jurors — have a propensity to overvalue the danger of low-probability [risks]. [Third], dreadful, salient, and emotionally resonant threats, [such as threats of "wars, riots, revolutions, and especially acts of terrorism," are especially likely to trigger these] powerful reactions. [The] probability threshold exists to curb our inclination to overvalue these low-probability threats and to deter the over-suppression of speech that might otherwise result.

Page 1098.   At the end of section 4c of the Note, add the following:

d. Note that *Herceg, Olivia N.,* and *Rice* all involved "crime-facilitating speech." That is, each involved speech that conveyed information that made it easier to others to commit crimes, torts, or other undesirable acts. Most "crime-facilitating speech" has both harmful and valuable uses, and it is "often impossible for the distributor to know which consumers will use the material in which way." In what circumstances may the government prohibit such speech? Consider Volokh, Crime-Facilitating Speech, 57 Stan. L. Rev. 1095, 1105-1106 (2005):

> [C]rime-facilitating speech ought to be constitutionally protected unless (1) it's said to a person or small group of people when the speaker knows these few listeners are likely to use the information for criminal purposes, (2) it's within one of the few classes of speech that has almost no noncriminal value, or (3) it can cause extraordinarily serious harm (on the order of a nuclear attack or a plague) even when it's also valuable for lawful purposes.

Page 1103. At the end of section 8 of the Note, add the following:

Consider also Morse v. Frederick, 127 S. Ct. 2618 (2007) (upholding the suspension of a high school student for displaying at a school-sponsored event a fourteen-foot long banner bearing the phrase "BONG Hits 4 JESUS" because *Tinker* does not apply when a student's speech does not contribute to political debate and "can reasonably be regarded as encouraging illegal drug use").

In a separate concurring opinion in *Morse*, Justice Thomas urged the Court to overrule *Tinker*: "[T]he standard set forth in *Tinker* is without basis in the Constitution. [The] history of public education suggests that the First Amendment, as originally understood, does not protect student speech in public schools. [If] students in public school were originally understood as having free-speech rights, one would have expected 19th century public schools to have respected those right and courts to have enforced them. They did not. [In] the earliest public schools, teachers taught, and students listened. Teachers commanded, and students obeyed. [*Tinker*'s] reasoning conflicted with the traditional understanding of the judiciary's role in relation to public schooling, a role limited by *in loco parentis*. [We should] dispense with *Tinker* altogether. . . ."

Page 1108. At the end of section 2, add the following:

Consider Karst, Threats and Meanings: How the Facts Govern First Amendment Doctrine, 58 Stan. L. Rev. 1337, 1392-93 (2006):

> The dissenters [in *ACLA*] criticize the majority for interpreting the posters as coded death threats by reference to other factors. . . . Applause for the killing of "abortionists" is, of course, protected advocacy, just as the

defendants' posters, considered literally, would be protected advocacy if they were published by some persons who had no knowledge of the previous posters. ... To the dissenters, [the] court abandoned the First Amendment when it used the earlier [posters] as aids in interpreting the recent ones. ... Apparently their view is that the First Amendment provides a *cordon sanitaire* around each statement; if each, considered alone, would be protected, then that is the end of the inquiry. [But] when the central question is the propriety of assigning a threatening meaning to a statement, the First Amendment does not command this tunnel vision. ...

Page 1122. At the end of section 4 of the Note, add the following:

Would the fighting words doctrine be more useful if the government were required to specify in advance the *particular* words, phrases, epithets, and symbols that could constitute fighting words? If so, which words, phrases, epithets, and symbols could constitutionally be included on the list? See Friedlieb, Comment, The Epitome of an Insult: A Constitutional Approach to Designated Fighting Words, 72 U. Chi. L. Rev. 385 (2005).

Page 1122. After section 5 of the Note, add the following:

6. *The actual facts of* Chaplinsky. Consider Blasi and Shiffrin, The Real Story of *West Virginia Board of Education v. Barnette*, in Constitutional Law Stories 433 (M. Dorf ed. 2004):

In April of 1940, Walter Chaplinsky, a vociferous Jehovah's Witness preaching in Rochester, New Hampshire, was surrounded by a group of men who scornfully invited him to salute the flag. While one veteran attempted to pummel Chaplinsky, the town marshal looked on, warned the Witness that things were turning ugly, but refused to arrest the assailant. After the marshal left, the assailant returned with a flag and attempted to impale Chaplinsky on the flagpole, eventually pinning him onto a car while other members of the crowd began to beat him. A police officer then arrived, not to detain or disperse members of the mob but to escort Chaplinsky to the police station. En route, the officer and others who joined the escort directed epithets at the hapless Witness. When Chaplinsky responded in kind, calling the marshal who had reappeared "a damn fascist and a racketeer," he was arrested for, and later convicted of, using offensive language in public.

Page 1137.   Before section 6 of the Note, add the following:

5a. *Disclosure of the NSA Surveillance Program.* In January 2006, the *New York Times* publicly disclosed that President George W. Bush had secretly authorized the National Security Agency to intercept international telephone calls and emails between individuals inside the United States and individuals outside the United States whenever the NSA had "a reasonable basis to conclude that one party to the communication is a member of al Qaeda, affiliated with al Qaeda, or a member of an organization affiliated with al Qaeda, or working in support of al Qaeda." Critics of the program charged that it violates the Foreign Intelligence Surveillance Act of 1978, which prohibits such surveillance in the absence of probable cause and a warrant. Defenders of the program argued that FISA violates the inherent authority of the "President as 'Commander in Chief of the Army and Navy'."

Attorney General Alberto Gonzales raised the possibility that the United States might prosecute the *New York Times* for violating the Espionage Act of 1917. Gonzales complained that the disclosure of the program seriously undermined the national security by alerting terrorists to its existence. Suppose the United States indicted the New York Times under section 793(e). What standard would apply in deciding whether the publication was protected by the First Amendment? Note that the United States has *never* criminally prosecuted the press for publishing secret government information.

Suppose that in 2003 the NSA secretly breaks the al Qaeda code, enabling the United States to thwart several terrorist attacks. Suppose further than in 2007 a newspaper publishes this information, with the result that the terrorists change their cipher. Can the newspaper be punished for publishing this information?

Consider Stone, Government Secrecy v. Freedom of the Press, 1 Harv. L. & Pol. Rev. 185, 203-04 (2007):

> [T]he reason for protecting the publication of the Pentagon Papers was not only that the disclosure would not "surely result in direct, immediate, and irreparable damage" to the nation, but also that the Pentagon Papers made a meaningful contribution to informed public discourse. Suppose a newspaper accurately reports that American troops in Iraq recently murdered twenty insurgents in cold blood. As a result of this publication, insurgents quite predictably kidnap and murder twenty Americans. Could the newspaper constitutionally be punished for disclosing the initial massacre? I would

argue that it could not. Even if there were a clear and present danger that the retaliation would follow, the information is simply too important to the American people to punish its publication.

What this suggests is that to justify the criminal punishment of the press for publishing classified information, the government must prove that the publisher knew that (a) it was publishing classified information, (b) the publication of which would result in likely, imminent, and serious harm to the national security, *and* (c) the publication of which would not meaningfully contribute to public debate.

Page 1138. After subsection e of the Note, add the following:

f. Stone, Government Secrecy v. Freedom of the Press, 1 Harv. L. & Pol. Rev. 185, 191-192 (2007):

[I]t seems reasonable to assume that a public employee who discloses classified information [to] a journalist [has] violated his position of trust and ordinarily may be discharged and/or criminally punished without violating the First Amendment. [But unlike] public employees, who have agreed to abide by constitutionally permissible restrictions of their speech, journalists and publishers have *not* agreed to waive their rights. [Moreover,] that the government has a legitimate reason to prohibit its employees from disclosing such information does not [mean] that the government's interest in confidentiality *outweighs* the public's interest in disclosure. [In] theory, of course, it would be possible for the courts to decide in each instance whether an unauthorized disclosure of confidential information by a public employee is protected by the First Amendment because the value of the information to the public outweighs the government's need for secrecy. But such an approach would put the courts in an extremely awkward position and effectively would convert the First Amendment into a constitutional Freedom of Information Act. The Supreme Court has sensibly eschewed that approach and granted the government considerable deference in deciding whether and when public employees may disclose confidential government information.

Page 1138. Before the last sentence in section 6 of the Note, add the following:

Consider Stone, Government Secrecy v. Freedom of the Press, 1 Harv. L. & Pol. Rev. 185, 196-97 (2007), suggesting that the government can constitutionally discipline, discharge, and/or criminally punish "a public employee who knowingly discloses classified information to a journalist for the purpose of publication ... if the information was not already in the public domain and its disclosure has the potential to harm the national security, *unless* the disclosure reveals *unlawful* government action and the employee has complied with reasonable whistleblower procedures governing the disclosure of such information." Suppose the disclosure reveals that the president misled the American people into invading another nation?

Page 1140. At the end of the paragraph beginning "Suppose a terrorist ... ," add the following:

Should it matter whether the individual's *intent* was to facilitate terrorism rather than to alert people to the danger? Consider Donohue, Terrorist Speech and the Future of Free Expression, 27 Cardozo L. Rev. 233, 335 (2005):

> One could convincingly argue to restrict speakers who intend to cause harm. However, [there] appears to be something unjust about allowing a Republican to publish bomb diagrams on the Internet, while denying the same venue to an anarchist. The intent test here punishes political belief — not the manner in which someone uses the information. If the state exhibits concern about the availability of the information, then neither ought to be allowed to place the data in the public domain. And this gets to the heart of the problem in trying to prevent knowledge-based speech: The dual use nature of such information makes it inevitable that in many instances the state will *want* the information available.

C. Overbreadth, Vagueness, and Prior Restraint

Page 1154. After section 1 of the Note, add the following:

1a. Lovell *and* Bush v. Gore. Was Bush v. Gore correctly decided, but for the wrong reason? Consider Greene, Is There a First Amendment Defense for *Bush v. Gore*?, 80 Notre Dame L. Rev. 1643, 1682 (2005):

> [T]he core problem with the Florida recount system is the core problem with the ordinances in the *Lovell* line of cases. Just as it is hard to monitor on a

case-by-case basis the broad discretion that parade permit ordinances vest in local political officials, so it is hard to monitor on either a case-by-case or county-by-county basis the broad discretion that the Florida 'voter intent' provisions vest in local political officials. Requiring the sub-standards to be set in the statute — in this setting as in the *Lovell* line of cases — helps to ensure against this hard to prove bias.

D. Content-Based Restrictions: *"Low" Value Speech*

Page 1179. At the end of section 3 of the Note, add the following:

Marshall, False Campaign Speech and the First Amendment, 153 U. Pa. L. Rev. 285, 299 (2004) ("authorizing the government to decide what is true or false in campaign speech opens the door to partisan abuse").

4. In a state law defamation action filed by attorney Johnnie Cochran, a California trial court found that defendant Tory had falsely claimed that Cochran owed him money, picketed Cochran's office with signs containing insults, and pursued him in public, chanting similar insults, in order to coerce Cochran into paying Tory money to get him to desist from such defamatory activity. Because Tory was judgment-proof, the California court enjoined him from continuing in this conduct. Is such a prior restraint permissible in these circumstances? See Tory v. Cochran, 544 U.S. 734 (2005) (vacating the injunction in light of Cochran's death).

Page 1180. Before Section 2, add the following:

Did the Court in *Hustler* give sufficient weight to Falwell's dignitary interests? Consider *Strauss Caricature*, 75 BVerfGE 369 (1987), in which the German Constitutional Court reviewed a civil action for damages brought by Bavarian Prime Minister Franz Josef Strauss against the magazine *Konkret*, which had published a series of disparaging cartoons portraying Strauss as a rutting pig. One cartoon, for example, depicted a pig, clearly drawn to be a caricature of Strauss, copulating with other pigs dressed in judicial robes. Noting that individual dignity is a "preferred constitutional value," the court held that the cartoons were not protected by Germany's constitutional guarantee of freedom of speech. The court explained that by depicting the Prime Minister as a pig engaged in bestial sexual conduct, the cartoons were clearly "intended to devalue the person concerned as a person, to deprive him of his dignity as a human being," and therefore went "too far" to merit constitutional protection. See Ronald Krotoszynski, The First Amendment in Cross-Cultural Perspective 112-114 (2006).

Consider Carmi, Dignity — The Enemy from Within: A Theoretical and Comparative Analysis of Human Dignity as a Free Speech Justification, 9 U. Pa. J. Const. L. 957, 967, 991(2007):

> Because of their relative youth, free expression doctrines in other Western democracies are still in the formative stage. [Unlike] the United States, their free expression doctrines may be characterized as non-rule-based. Instead of rules, these countries frequently utilize concepts of balancing and proportionality. [A concern with] human dignity surfaces prominently in many Western democracies, particularly in Germany, where it receives heightened status vis-à-vis other rights. [While] the United States views freedom of speech through the lens of "liberty," other Western democracies [define] freedom of expression in dignity terms. [In] these countries, human dignity may serve as [an important] limitation on freedom of expression. . . .
>
> . . . World War II was a formative experience [in creating the constitutional cultures of most Western democracies, analogous in some ways to the role slavery played in the United States]. One of the reactions to [the World War II] experience was the adoption of human dignity as a leading constitutional value. [In the light of this history,] the restriction of [hateful] speech [is seen as] justified from a communitarian viewpoint. A restriction of such speech is [thought] desirable "[for] the well-being of the society as a whole." Maintaining a minimum of civility in public discourse may be viewed as [a fundamental goal because] permitting vilification harms the society as a whole.

Page 1185.   After section 4 of the Note, add the following:

5. *Data privacy.* Technological advances have enabled businesses to compile extraordinarily detailed databases about millions of individuals. The information comes from many different sources, including publicly available government records, transactional data from non-cash purchases, human resource databases, frequent shopper programs, promotional activities such as contests and mass mailings, and Internet and telephone use. Using such sources, "profiling" companies aggregate personal information about indivi-

duals dealing with such matters as shopping preferences, financial data, health issues, arrest records, charitable and political contributions, reading preferences, homeownership, chat room participation, mail order purchases, and so on, and then sell those databases to interested parties, both private and public. Can the government constitutionally regulate the sale of such databases, or would such regulation violate the First Amendment? Compare Richards, Reconciling Data Privacy and the First Amendment, 52 UCLA L. Rev. 1149 (2005) (such regulations are constitutional); Volokh, Freedom of Speech and Information Privacy: The Troubling Implications of a Right to Stop People From Speaking About You, 52 Stan. L. Rev. 1049 (2000) (such regulations are unconstitutional).

Page 1208. At the end of section 9 of the Note, add the following:

In Johanns v. Livestock Marketing Association, 544 U.S. 550 (2005), the Court distinguished *United Foods* and upheld the Beef Promotion and Research Act of 1985, which creates a Beef Board and imposes an assessment on all sales and importation of cattle. The assessment funds, among other things, beef promotional campaigns approved by the Secretary of Agriculture. The Court held that *United Foods* was inapplicable because in this case the promotional materials are "government speech," rather than government-compelled private speech. This is so because the Secretary of Agriculture directly controls "every word" in the promotional materials. Although the objecting beef producers argued that they should not be assessed to support speech that conflicts with their interests, the Court held that this is no different than any time taxpayers are compelled to pay taxes that enable the government to convey its own messages. Justices Stevens, Kennedy, and Souter dissented. For more on the problem of government speech, see pages 1343-1367 of the main volume. See Post, Compelled Subsidization of Speech: *Johanns v. Livestock Marketing Association*, 2005 Sup. Ct. Rev 195.

Page 1211. After subsection a of the Note, add the following:

aa. Stone, Sex, Violence, and the First Amendment, 74 U. Chi. L. Rev. 1857, 1861-63 (2007):

In *Roth*, the Court maintained that "implicit in the history of the First Amendment is the rejection of obscenity as utterly without redeeming social importance." [The] Court's reasoning apparently was that because the states prohibited certain categories of expression despite their own state constitutional guarantees of free speech, the Framers of the First Amendment must have assumed that the those classes of speech were also unprotected by the First Amendment. This makes sense. But, unfortunately, it tells us nothing about obscenity, for unlike libel, blasphemy, and profanity, obscenity was not unlawful under either English or American law in 1792.

In England, the state first punished an obscene publication in 1727. In *King v. Curll* [2 Stra. 788], the court sustained the conviction of Edward Curll for publishing *Venus in the Cloister or the Nun in her Smock*, an English translation of a French anti-Catholic tract written around 1682. *Venus in the Cloister* was a sexually explicit depiction of supposedly rampant sex among monks and nuns in a convent. It dealt quite graphically with voyeurism, masturbation, fornication, dildos, and flagellation. In a two-to-one decision, the King's Bench held that Curll's publication was "punishable at common law, as an offense against the peace, in tending to weaken the bonds of civil society, virtue, and morality." In fact, the prosecution had less to do with the sexual nature of the material than to Curll's long-running feud with the authorities and his recent publication of several politically libelous works that had infuriated public officials.

Thereafter, obscenity prosecutions remained essentially unknown in England throughout the eighteenth century, despite a profusion of sexually explicit writings. *The Toast*, a satirical work [published] in 1736, has been described "as one of the most obscene works ever printed" in England, and Gervaise de Latouche's *History of Dom B*, published in England in 1743, portrayed in graphic detail the hero's nocturnal orgies with monks and nuns.[*]

---

[*] Lest you think eighteenth-century pornography was tame, here is an excerpt from *History of Dom B*:

Sometimes I was put on a bench, completely naked; one Sister placed herself astride my throat is such a way that my chin was hidden in her pubic hair, another one put herself on my belly, a third one, who was on my thighs, tried to introduce my prick into her cunt; two others again were placed at my sides so that I could hold a cunt in each hand; and finally another one, who possessed the nicest breasts, was at my head, and bending forward, she pushed my face between her bubbies; my thighs, my belly, my chest, my prick, everything was wet, I floated while fucking.

Quoted in P. Wagner, Eros Revived: Erotica of the Enlightenment in England and America 236 (Secker and Warburg 1988).

English readers in the eighteenth century also had ready access to a constant stream of sexually explicit ballads, poems, law reports, whore catalogues, sex guides, prints, and anti-Catholic and anti-government tracts.

For almost a century after the decision in *Curll*, English law yielded nothing of consequence on the concept of obscenity. There was no definition of the concept, no rationale for its regulation, and only sporadic skirmishes over the matter. In the 1790s, when the United States was contemplating the First Amendment, England was awash with all sorts of sexually explicit material, including lewd novels, racy poems, bawdy songs, erotic prints, and licentious newspapers and magazines. [The] first prosecution for obscenity in the United States [Commonwealth v. Sharpless] did not occur until 1815, almost a quarter-century *after* the adoption of the First Amendment. ...

Page 1213.   At the end of section 3b of the Note, add the following:

But consider Koppelman, Does Obscenity Cause Moral Harm?, 105 Colum. L. Rev. 1635 (2005): "The status of 'moral harm' is somewhat analogous to the constitutional status of 'religion.' The state can recognize it and try to take account of it — at a very high level of abstraction. What it cannot do is try to make fine distinctions among instances of it. That is beyond its competence. And the idea of state incompetence is as important to free speech doctrine as it is to religion clause doctrine. It has particular bite here. Just as government should not be able to decide for us the path to salvation, so it should not be able to decide for us what our sexual fantasies should be."

Page 1215.   At the end of section 2b of the Note, add the following:

Is there really anything to the notion that children need to be protected from exposure to sexual images? Consider Garfield, Protecting Children from Speech, 57 Fla. L. Rev. 565 (2005): "[T]he concept of sheltering children from [sexual] speech is largely a modern conceit. The concept, after all, presupposes a 'childhood' — a prolonged period of innocence — that was rare in premodern times and continues to be rare in many parts of the world. Put bluntly, children in the Middle Ages, who slept in their parents' beds ... did not need sheltering from sexually-explicit speech."

Page 1228. Before section 2 of the Note, add the following:

1a. *Sex, violence, and tradition.* Consider Stone, Sex, Violence and the First Amendment, 74 U. Chi. L. Rev. 1857, 1866-67 (2007):

> [A]lthough the United States has a long history of regulating obscene expression, it has no similar tradition of regulating violent speech. Not only was violent expression not included in the *Chaplinsky* list, but the Court made clear almost sixty years ago [in Winters v. New York, 333 U.S. 507, 513 (1948)] that speech focusing on "deeds of bloodshed, lust or crime" is "as much entitled to the protection of free speech as the best of literature." Indeed, in the entire history of American law there have been almost no efforts to regulate the depiction of violence. As a consequence, whereas we have had almost 150 years of experience with the regulation of obscenity, we have had no experience with censorship of violent themes or images. [We] have no shared understanding of what we might mean by low value violent speech, or even a word analogous to "obscenity" with which to describe the concept. "I know it when I see it" has never been a sound basis for First Amendment doctrine.
>
> ... At least with obscenity, we have managed over many years to develop reasonably workable standards. To start from scratch in the realm of violence, after eschewing that approach for more than two centuries, is simply a bad idea. This analysis suggests that the list of low value categories is effectively frozen in time. There are obvious objections to such an approach. There may be good reasons to recognize new categories of law value speech as society, technology, First Amendment theory, and our understanding of human behavior change over time. But the recognition of novel categories of low value speech also poses real dangers. The very concept of low value speech is problematic. [Placing] great weight on history in this context is a sound way to capture the benefits of the doctrine without opening the door to wide-ranging judicial judgments about constitutional "value."

Page 1234. After the Note, add the following:

UNITED STATES v. WILLIAMS, 128 S. Ct. 1830 (2008). In response to *Ashcroft v. Free Speech Coalition*, Congress in 2003 enacted the Prosecutorial Remedies and Other Tools to end the Exploitation of Children Today Act (the "PROTECT Act"), which made it a crime for any person "knowingly" to "advertise, promote, present, distribute, or solicit through the mails, or in interstate or foreign commerce by any means, including by computer, any material or purported material in a manner that reflects the belief, or that is intended to cause another to believe, that the material or purported material is, or contains [a] visual depiction of an actual minor engaging in sexually explicit conduct." The Act defined "sexually explicit conduct" in a manner consistent with the New York law upheld in *Ferber*.

Congress enacted the Act because it was concerned that "limiting the child-pornography prohibition to material that could be *proved* to feature actual children would enable many child pornographers to evade conviction." Congress found that the "emergence of new technology and the repeated retransmission of picture files over the Internet could make it nearly impossible to prove that a particular image was produced using real children — even though '[t]here is no substantial evidence that any of the child pornography images being trafficked today were made other than by the abuse of real children.'"

Williams was convicted under the Act for making available on the Internet "seven pictures of actual children, aged approximately 5 to 15, engaging in sexually explicit conduct and displaying their genitals." The Court of Appeals for the Eleventh Circuit held the Act unconstitutionally overbroad and vague. In a seven-to-two decision, the Supreme Court reversed. Justice Scalia delivered the opinion of the Court.

In holding the Act overbroad, the Eleventh Circuit emphasized that the Act makes it unlawful knowingly to distribute material that *appears* to be child pornography, with the intent to cause others to *believe* it to be child pornography, even if it is *not* child pornography within the meaning of *Free Speech Coalition*. In the view of the Eleventh Circuit, Congress could constitutionally go no further than prohibiting the knowing sale or distribution of *actual* child pornography.

Justice Scalia rejected this argument: "The statute does not require the actual existence of child pornography. [Rather] than targeting the underlying material, this statute bans the collateral speech that introduces such material into the child-pornography distribution network. Thus, [a] person who advertises virtual child pornography as depicting actual children falls within the reach of the statute. [This is not unconstitutional. Offers] to engage in illegal transactions are categorically excluded from First Amendment protection. One would think that this principle resolves the present case, since the statute criminalizes only offers to provide or requests to obtain contraband — child [pornography] involving actual children. . . .

"The Eleventh Circuit, however, believed that the exclusion of First Amendment protection extended only to *commercial* offers to provide or receive contraband. [The] categorical exclusion [is] based not on the less privileged First Amendment status of commercial speech, but on the principle that offers to give or receive what it is unlawful to possess have no value and thus [enjoy] no First Amendment protection. Many long-established criminal proscriptions — such as laws against conspiracy, incitement, and solicitation — criminalize speech (commercial or not) that is intended to induce or commence illegal activities. [It] would be an odd constitutional principle that permitted the government to prohibit offers to sell illegal drugs, but not offers to give them away for free. To be sure, there remains an important distinction between a proposal to engage in illegal activity and the abstract advocacy of illegality. [See *Brandenburg*.] The Act [does] not prohibit advocacy of child pornography, but only offers to provide or requests to obtain it. [In] sum, we hold that offers to provide or requests to obtain child pornography are categorically excluded from the First Amendment. . . .

"The Eleventh Circuit believed it a constitutional difficulty that no child pornography need exist to trigger the statute. [That] seems to us a strange constitutional calculus. Although we have held that the government can ban *both* fraudulent offers *and* offers to provide illegal products, the Eleventh Circuit would forbid the government from punishing *fraudulent offers to provide illegal products*. We see no logic in that position. [The] Eleventh Circuit found 'particularly objectionable' the fact that the 'reflects the belief' prong of the statute could ensnare a person who mistakenly believes that material is child pornography. [The] Eleventh Circuit thought that it would be unconstitutional to punish someone for mistakenly distributing virtual child pornography as real child pornography. We disagree. Offers to deal in illegal products [do] not acquire First Amendment protection when the offeror is mistaken about the factual predicate of his offer. [As] with other inchoate crimes — attempt and conspiracy, for example — impossibility of completing the crime because the facts were not as the defendant believed is not a defense. [Justice Scalia cited the example of a person who intentionally offers to sell an unlawful drug without realizing that the substance in his possession is not in fact an unlawful drug.]

"Finally, the dissent accuses us of silently [overruling] *Ferber* and *Free Speech Coalition*. According to the dissent, Congress has made an end-run around the First Amendment's protection of virtual child pornography by prohibiting proposals to transact in such images rather than prohibiting the images themselves. But an offer to provide or request to receive virtual child pornography is not prohibited by the statute. A crime is committed only when the speaker believes or intends the listener to believe that the subject of the proposed transaction depicts *real* children. [Simulated] child pornography will be as available as ever, so long as it is offered and sought *as such*, and not as real child pornography. The dissent would require an exception from the statute's prohibition when, unbeknownst to one or both of the parties to the proposal, the completed transaction would not have been unlawful because it is (we have said) protected by the First Amendment. [There] is no First Amendment exception from the general principle of criminal law that a person

240

attempting to commit a crime need not be exonerated because he has a mistaken view of the facts." The Court also rejected the vagueness claim.

Justice Stevens, joined by Justice Breyer, filed a concurring opinion. Although conceding that the statute "covers proposals to transact in constitutionally protected material," Justice Stevens explained that he was satisfied that, in light of "the construction the Court gives the statute's operative [provisions], proposing a transaction in such material would not give rise to criminal liability [unless] the defendant actually believed, or intended to induce another to believe, that the material in question depicted real children."

Justice Souter, joined by Justice Ginsburg, dissented: "What justification can there be for making independent crimes of proposals to engage in transactions that [actually distribute] constitutionally protected materials? [The Court argues] that a proposal to commit a crime enjoys no speech protection. [But why] should [this] general rule [cover] a case like the proposal to transfer what [turns] out to be [constitutional protected speech]? [The Court offers the] example of a drug dealer who sells something else. (A package of baking powder, not powder cocaine, would be an example.) [This analogy] does not suffice, however, because [powder] sales are [not] constitutionally privileged. [When] baking powder [is] involved, deterrence can be promoted without compromising any other important policy, which is not true [here].

"No one can seriously assume that after today's decision the Government will go on prosecuting defendants for selling child pornography (requiring a showing that a real child is pictured); it will prosecute for merely proposing a pornography transaction manifesting or inducing the belief that a photo is real child pornography, free of any need to demonstrate that any extant [photo] does show a real child. If the Act can be enforced, it will function just as it was meant to do, by merging the whole subject of child pornography into the offense of proposing a transaction, dispensing with the real-child element in the underlying subject. [If] the deluded drug dealer is held liable for an attempted crime there is no risk of eliminating baking powder from trade in lawful commodities. [But] if the Act can effectively eliminate the real-child requirement, [a] class of protected speech will disappear. . . .

"There is no justification for saving the Act's attempt to get around our holdings. We should hold that a transaction in what turns out to be [constitutionally protected speech] is better understood, not as an incomplete attempt to commit a crime, but as a completed series of intended acts that simply do not add up to a crime, owing to the privileged character of the material the parties were in fact about to deal in. [The] Court is going against the grain of pervasive First Amendment doctrine that tolerates speech restriction not on mere general tendencies of expression, or the private understandings of speakers or listeners, but only after a critical assessment of practical consequences. [Citing *Brandenburg*.]"

Page 1243.   After *Pacifica*, add the following:

In light of *Cohen* and *Pacifica*, to what extent can the government constitutionally regulate profanity at sporting events, where fans, including children, may be "captive auditors"? Can the state prohibit a fan from repeatedly shouting "Fuck the Dragons"? Does it matter if it is a privately or publicly owned stadium? See Wasserman, Fans, Free Expression, and the Wide World of Sports, 67 U. Pitt. L. Rev. 525 (2006).

Page 1249.   Before section 2 of the Note, add the following:

Consider also Kende, Filtering Out Children: The First Amendment and Internet Porn in the U.S. Supreme Court, 2005 Mich. St. L. Rev. 843, 851-852:

> [In *Ashcroft*, Justice] Kennedy misunderstands the concept of less restrictive alternative. For such an alternative to exist, there must be some other proposed legislation or regulation that is just as effective, but that burdens less speech. Otherwise the term is devoid of significance. Kennedy, however, has no alternative legislative plan. [Kennedy] simply assumes that government need not do anything because more parents will magically start installing filter software. [Kennedy] is also wrong in assuming that filters would protect children as effectively as COPA. After all, COPA would still permit parents to install filters. And COPA *plus* filters would be far more effective than filters alone.

Page 1251.   After section 6 of the Note, add the following:

7. *Indecent expression and public employees.* In City of San Diego v. Roe, 543 U.S. 77 (2004), the Court unanimously upheld the discharge of a police officer for selling on the adults only section of eBay videotapes of himself stripping off a police uniform (not his official uniform) and then masturbating. His eBay user profile identified him as a person "employed in the field of law enforcement." The Court explained that "a governmental employer may impose certain restraints on the speech of its employees, restraints that would not be constitutional if applied to the general public." Indeed, when such an employee speaks on matters unrelated to his employment and of no "public concern," the governmental employer may discipline or discharge him if "legitimate and substantial interests [are] compromised by his speech."

The Court held that the police officer's speech "does not qualify as a matter of public concern under any view of the public concern test." Because the officer "took deliberate steps to link his videos [to] his police work," and because his "debased parody of an officer performing indecent acts while in the course of his official duties brought the mission of the employer and the professionalism of its officers into serious disrepute," he could be discharged consistent with the First Amendment.

To what extent does this decision turn on the officer's sexual activity? Suppose he had performed in a skit mocking the police department's respect for the Constitution? Suppose he had performed in black-face in order to parody the department's treatment of African-Americans?

Page 1255. After section 2 of the Note, add the following:

2a. *Modes of expression.* Would it be helpful to think of the laws in *Cohen, Pacifica, Erznoznik, Reno, Ashcroft, Sable, Young, Renton,* and *Alameda* as regulations of the "mode" of expression, rather than as regulations that are either content-based or content-neutral, where "mode" refers to "the particular words, musical notes, pictures and the like that a speaker uses to convey his or her ideas and feelings"? See Howard, The Mode in the Middle: Recognizing a New Category of Speech Regulations for Modes of Expression, 14 UCLA Entertain. L. Rev. 47, 58 (2007) (arguing that the Court should distinguish between regulations of the message (e.g., "no one may criticize the war"), the mode (e.g., "no one may use profanity or sexually explicit images"), and the method (e.g., "no one may use billboards or loudspeakers in residential neighborhoods") of speech, and that regulations of the mode of expression should be tested by a form of intermediate scrutiny).

Page 1262. Before section 4e of the Note, add the following:

Consider also Krotoszynski, A Comparative Perspective on the First Amendment: Free Speech, Militant Democracy, and the Primacy of Dignity as a Preferred Constitutional Value in Germany, 79 Tulane L. Rev. 1549, 1550-1551, 1563, 1595, 1608-1609 (2004):

Critics of the United States Supreme Court's protection of racist speech point to the experience of other constitutional democracies in support of their position. [But at] least in the case of Germany, it is very difficult to

243

claim plausibly that "limited regulation of hate speech does not ... cause deterioration of the respect accorded free speech." [For] example, the German Constitutional Court has found that preserving the dignity of a dead man outweighed the free expression rights of a living novelist; it has prohibited the publication of a fictional interview involving the wife of the Shah of Iran; it has also enjoined distribution of a docudrama about a gay robber and refused to protect political satire that presented a politician as a rutting pig. [Similarly, it is a crime in Germany for anyone to advocate the violent overthrow of government or to display a swastika in any way that appears] to sympathize with the Third Reich. ... As a matter of causation, Germany's adoption and enforcement of hate speech laws probably reflect the subordinated position that free speech enjoys vis-à-vis other interests.

Page 1284.　Before the Note, add the following:

Consider the following views:

a. Schauer, Intentions, Conventions, and the First Amendment: The Case of Cross-Burning, 2003 Sup. Ct. Rev. 197, 206-208:

[B]ecause Justice O'Connor saw the Virginia statute as singling [out] intimidation with special intimidating power, she concluded [that] the statute was [a] constitutionally permissible prohibition on unprotected intimidation. [But] a closer look at the dynamics of what causes cross-burning to be especially intimidating [makes] the Court's distinction between *Black* and *R.A.V.* difficult to accept. What makes cross-burning more intimidating than, say, flag-burning or leaf-burning [is] a function of the racist [point] of view it embodies. [Virginia's] belief that burning a cross is especially intimidating is based solely on the viewpoint-based judgment that symbols with one point of view have effects that symbols with another point of view do not have.

b. Gey, A Few Questions About Cross Burning, Intimidation, and Free Speech, 80 Notre Dame L. Rev. 1287, 1373-1374 (2005):

Black is just one example of a disturbing [proliferation] of alternative First Amendment constructs to regulate antisocial speech. These constructs appear uncoordinated by any central principle and seem limited only by the ingenuity of plaintiffs and prosecutors in fitting familiar examples of antisocial speech into the new regulatory patterns. [Some] overriding constitutional framework is needed to limit the expansion of the new categories and constrain the use of flexible terms such as "intimidation" and "terrorism." The *Brandenburg* [explicitness and immediate harm] paradigm was devised to serve precisely that function, if the courts would only use it.

c. Charles, Colored-Speech: Cross-Burnings, Epistemics, and the Triumph of the Crits?, 93 Geo. L. J. 575 (2005):

If the statute in *R.A.V.* is unconstitutional, so is the one in *Black*. ... *Black* cannot be squared with *R.A.V.* [*Black*'s] doctrinal divergence from *R.A.V.* [must be understood as a triumph of critical race theory.] Critical race theorists have argued that cross-burning legislation, and hate speech legislation more generally, should be understood within the historical context from which they arise, [that] the Court should use the historical context to frame its doctrinal analysis, [and that] First Amendment doctrine is sufficiently capacious to protect speech and accommodate legislation targeting cross burnings. Each of these perspectives is reflected in the majority opinion in *Black*. ...

For critical race theorists, appeals to legal authority are political. That is, these appeals cannot be understood as objective, reasonable appeals to logic or legal doctrine. They are sociological, cultural, political, economic, and racial. That they are so does not make them any less legitimate. ... Disputes over legal authority tell us about who matters in our society. They tell us about whose injury counts as harm. Legal doctrine, in this case the First Amendment, is part of the rhetoric. Doctrine masks these disputes and cloaks their political resolution. [What] critical race theory [helps] explain is how the First Amendment, which formerly could not countenance cross-burning statutes, has become less absolute in scope. Whereas *R.A.V.* appears to be a complete repudiation of the approach to hate speech advocated by the crits, *Black* seems to embrace it.

Page 1290.   After the quotation from Sunstein, add the following:

For a slightly different formulation, consider Stone, Sex, Violence and the First Amendment, 74 U. Chi. L. Rev. 1857, 1863-64 (2007):

The Supreme Court has never offered a clearly-defined theory of low-value speech. The case law, however, suggests that several factors are relevant to the analysis. First, categories of low-value speech (for example, false statements of fact, threats, commercial advertising, fighting words, express incitement of unlawful conduct, and obscenity) do not primarily advance political discourse. Second, categories of low-value speech are not defined in terms of disfavored ideas or political viewpoints. Third, low-value speech usually has a strong noncognitive impact on its audience. Fourth, categories of low-value speech have long been regulated without undue harm to the overall system of free expression.

E. Content-Neutral Restrictions: Limitations on the Means of Communication and the Problem of Content-Neutrality

Page 1299. At the end of section 1 of the Note, add the following:

For a critique of the Court's use of "intermediate scrutiny" across a broad range of First Amendment issues, see Bhagwat, The Test that Ate Everything: Intermediate Scrutiny in First Amendment Jurisprudence, 2007 U. Ill. L. Rev. 783.

Page 1302. At the end of section 3 of the Note, add the following:

Consider McDonald, Speech and Distrust: Rethinking the Content Approach to Protecting the Freedom of Expression, 81 Notre Dame L. Rev. 1347, 1387 (2006):

Consider [laws] currently being enacted by states that prohibit picketing and demonstrating within a certain distance of funerals shortly before and after a service. These laws are being passed in response to an alleged pastor and members of a church who are using funerals of American soldiers killed in Iraq as opportunities to get out their message that the war and soldiers' deaths constitute divine retribution for the country's tolerant attitude towards homosexuals. Apparently, the church group assembles across the street from such funerals, engaging in expletive-laden chants and displaying signs containing messages such as "Thank God for Dead Soldiers,"

"Thank God for IEDs" (improvised explosive devices that frequently kill soldiers), and "God Hates Fags."

Should such laws be analyzed as content-based or content-neutral?

Page 1310.   After section 8 of the Note, add the following:

8a. *Picketing near military funerals.* In recent years, members of the Westboro Baptist Church have protested at the funerals of American soldiers, carrying placards and shouting such phrases as "Thank God for Dead Soldiers," "God is Your Enemy," and "Thank God for 9/11." The church's predominant message is one of virulent antihomosexuality, and these protests are designed to convey the message that the United States is being punished for its toleration of such conduct.

To rein in such protests, most states have enacted laws designed to restrict demonstrations near military funerals. What do you think of the constitutionality of the federal Respect for America's Fallen Heroes Act, which was enacted in 2006? The act, which governs funerals at national cemeteries, prohibits any "demonstration" "during the period beginning 60 minutes before and ending 60 minutes" after a funeral at a national cemetery if the demonstration is "within 150 feet of a road pathway, or other route of ingress to or egress from such cemetery property" and the demonstrators willfully make "any noise or diversion that disturbs or tends to disturb the peace or good order" of the funeral or is "within 300 feet of such cemetery" if the demonstration "impedes the access to or egress from such cemetery." The act defines "demonstration" to include "any picketing or similar conduct," "any oration, speech, use of sound amplification equipment" that is not part of the funeral, "the display of any placard, banner, flag, or similar device" that is not part of the funeral, and the "distribution of any handbill, pamphlet, or other written or printed matter" that is not part of the funeral. Is this law a reasonable regulation of public property? Is it content-neutral? See McAllister, Funeral Picketing Laws and Free Speech, 55 U. Kan. L. Rev. 575 (2007).

Page 1310.   After section 9 of the Note, add the following:

10. *Free speech zones.* Consider Note, Crowd Control: The Troubling Mix of First Amendment Law, Political Demonstrations, and Terrorism, 73 Geo. Wash. L. Rev. 395, 396 (2005):

When President Bush visits a city or town, local law enforcement, often under the direction of the Secret Service, sets up "free speech zones" —

areas at a distance from the President's destination where demonstrators are permitted to protest. The areas [are] often placed within or behind fences, barricades, or "Greyhound-sized buses." The distances between the "zones" and the sites [of the President's appearances and the media] vary from a city block to [a] quarter mile. [In] defense of their actions, "officials point to a post-9/11 need for crowd control and security." [W]hen the state raises powerful antiterrorism concerns within the weak First Amendment time, place, manner framework it will almost always prevail. As a result, the First Amendment rights of demonstrators are being materially altered.

Consider also Zick, Speech and Spatial Tactics, 84 Tex. L. Rev. 581, 584-89 (2006):

> Governments have learned to manipulate geography in a manner that now seriously threatens basic First Amendment principles. [The] state has moved from *regulating* place to actually ... *creating* places [such as "buffer zones," "free speech zones," and "speech-free zones"] for the express purpose of controlling and disciplining protest and dissent. [By] design, these places mute and even suppress messages, depress participation in social and political protests, and send negative signals to those on the outside regarding those confined within. [Protests in such] places are docile; they are tightly scripted and ineffectual imitations of past social and political movements. [Passively] filing into cages, zones, and other tactical places is an utter capitulation to the status quo. [Such places are] being used to marginalize dissent, to capture and confine it. [Courts] should view [such manipulation of protests] with far greater skepticism than they currently do [and should] take far more seriously the notion that "one is not to have the exercise of his liberty of expression in appropriate places abridged on the please that it may be exercised elsewhere." [Quoting Schneider v. State.]

Page 1327. After section 1 of the Note, add the following:

1a. *Does* Mosely *make sense?* Consider Fee, Speech Discrimination, 85 B.U.L. Rev. 1103, 1106 (2005):

> The central guarantee of the freedom of speech is to secure for all citizens plentiful places and means to communicate their ideas to the public. Provided that this basic floor of expressive freedom requirement is protected, the Constitution does not prohibit government from using [its]

resources and forums to promote communication that the majority favors or to counter communication that the majority deems harmful, distasteful, or misguided. In other words, there is nothing inherently illegitimate about government-imposed speech discrimination. . . .

Page 1352.   After section 3 of the Note, add the following:

3a. *Government speech or government-controlled private speech?* In Johanns v. Livestock Marketing Association, 544 U.S. 550 (2005), the Court, in an opinion by Justice Scalia, upheld the Beef Promotion and Research Act of 1985, which creates a Beef Board and imposes an assessment on all sales and importation of cattle. The assessment funds, among other things, beef promotional campaigns approved by the Secretary of Agriculture. The Court upheld the Act because the promotional materials were government speech rather than government-compelled private speech. This is so because the Secretary of Agriculture directly controls "every word" in the promotional materials.

Justice Souter, joined by Justices Stevens and Kennedy, dissented. Souter argued that "if government relies on the government-speech doctrine to compel specific groups to fund speech with targeted taxes, it must make itself politically accountable by indicating that the content actually is a government message." That is, government must label "the speech as its own." Because the Act "fails to require the Government to show its hand," Souter concluded that the government speech doctrine was inapplicable because "the First Amendment cannot be implemented by sanctioning government deception."

In response, the Court maintained that it needn't reach this question because the only question properly before the Court was whether the Act was constitutional on its face. The Court put aside for another day whether the government speech doctrine would apply if the promotional materials credited the advertising to "America's Beef Producers" rather than to the Department of Agriculture.

3b. *When is government speech unconstitutional?* Consider Lee, Persuasion, Transparency, and Government Speech, 56 Hasting L. J. 983, 988, 1018-1019 (2005):

> Hundreds of local television news stations reaching tens of millions of households [ran] prepackaged video news segments produced and distributed by the federal government. The segments lauded a broad range of government policies [but included no] attribution to the government. [When] the government participates in public debate, it should make the fact of its participation transparent. [Whereas] private parties may generally decide to express their views anonymously, [government] ought to speak in

a manner that permits the polity to hold it accountable. [The] argument here is neither that the government is dominating people's minds [nor] that the government is exercising unique or heightened persuasive powers. Indeed, any speaker can engage in such non-transparent communications. [The] argument [rests instead] on the claim that government speakers [operate] under obligations that do not constrain private speakers.

See also Morse, Managing the News: The History and Constitutionality of the Government Spin Machine, 81 N.Y.U. L. Rev. 843, 872 (2006) ("By concealing government as the true speaker, covert payments to columnists and prepackaged newscasts intrude on the media's editorial independence and impair its ability to call government to account for wrongdoing.").

Page 1352. At the end of section 3 of the Note, add the following:

3c. *Does the government have First Amendment rights?* Consider Fagundes, State Actors as First Amendment Speakers, 100 Nw. U. L. Rev. 1637 (2006): "Imagine that the Vermont Agency of Transportation uses state funds to erect a series of highway billboards critical of the Iraq War, and that the United States Congress — in an attempt to end the practice in Vermont and deter it elsewhere — responds by passing a law that levies substantial fines on any state that engages in such expression."

Page 1359. Before *United States v. American Library Association,* add the following:

Are Institutional Review Boards (IRBs) constitutional? Consider Hamburger, The New Censorship: Institutional Review Boards, 2004 Sup. Ct. Rev. 271:

Institutional Review Boards [license] research in accord with federal policy. The federal government seeks to minimize the risk that research performed on human subjects will cause them harm, and the government therefore has [required] universities and other research institutions to establish IRBs [as a condition of federal funding]. [Thus,] a professor who wants to study human subjects must first submit a proposal to the IRB, which will review the proposal and evaluate its risk and on this basis will grant or deny him permission to do his research.

Page 1376.   After section 6 of the Note, add the following:

6a. *Banning military recruiters.* Suppose law schools exclude from their placement facilities any employer, including the military, who discriminates against gays and lesbians. Suppose also that the government makes it a crime for any institution of higher education to discriminate against the military in the use of its placement facilities. Is the exclusion of military recruiters "speech" within the meaning of the First Amendment? Is the constitutionality of the statute governed by *O'Brien*?

In Rumsfeld v. FAIR, 547 U.S. 47 (2006), the Court, in an opinion by Chief Justice Roberts, declared that "we have extended First Amendment protection only to conduct that is *inherently* expressive." Unlike burning a draft card, the exclusion by law schools of military recruiters "is not inherently expressive," because such conduct has meaning only if the law schools accompany "their conduct with speech explaining it." Indeed, "an observer who sees military recruiters interviewing away from the law school has no way of knowing whether the law school is expressing its disapproval of the military, all the law school's interview rooms are full, or the military recruiters decided for reasons of their own that they would rather interview someplace else." The Court concluded that the fact that "explanatory speech is necessary" to give content to the act "is strong evidence that the conduct [is] not so inherently expressive that it warrants protection under *O'Brien*." In any event, the Court held that even if the law were regarded as incidentally burdening speech it would satisfy *O'Brien* because it serves the government's legitimate interest in facilitating military recruitment. For more on Rumsfeld v. FAIR, see the insert for page 1439 in this Supplement.

Page 1386.   Before the Note, add the following:

Consider Adler, Girls! Girls! Girls!: The Supreme Court Confronts the G-String, 80 NYU L. Rev. 1108, 1124, 1109 (2005):

Why is nude dancing so dangerous? And if it is so dangerous, why would the Court and the legislature take solace in a mere piece of string to ward off this threat? [What] is it about the nude female body that inspires irrationality, fear, and pandemonium, or at least inspires judges to write bad decisions? In [*Erie* and *Barnes*], the Court accepted and acted upon culturally entrenched views of the nude female form: that the female body is a site of unreason; that it is barely intelligible; that it is inviting yet dangerous; and that it causes mayhem, disease, and destruction. This view of the seductive, dangerous, writhing woman ... has a long and feverish history in Western culture. ...

Page 1403. Before section 3 of the Note, add the following:

2a. *Expanding the "donor class."* Consider Overton, The Donor Class: Campaign Finance, Democracy, and Participation, 153 U. Pa. L. Rev. 74, 75-76, 103, 107 (2004):

> Although approximately 51.3% of voting-age Americans cast a ballot in the 2000 general presidential election, less than 2% contributed $200 or more to a presidential or congressional candidate. [For those who cannot afford to contribute $200 or more, the system] may tap into a reservoir of suspicion that they do not count as full citizens. [Rather] than focus on candidate corruption or candidate equalization, campaign reform should empower more citizens to participate in the funding of campaigns. [Lawmakers] should provide incentives for a broader and more diverse group of Americans to make small contributions and enhance the effect of their participation by adopting matching funds and tax credits for contributions of $100 or less.

Page 1410. At the end of section 5 of the Note, add the following:

Clingman v. Beaver, 544 U.S. 581 (2005) (upholding a state law prohibiting a political party to invite registered members of other political parties to vote in its primary); Washington State Grange v. Washington State Republican Party, 128 S. Ct. 1184 (2008) (rejecting a facial challenge to a law providing that candidates for office shall be identified on the primary ballot by their self-designated "party preference," that voters may vote for any candidate, and that the top two votegetters for each office, regardless of party affiliation, advance to the general election); New York State Board of Elections v. Lopez Torres, 128 S. Ct. 791 (2008) (rejecting a challenge to a law requiring parties to select judicial nominees by a convention composed of delegates elected by party members).

Page 1420. Before the Note, add the following:

RANDALL v. SORRELL, 548 U.S. 230 (2006). Vermont's Act 64 stringently limited both the amount that candidates for state office could spend on their campaigns and the amount that individuals, organizations, and political parties could contribute to those campaigns. The Court held both the expenditure and contributions limits unconstitutional.

The expenditure regulation provided that candidates for governor could spend no more than $300,000, candidates for other statewide offices no more than $45,000, candidates for state senator no more than $4,000, and candidates for state representative no more than $2,000 in the primary and general elections combined. In a six-to-three decision, the Court invalidated these limitations. Justice Breyer, joined by Chief Justice Roberts and Justice Alito, concluded that the expenditure limitations were governed by *Buckley*. They rejected the argument that *Buckley* had not addressed a new justification for the Vermont expenditure regulations: That these limitations were necessary "to protect candidates from spending too much time raising money." Breyer held that this argument had implicitly been rejected in *Buckley* and did not merit reconsideration. Breyer, joined only by Chief Justice Roberts, also rejected the contention that *Buckley* should be overruled insofar as it invalidated expenditure limitations. Invoking the doctrine of *stare decisis*, Breyer reasoned that "departure from precedent is exceptional, and requires 'special justification.'" He maintained that this principle is particularly strong when, as in this context, the earlier decision "has become settled through iteration and reiteration over a long period of time." Breyer argued that there was no "special justification that would require us to overrule *Buckley*." There had been no showing "that circumstances have changed so radically as to undermine *Buckley*'s critical factual assumptions." Moreover, both Congress and state legislatures "have used *Buckley* when drafting campaign finance laws," and a decision overruling *Buckley* would therefore "dramatically undermine this reliance on our settled precedent." In light of these circumstances, Breyer declined the "invitation to reconsider *Buckley*." Justice Alito found it unnecessary to reconsider *Buckley* one way or the other because, in his view, the parties had not made a sufficient case to justify such a reexamination. He therefore concurred with Breyer's reasoning on the assumption that *Buckley* was good law. Justices Kennedy, Scalia, and Thomas reaffirmed their view that *Buckley* had properly held that expenditure limitations violate the First Amendment, and they concurred with Breyer that Act 64 clearly fell within *Buckley*'s proscription.

Justices Stevens, Souter, and Ginsburg dissented on the expenditure limitations. Writing only for himself, Stevens concluded that "*Buckley*'s holding on expenditure limitations is wrong, and [the] time has come to overrule it." Stevens argued that although "*stare decisis* is a principle of 'fundamental importance,' [it] is not an inexorable command." He identified several factors that, in his view, justified the overruling of *Buckley*'s analysis of expenditure limitations, including that it "upset a long-established practice," that the Court had not previously had occasion to reexamine or reaffirm *Buckley*'s holding with respect to expenditure limitations (unlike its holding with respect to contribution limitations), that the Court had been wrong in *Buckley* to "equate money with speech," and that "limits on expenditures are far more akin to time, place, and manner restrictions than to restriction on the content of speech" and should therefore be upheld "so long as the purposes they serve are legitimate and sufficiently substantial." Applying that standard, Stevens found that the state interests in reducing corruption, freeing candidates from the burdens of fundraising, and protecting "equal access to the political arena" were sufficiently important to justify Act 64's expenditure limitations. Finally, Stevens rejected the contention that expenditure limits "are fronts for incumbency protection," noting that only by permitting states "to experiment with these critically needed reforms [will] we enable further research on how expenditure limits relate to our incumbent reelection rates."

Justice Souter, joined by Justice Ginsburg, noted that *Buckley* had not categorically foreclosed "the possibility that some spending limit might comport with the First Amendment," but had held that "the constitutionality of an expenditure limitation 'turns on whether the governmental interests advanced in its support satisfy the [applicable] exacting scrutiny.'" Because he disagreed with Justice Breyer that Vermont's interest in protecting candidates from the demands of endless fundraising had been considered in *Buckley*, Souter argued that the case should be remanded to the district court to enable it to consider the state's evidence on that question.

The Court, in a six-to-three decision, also invalidated Act 64's contribution limitations. The Act limited contributions to candidates for governor to $200 over a two-year period, with substantially lower limits for contributions to candidates for state senator and state representative. In an opinion joined by Chief Justice Roberts and Justice Alito, Justice Breyer observed that although in the more than twenty-five years since *Buckley* the Court had consistently upheld contributions limits of varying amounts, it had consistently maintained that it must determine whether contribution limitations prevent candidates from amassing "the resources necessary for effective campaign advocacy" and whether they "magnify the advantages of incumbency to the point where they put challengers to a significant disadvantage." Breyer noted that although the Court ordinarily "deferred to the legislature determination of such matters," it recognized that there must be "some lower bound." To make that determination, courts must exercise "independent judicial judgment." In this instance, Breyer concluded that Act 64's limits were so "low as to generate suspicion" that they were "not closely drawn" to serve the state's legitimate interest in preventing the reality and appearance of corruption. Breyer pointed out that Vermont's contribution limits were not only lower than the limits the Court had upheld in *Buckley* and subsequent decisions, but that they were the lowest in the nation, viewed both for the state as a whole and on a per capita basis.

Five factors led Breyer to the conclusion that Vermont's contribution limits were "too restrictive": (1) The "record suggests [that] Act 64's contribution limits will significantly restrict the amount of funding available for challengers to run competitive campaigns." (2) The Act's insistence that "political parties abide by exactly the same low contribution limits that apply to other contributors threatens harm to [the] right to associate in a political party." (3) The Act includes as contributions "the expenses volunteers incur, such as travel expenses, in the course of campaign activities." (4) The Act's contribution limits "are not adjusted for inflation" over time. (5) The record includes no "special justification that might warrant a contribution limit so low." Breyer concluded that, "taken together," these factors justify the conclusion that the Vermont contribution limits "are not narrowly tailored" and therefore violate the First Amendment.

In a separate concurring opinion, Justice Kennedy reiterated his view that contribution limits violate the First Amendment. Justice Thomas, joined by Justice Scalia, also concurred in the judgment. Thomas argued that *Buckley's* treatment of contribution limits should be overruled. In his view, contribution limits are just as severe "an infringement on First Amendment rights" as expenditure limits, and the Court in *Buckley* had erred in holding otherwise. Moreover, Thomas contended that the Breyer opinion had demonstrated that "*Buckley's* limited scrutiny of contribution limits is 'insusceptible of principle application,' and accordingly is not entitled to *stare decisis* effect." He maintained that the plurality's "newly minted, multifactor test [places] this Court in the position of addressing the propriety of regulations of political speech based upon little more than its *impression* of the appropriate limits."

Justice Souter, joined by Justices Stevens and Ginsburg, dissented. Although conceding that Act 64's contribution limitations are low, he concluded that they are not "so radical in effect as to render political association ineffective, drive the sound of a candidate's voice below the level of notice, [or] render contributions pointless." The Court, he admonished, should not indulge in "second-guessing legislative judgments about the risk of corruption." Although "we can all imagine dollar limits that would be laughable," Souter maintained that that was not at all the case here.

Is the debate over contribution limits in *Randall* any less principled or more troubling than the debate over the size and number of campaign signs that might arise in a case like Ladue v. Gilleo?

FEDERAL ELECTION COMMISSION v. WISCONSIN RIGHT TO LIFE, 127 S. Ct. 2652 (2007) In a five-to-four decision, the Court held § 203 of the BCRA unconstitutional *as applied* to Wisconsin Right to Life's televised political advertisements that criticized Wisconsin's senators for participating in a filibuster to block the confirmation of several of President Bush's judicial nominees. Because the ads expressly mentioned Senator Russ Feingold by name and called upon viewers to contact Feingold and urge him to oppose the filibuster, they clearly violated § 203, which prohibits "electioneering communications" by corporations and labor unions paid for out of treasury funds within thirty days of a primary election.

In an opinion joined only by Justice Alito, Chief Justice Roberts argued that the Court in *McConnell* had upheld § 203 only insofar as it regulated political advertising that "was the 'functional equivalent'of express campaign speech." The question in this case, Roberts declared, was whether the WRTL ads were "the 'functional equivalent' of speech expressly advocating the election or defeat of a candidate for federal office," which could constitutionally be regulated under *McConnell*, or whether they were "genuine" issue ads, which, he maintained, could not be regulated consistent with the First Amendment:

"In drawing that line, the First Amendment requires us to err of the side of protecting political speech rather than suppressing it. We conclude that the speech at issue in this as-applied challenge is not the 'functional equivalent' of express campaign speech. We further conclude that the interests held to justify restricting corporate campaign speech or its functional equivalent do not justify restricting issue advocacy, and accordingly we hold that BCRA § 203 is unconstitutional as applied to the advertisements at issue. ...

"Because BCRA § 203 burdens political speech, it is subject to strict scrutiny. Under strict scrutiny, the Government must prove that applying BCRA to WRTL's ads furthers a compelling interest and is narrowly tailored to achieve that interest. [This] Court has already held [in *McConnell*] that [§ 203] survives strict scrutiny to the extent it regulates express advocacy or its functional equivalent. [But] no precedent of this Court has yet [decided whether the government may constitutionally regulate ads that] are *not* express advocacy or its equivalent [nor has the Court decided on the definition of 'functional equivalent.' [The dissent contends] that *McConnell* already established the constitutional test for determining if an ad is the functional equivalent of express advocacy: whether the ad is intended to influence elections and has that effect. [We disagree.] *McConnell* did not adopt any test as the standard for future as-applied challenges. ...

"[W]e decline to adopt a test for as-applied challenges turning on the speaker's intent to affect an election. [An] intent-based test would chill core political speech. [No] reasonable speaker would choose to run an ad covered by [§ 203] if its only defense to a criminal prosecution would be that its motives were pure. An intent-based [test] 'offers no security for free discussion.' [The] proper standard for an as-applied challenge to [§ 203] must be objective, focusing on the substance of the communication rather than amorphous considerations of intent and effect. [A] court should find that an ad is the functional equivalent of express advocacy only if the ad is susceptible of no reasonable interpretation other than as an appeal to vote for or against a specific candidate. Under this test, WRTL's [ads] are plainly not the functional equivalent of express advocacy. First, their content is consistent with that of a genuine issue ad: The ads focus on a legislative issue, take a position on the issue, exhort the public to adopt that position, and urge the public to contact public officials with respect to the matter. Second, their content lacks indicia of express advocacy: The ads do not mention an election candidacy, political party, or challenger; and they do not take a position on a candidate's character, qualifications, or fitness for office. . . .

"Looking beyond the content of WRTL's ads, the FEC [argues] that several 'contextual factors' prove that the ads are the equivalent of express advocacy. [For example, the FEC noted that WRTL actively opposed Feingold's reelection, identified filibusters as a campaign issue to be used against, and aired the ads near the election rather than during the filibuster. But this] evidence goes to WRTL's subjective intent in running the ads, and we have already explained that WRTL's intent is irrelevant. . . .

BCRA § 203 can be constitutionally applied to WRTL's ads only if it is narrowly tailored to further a compelling interest. This Court has never recognized a compelling interest in regulating ads, like WRTL's, that are neither express advocacy nor its functional equivalent. [This] Court has long recognized 'the governmental interest in preventing corruption and the appearance of corruption' in election campaigns [and] *McConnell* arguably applied this interest [to] ads that were the 'functional equivalent of express advocacy.' But to justify regulation of WRTL's ads, this interest must be stretched yet another step. . . . Enough is enough. . . . A second possible compelling interest recognized by this Court lies in addressing [the] 'corrosive and distorting effects of immense aggregations of wealth that are accumulated with the help of the corporate form and that have little or no correlation to the public's support for the corporation's political ideas.' [Quoting *Austin*.]. *McConnell* also relied on this interest. . . . We hold that the interest recognized in *Austin* as justifying regulation of corporate campaign speech and extended in *McConnell* to the functional equivalent of such speech has no application to issue advocacy of the sort engaged in by WRTL."

Justice Scalia, joined by Justices Kennedy and Thomas, concurred in the result: "In this critical area of political discourse, the speaker cannot be compelled to risk felony prosecution with no more assurance of impunity than his prediction that what he says will be found susceptible of some 'reasonable interpretation other than as an appeal for or against a specific candidate.' [Though the Chief Justice's] opinion purports to recognize the 'imperative for clarity' in this area of First Amendment law, its attempt [falls] far short. [I] recognize the practical reality that corporations can evade the express-advocacy standard. [But any test short of express advocacy is either too vague or too broad.] Section 203's line is bright, but it bans vast amounts of political advocacy. [It] was adventurous for *McConnell* to extend *Austin* beyond corporate speech constituting express advocacy. Today's cases make it apparent that the adventure is a flop. [Which] brings me to the question of *stare decisis*. [*Stare decisis* carries] little weight when an erroneous 'governing decision[n]' has created an 'unworkable' regime. [The] *McConnell* regime is unworkable because of the inability of any acceptable as-applied standard to validate the facial constitutionality of § 203. [Neither] do any of the other considerations relevant to *stare decisis* suggest adherence to *McConnell*. These cases do not involve property or contract rights, where reliance interests are involved. And *McConnell*'s § 203 holding has assuredly not become 'embedded' in our 'national culture.' [I] would overrule that part of the Court's decision in *McConnell* upholding § 203(a) of the BCRA."

Justice Souter, joined by Justices Stevens, Ginsburg, and Breyer, dissented: "[This Court's decisions that interpreted federal legislation to narrow] the corporate-union electioneering limitation to magic words [reduced] it to a nullity [and] the 'ingenuity and resourcefulness' of political financiers revealed the massive regulatory gap left by the 'magic words' test. [Experience] showed [that] the line between 'issue' broadcasts and outright electioneering was a patent fiction. [During the 2000 election cycle,] spending on issue ads [climbed] to $500 million. [The] congressional response was § 203. [In] *McConnell*, we found [§ 203] to be 'easily understood and objective[e]' [and] we held that the [line] separating regulated election speech from general political discourse does not, on its face, violate the First Amendment. [We] found '[l]ittle difference ... between an ad that urged viewers to "vote against Jane Doe" and one that condemned Jane Doe's record on a particular issue before exhorting viewers to "call Jane Doe and tell her what you think"'. ...

"Campaign finance reform has been a series of reactions to documented threats to electoral integrity [posed] by large sums of money from corporate or union treasuries, with no redolence of 'grassroots' about them. [From] early in the 20th century through the decision in *McConnell*, we have acknowledged that the value of democratic integrity justifies a realistic response when corporations and labor organizations commit the concentrated moneys in their treasuries to electioneering. ...

"*McConnell*'s holding that § 203 is facially constitutional is overruled. By what steps does the principal opinion reach this unacknowledged result less than four years after *McConnell* was decided? First, it lays down a new test to identify a severely limited class of ads that may constitutionally be regulated as electioneering communications, a test that is flatly contrary to *McConnell*. [Second], the principal opinion seems to defend this inversion of *McConnell* as a necessary alternative to an unadministrable subjective test for the equivalence of express (and regulable) electioneering advocacy. [But] *McConnell* did not [purport] to draw constitutional lines based on the subjective motivations of corporations. [Rather, it reasonably assumed that the "electioneering purpose" political ads falling under § 203 would] be objectively apparent from those ads' content and context. ...

"[It] is hard to imagine the Chief Justice would ever find an ad to be 'susceptible of reasonable interpretation other than as an appeal to vote for or against a specific candidate' unless it contained words of express advocacy. The Chief Justice thus effectively reinstates the same toothless 'magic words' criterion [that] led Congress to enact BCRA in the first place. [The] price of *McConnell*'s demise [seems] to me a high one. The Court (and I think the country) loses when important precedent is overruled without good reason, and there is no justification for departing from our usual rule of *stare decisis* here."

DAVIS v. FEDERAL ELECTION COMMISSION, 554 U.S. __ (2008). Section 319(a) of the Bipartisan Campaign Reform Act of 2002, the so-called "Millionaire's Amendment," provides that if a candidate for Congress spends $350,000 or more of his own money in order to secure his own election, the opposing candidate is then permitted to accept individual campaign contributions up to three-times larger than would otherwise be allowed. (The opposing candidate cannot accept additional contributions under this provision that would in total exceed the "millionaire" candidate's personal expenditures.) The Court, in a five-to-four decision, held the provision unconstitutional.

Justice Alito delivered the opinion of the Court: "In *Buckley*, we soundly rejected a cap on a candidate's expenditure of personal funds to finance campaign speech. [We] rejected the argument that [such] an expenditure cap could be justified on that ground that it served [the] 'interest in equalizing the relative financial resources of candidates competing for elective office.' [While § 319(a)] does not impose a cap on a candidate's expenditure of personal funds, it imposes a penalty on any candidate who robustly exercises that First Amendment right. Section 319(a) requires a candidate to choose between the First Amendment right to engage in unfettered political speech and subjection to discriminatory fundraising limitations. [Under] § 319(a), the vigorous exercise of the right to use personal funds to finance campaign speech produces fundraising advantages for opponents in the competitive context of electoral politics. [Because] § 319(a) imposes a substantial burden on the exercise of the First Amendment right to use personal funds for campaign speech, [it] cannot stand unless it is 'justified by a compelling state interest.' No such justification is present here. ...

"The Government maintains that § 319(a)'s asymmetrical limits are justified because they 'level electoral opportunities for candidates of different personal wealth,' [but our decisions] provide no support for the proposition that this is a legitimate government objective. [The] argument that a candidate's speech may be restricted in order to 'level electoral opportunities' has ominous implications. [Different] candidates have different strengths. Some are wealthy; others have wealthy supporters who are willing to make large contributions. Some are celebrities; some have the benefit of a well-known family name. Leveling electoral opportunities means making and implementing judgments about which strengths should be permitted to contribute to the outcome of an election. [It] is a dangerous business for Congress to use the election laws to influence the voters' choices. ...

"[The] Government contends that § 319(a) is justified because it ameliorates the deleterious effects that result from the tight limits that federal election law places on individual campaign contributions. [These] limits, it is argued, make it harder for candidates who are not wealthy to raise funds and therefore provide a substantial advantage for wealthy candidates. Accordingly, § 319(a) can be seen, not as a legislative effort to interfere with the natural operation of the electoral process, but as a legislative effort to mitigate the untoward consequences of Congress' own handiwork and restore 'the normal relationship between a candidate's financial resources and the level of popular support for his candidacy.'

"Whatever the merits of this argument as an original matter, it is fundamentally at war with the analysis of expenditure and contribution limits that this Court adopted in *Buckley* and has applied in subsequent cases. The advantage that wealthy candidates now enjoy and that § 319(a) seeks to reduce is an advantage that flows directly from *Buckley's* disparate treatment of expenditures and contributions. If that approach is sound [it] is hard to see how undoing the consequences of that decision can be viewed as a compelling interest. If the normally applicable limits on individual contributions [are] seriously distorting the electoral process, if they are feeding a 'public perception that wealthy people can buy seats in Congress,' and if those limits are not needed in order to combat corruption, then the obvious remedy is to raise or eliminate those limits. But the unprecedented step of imposing different contribution [limits] on candidates vying for the same seat is antithetical to the First Amendment."

Justice Stevens, joined by Justices Souter, Ginsburg and Breyer, dissented: "The Millionaire's Amendment [is] the product of a congressional judgment that candidates who are willing and able to spend over $350,000 of their own money in seeking election to Congress enjoy an advantage over opponents who must rely on contributions to finance their campaigns. To reduce that advantage, and to combat the perception that congressional seats are for sale to the highest bidder, Congress has relaxed the amount of contributions that the opponents of self-funding candidates may accept from their supporters. [Because] the Millionaire's Amendment does not impose any burden [on] the self-funding candidate's freedom to speak [and] because it does no more than diminish the unequal strength of the self-funding candidate, it does not violate the [Constitution]. ...

"According to [*Buckley*], the vice that condemns expenditure limitations is that they 'impose direct quantity restrictions' on political speech. [I have come to the judgment that this facet of *Buckley* was incorrect.] In my view, a number of purposes [justifies] the imposition of reasonable limitations on [expenditures]. Quantity limitations are commonplace in [other] contexts in which high-value speech occurs. Litigants in this Court [are] allowed only a fixed time for oral debate and a maximum number of pages for written argument. [In] the context of elections, the notion that rules limiting the quantity of speech are just as offensive to the First Amendment as rules limiting the content of speech is plainly incorrect. . . .

"Even accepting [*Buckley's*] holding that expenditure limits as such are uniquely incompatible with the First Amendment, [the] Millionaire's Amendment represents a [constitutionally permissible] attempt to regulate one particularly pernicious feature of many contemporary political campaigns. [The] twin rationales at the heart of the Millionaire's Amendment — reducing the importance of wealth as a criterion for public office and countering the perception that seats in the United States Congress are available for purchase by the wealthiest bidder — are important Government interests. [The] thrust of [the challenge to § 319(a)] is that by relaxing the contribution limits applicable to the opponent of a self-funding candidate, the Millionaire Amendment punishes the candidate who chooses to self-fund. [But § 319(a)] quiets no speech at all. [Enhancing] the speech of the millionaire's opponent, far from contravening the First Amendment, actually advances its core principles. If only one candidate can make himself heard, the voter's ability to make an informed choice is impaired. And the self-funding candidate's ability to engage meaningfully in the political process is in no way undermined by this provision.

"Even were we to credit [the] view that the benefit conferred on the self-funding candidate's opponent burdens the self-funder's First Amendment rights, the purposes of the Amendment surely justify its effects. [We] have long recognized the strength of an independent governmental interest in reducing both the influence of wealth on the outcomes of elections, and the appearance that wealth alone dictates those results. [Citing, e.g., *Austin*; *McConnell*.] Although the focus of our cases has been on the aggregations of corporate rather than individual wealth, there is no reason that their logic — specifically their concerns about the corrosive and distorting effects of wealth on our political process — is not equally applicable in the context of individual wealth."

Consider BeVier, Full of Surprises (And More to Come: Randall v. Sorrell, The First Amendment, and Campaign Finance Regulation, 2006 Sup. Ct. Rev. 173, 195-196:

[D]ebate on these issues has reached an impasse. [The] chasm that separates the Justices from one another appears unbridgeable. After all that has been written on the issue already, one who thinks that basic freedoms are not at stake when campaign finance regulations are enacted is not likely to become persuaded that they are. On the other hand, one who embraces the intuition that legislative judgments tend to be hostages to incumbent self-interest is unlikely to think that legislators are trustworthy rule-makers when it comes to deciding how much their challengers may spend in future elections. And one who believes that the integrity of the very democratic process that the First Amendment protects is put at risk by excessive and unregulated spending on political campaigns and that the rights of the entire electorate cannot be secured without limiting the rights of some within it is likely to find the threat to political freedom too abstract and in any case too trivial in a state as active as ours to stand in the way of campaign finance reform efforts. There would seem to be little if anything that could be said and little if any evidence that could be marshaled, by either side, which would stand much of a chance of persuading those on the other to reconsider their positions.

Page 1422.   At the end of section 2 of the Note, add the following:

2a. *Voluntary associations.* The Tennessee Secondary School Athletic Association regulates interscholastic sports among its members, Tennessee public and private high schools. Brentwood Academy is a private school that voluntarily joined the TSSAA. Brentwood was held to have violated a TSSAA rule prohibiting member schools from using "undue influence" in recruiting middle school students for their athletic programs. The violation consisted of a letter from Brentwood's football coach to a group of eighth-grade boys inviting them to attend spring football practice sessions. In Tennessee Secondary School Athletic Association v. Brentwood Academy, 127 S. Ct. 2489 (2007), the Court unanimously rejected Brentwood's claim that the enforcement of this rule violated the school's First Amendment rights. Although recognizing that the First Amendment "protects Brentwood's right to publish truth information about the school and its athletic programs" and its "right to try to persuade prospective students and their parents that its excellence in sports is a reason for enrolling," the Court nonetheless held that the rule could constitutionally be applied to Brentwood because (a) Brentwood had "made a voluntary decision to join TSSAA and to abide by its antirecruiting rule" and (b) TSSAA, like a public employer, can constitutionally impose conditions on the speech of its voluntary members that "are necessary to managing an efficient and effective state-sponsored high school athletic league." Is the extension of *Pickering* balancing from public employment to public associations warranted? How does this reasoning relate to such cases as Rust v. Sullivan, Rumsfeld v. FAIR, and National Endowment for the Arts v. Finley?

Page 1422.   At the end of section 2 of the Note, add the following:

Consider Kozel, Reconceptualizing Public Employee Speech, 99 Nw. U. L. Rev. 1007, 1019 (2005):

> The *Pickering/Connick* doctrine collapses into little more than the constitutionalization of a heckler's veto. Speech that sparks too much opposition will be vulnerable to public employer restriction and retaliation, whereas speech that is sufficiently in line with mainstream beliefs to be unobjectionable will be protected.

Page 1422.   After section 2 of the Note, add the following:

2a. *What if a public employee speaks pursuant to official duty?* Suppose Pickering was Administrative Assistant to the Chair of the State Board of Education and that his job was, among other things, to bring to the Chair's attention problems that arose within the state educational system. Suppose he wrote a memorandum to the Chair similar to the letter he actually wrote to the press in *Pickering*, and suppose also the Chair found that the memorandum was incomplete, inaccurate, inflammatory, or unprofessional. Could the Chair fire Pickering for doing his job poorly, or could Pickering assert the First Amendment in his defense? In Garcetti v. Ceballos, 547 U.S. 410 (2006), the Court, in a five-to-four decision, held that "when public employees make statements pursuant to their official duties, the employees are not speaking as citizens for First Amendment purposes, and the Constitution does not insulate their communications from employer discipline." Thus, in the hypothetical variation of *Pickering,* "[r]estricting speech that owes its existence to a public employee's professional responsibilities does not infringe any liberties the employee might have enjoyed as a private citizen. It simply reflects the exercise of employer control over what the employer itself has commissioned or created." The First Amendment, the Court concluded, "does not invest" public employees "with a right to perform their job however they see fit."

Is it ironic, as the dissenters argued, that Pickering would be protected by the First Amendment if he had sent his letter to the press, but would not be protected by the First Amendment if he sent exactly the same letter to his boss, the Chair of the Board of Education? In dissent, Justice Souter, joined by Justices Stevens and Ginsburg, argued that "a public employee's speech unwelcome to the government but on a significant public issue [is] protected from reprisal unless the statements are too damaging to the government's capacity to conduct public business." How does the principle of *Garcetti* apply to cases like Rust v. Sullivan and Legal Service Corporation v. Velazquez?

Page 1435.   Replace the third paragraph of the quotation in Note c with the following:

The answer to all these questions is no, and the reason is that there is no such thing as a free speech immunity based on the claim that someone wants to break an otherwise constitutional law for expressive purposes. [When] a law is otherwise constitutional, and when an actor has not been singled out *because* of his expression, the actor has no free speech claim. The Boy Scouts were not singled out in this way. As a result, the Scouts' claim should have been taken no more seriously than that of a tax protestor or that of a racist employer who demanded an exemption from Title VII on the theory that he wanted to discriminate for expressive, rather than merely commercial, reasons.

Page 1439.   After section 4 of the Note, add the following:

4a. *Military recruiting in law schools.* Most law schools do not permit employers who discriminate on the basis of race, religion, gender, national origin, or sexual orientation to use their placement facilities. In the 1980s, most law schools extended this policy to the U.S. military, because it discriminates on the basis of sexual orientation. In response, Congress enacted the Solomon Amendment, which provides that if any part of an institution of higher education denies military recruiters access equal to that provided other recruiters, the entire institution will lose access to federal funds. Because most universities are heavily depending on federal support for research and financial aid, most law schools waived their non-discrimination policy as applied to the military. The Forum for Academic and Institutional Rights (FAIR), an association of law schools and law faculties, filed suit to enjoin the application of the Solomon Amendment on the ground that it violates the First Amendment.

In a unanimous decision, the Court rejected this argument in Rumsfeld v. FAIR, 547 U.S. 47 (2006). In his opinion for the Court, Chief Justice Roberts observed that the Solomon Amendment "gives universities a choice: Either allow military recruiters the same [access] afforded any other recruiter or forgo certain federal funds." Although this seemed to be a question of "unconstitutional conditions," Roberts concluded that because the government could constitutionally *require* universities to grant military recruiters equal access there was no need even to consider the unconstitutional conditions issue.

Roberts conceded that the Solomon Amendment compels some "elements of speech," because law schools "may send e-mails or post notices on bulletin boards on an employer's behalf." But Roberts reasoned that this "sort of recruiting assistance [is] a far cry from the compelled speech in [cases like] *Barnette* and *Wooley*," because the Solomon Amendment does not compel the communication of any specific *content*. Rather, it requires only that a law school communicate for military recruiters those messages it voluntarily chooses to communicate for all other recruiters.

Roberts distinguished *Hurley* on the ground that in that situation "the complaining speaker's own message was affected by the speech it was forced to accommodate." Indeed, he explained, the "expressive nature of a parade was central" to the result in *Hurley*. In this case, however, "accommodating the military's message does not affect the law schools' speech, because the schools are not speaking when they host interviews and recruiting receptions. Unlike a parade organizer's choice of parade contingents, a law school's decision to allow recruiters on campus is not inherently expressive." Roberts concluded that, in this respect, the case was governed by *PruneYard*.

Finally, Roberts rejected the claim that this case was similar to *Dale*. He maintained that although the Solomon Amendment requires law schools to "associate" with military recruiters in the sense that they must "interact with them" to the same extent that they interact with other recruiters, those recruiters "are not part of the law school." Rather, they are "outsiders who come onto campus for the limited purpose of trying to hire students — not to become members of the school's expressive association. This distinction is critical. Unlike the public accommodations law in *Dale*, the Solomon Amendment does not force a law school 'to accept members it does not desire.'" In sum, a "military recruiter's mere presence on campus does not violate a law school's right to associate, regardless of how repugnant the law school considers the recruiter's message."

If the government required law schools that receive federal funds to hire members of the military to teach a course on military law, would it violate the First Amendment? In what circumstances, if any, would this be (un)constitutional? See Horwitz, *Grutter*'s First Amendment, 46 B.C.L. L. Rev. 461 (2005).

Page 1439.   At the end of section 5 of the Note, add the following:

See also Davenport v. Washington Education Association, 127 S. Ct. 2372 (2007) (a state may constitutionally require public-sector unions to receive affirmative authorization from non-members before spending their agency fees for election-related purposes).

Page 1441.   Before the last full paragraph on the page, add the following:

Consider McDonald, Speech and Distrust: Rethinking the Content Approach to Protecting the Freedom of Expression, 81 Notre Dame L. Rev. 1347, 1430 (2006):

> [Although the content-based/content-neutral distinction] was a well intentioned effort to stave off instances of improper government censorship and control over the marketplace of public debate, it has taken on a life of its own in many ways divorced from these original concerns. The rigid and woodenly applied analytical framework it has devolved into actually threatens a healthy and vibrant system of free expression, because it renders the government powerless to address content-related problems with certain types of expression and unduly empowers it to threaten that system in noncontent related ways. It has also caused the Court to develop and employ often inconsistent, unprincipled, or ad hoc rules to allow it to reach common sense results in many cases where those results would otherwise be elusive under current doctrine.

F. Freedom of the Press

Page 1447.   In section 1 of the Note, after "Can the reporter be prosecuted?," add the following:

Note that this query implicates the incidental effects doctrine. See Stone, Government Secrecy v. Freedom of the Press, 1 Harv. L. & Pol. Rev. 185

(2007) (arguing that journalists do not have a First Amendment right to commit otherwise unlawful fraud, bribery, wiretapping, or burglary in order to obtain information).

Suppose a reporter encourages a public employee unlawfully to leak classified information. Can the reporter be punished for soliciting a crime? Consider Stone, supra, at 213: "The most sensible course is to hold that the government cannot constitutionally punish journalists for encouraging public employees unlawfully to disclose classified information, unless the journalist (a) expressly incites the employee unlawfully to disclose classified information, (b) knows that publication of this information would likely cause imminent and serious harm to the national security, and (c) knows that publication of the information would not meaningfully contribute to public debate."

Page 1447. At the end of section 2 of the Note, add the following:

For an excellent review of the journalist's privilege, see Papandrea, Citizen Journalism and the Reporter's Privilege, 91 Minn. L. Rev. 515 (2007).

Page 1448. After section 2 of the Note, add the following:

2a. *Valerie Plame and Judith Miller.* In 2006, the former *New York Times* reporter Judith Miller was jailed for eighty-five days for contempt of court for refusing to disclose to a grand jury the identity of the individual in the White House who revealed to her Valerie Plame's status as a covert CIA agent. Forty-nine states and the District of Columbia have adopted some form of journalist-source privilege, but the federal government has no such privilege. For analysis of whether the federal government should enact such a privilege, see Stone, Why We Need a Federal Reporter's Privilege, 34 Hofstra L. Rev. 39 (2005).

Three questions are especially vexing in crafting such a privilege: (1) Should the privilege be absolute or qualified? That is, should the government be able to overcome the privilege with a sufficient showing of need? (2) Should the privilege protect the confidentiality of a source whose disclosure is *unlawful*? If the purpose of the privilege is to encourage a source to communicate, does it make any sense to extend the privilege to unlawful communications? Note that this query has particular relevance to unlawful leaks of classified information. (3) Who should be able to assert the privilege? Presumably, the privilege would cover disclosures to a reporter for the Washington Post or CNN, but what about disclosures to a professor who is writing a book, to a blogger, or to the editor of a high school newspaper?

Consider Stone, supra, at 50-51: "[I]t must be recalled that the privilege belongs to the source, not to the reporter. When the reporter invokes the privilege, she is merely acting as the agent of the source. With that in mind, the question should properly be rephrased as follows: To whom may a source properly disclose information in reasonable reliance on the belief that the disclosure will be protected b the journalist-source privilege? The answer should be a functional one. The focus should not be on whether the reporter fits within any particular category. Rather, the source should be protected whenever he makes a confidential discosure to an individual, reasonably believing that the individual regularly disseminates information to the general public, when the source's purpose is to enable that individual to disseminate the information to the general public."

Page 1449. After the block quotation from *Eldred*, add the following:

Consider R. Tushnet, Copy This Essay: How the Fair Use Doctrine Harms Free Speech and How Copying Serves It, 114 Yale L.J. 535, 562-565 (2004):

> [*Eldred*] treated copiers' interests with indifference. [But] copying is of value to audiences who have access through copying to otherwise unavailable speech. It also enhances copiers' ability to express themselves; to persuade others; and to participate in cultural, religious, and political institutions. [Imagine] that the government, in the name of promoting creativity and deterring imitativeness, banned speakers from copying directly from the public domain. This would be an enormous, intolerable burden on speech. . . . Copying promotes democracy by literally putting information in citizens' hands.

Page 1450. After section 6 of the Note, add the following:

7. Scientific research. Related to the issue of newsgathering is the question of scientific research. Even if scientific expression is protected by the First Amendment, to what extent does the First Amendment also protect the right "to conduct experiments, make observations, or otherwise employ empirical methods of testing and data collection"? See McDonald, Government Regulation or Other "Abridgments" of Scientific Research: The Proper Scope of Judicial Review Under the First Amendment, 54 Emory L. J. 979, 993 (2005).

Page 1451.   After section 2 of the Note, add the following:

2a. *Access to the military.* See Anderson, Freedom of the Press in Wartime, 77 U. Colo. L. Rev. 49, 66, 95-98 (2006) ("So far as existing case law is concerned, there appears to be nothing to prevent the Pentagon from eliminating on-scene coverage of military operations, detention facilities, military hospitals, and other auxiliaries of war. [A] judicial response that leaves news about the conduct of war at the sufferance of the military is an abdication of constitutional responsibility.") For analysis of the press embed program used during the war in Iraq, see Zeide, In Bed with the Military: First Amendment Implications of Imbedded Journalism, 80 NYU L. Rev. 1309 (2005).

Page 1458.   After section 2 of the Note, add the following:

2a. *Defining First Amendment access rights by drawing on nonconstitutional regulations.* Might the Supreme Court hold that the First Amendment compels state governments to share information with the press or public by drawing on the analogy of the federal Freedom of Information Act? Consider Samaha, Government Secrets, Constitutional Law, and Platforms for Judicial Intervention, 53 U.C.L.A. L. Rev. 909 (2006):

> For both executive secrecy and public access, which are points along a single axis, constitutional status turns on structural logic. Every democracy develops a system for distributing and withholding information about government operations. Popular accountability depends on information access, while effective and sensible action requires secrecy on occasion. In addition, information about government facilitates a central function of the First Amendment: public discussion of public issues. [It is] conceivable that executive discretion to withhold information is more critical to executive operations than public disclosure is to democratic governance. But this is a very ambitious claim with contestable normative and descriptive aspects. [Critics] on and off the bench assert that courts are incompetent to grapple

with the delicate issue of information access. [J]udicial design of an access system does seem difficult at best. A foundation already exists, however. [S]tatutes and regulations [such as the Freedom of Information Act] can be used as a baseline for substantive judgment, they already have been the basis for judicial training in the field, and they indicate that widespread public access rights are feasible and valuable. Of course, borrowing from nonjudicial sources to construct constitutional law departs from some traditional thinking. But the integration of constitutional and nonconstitutional law can be powerfully useful. . . .

Page 1463. At the end of section 5 of the Note, add the following:

6. *Intermedia discrimination: Shield laws.* Suppose a journalist-shield law allows reporters for mainstream newspapers and television and radio stations to invoke the journalist-source privilege, but does not extend to bloggers. Does such intermedia discrimination violate the first amendment? Consider Stone, Why We Need a Federal Reporter's Privilege, 34 Hofstra L. Rev. 39, 48 (2005):

[Although the issue of "who is a member of the press"] was a serious constraint on the Court in *Branzburg*, it poses a much more manageable issue in the context of legislation. Government often treats different speakers and publishers differently from one another. Which reporters are allowed to attend a White House briefing? Which are eligible to be embedded with the military? Broadcasting is regulated, but print journalism is not. Legislation treats the cable medium differently from both broadcasting and print journalism. These categories need not conform perfectly to the undefined phrase " the press" in the First Amendment. Differentiation among different elements of the media is constitutional, as long as it is not based on viewpoint or any other invidious consideration, and as long as the differential is reasonable.

8
THE CONSTITUTION AND RELIGION

A. Introduction: Historical and Analytical Overview

Page 1495.   At the end of section 4 of the Note, add the following:

Dissenting in McCreary County v. ACLU of Kentucky, 545 U.S. 844 (2005), Justice Scalia, joined on this point by Chief Justice Rehnquist and Justice Thomas, argued:

> With respect to public acknowledgment of religious belief, [the] Establishment Clause permits [disregard] of polytheists and believers in unconcerned deities, just as it permits the disregard of devout atheists. [Historical] practices [demonstrate] that there is a distance between the acknowledgment of a single Creator and the establishment of a religion. [The] three most popular religions in the United States, Christianity, Judaism, and Islam — which combined account for 97.7% of all believers — are monotheistic. All of them [believe] that the Ten Commandments were given by God to Moses, and are divine prescriptions for a virtuous life. Publicly honoring the Ten Commandments is thus indistinguishable, insofar as discriminating against other religions is concerned, from publicly honoring God. Both practices are recognized across such a broad and diverse range of the population [that] they cannot be reasonably be understood as a government endorsement of a particular religious viewpoint.

Justice Stevens responded to this argument in dissenting in Van Orden v. Perry, 545 U.S. 677 (2005): "[Many] of the Framers understood the word 'religion' in the Establishment Clause to encompass only the various sects of

Christianity," citing, among other sources, Justice Joseph Story's Commentaries on the Constitution. "The original understanding of the type of 'religion' that qualified for constitutional protection under the Establishment Clause likely did not include [followers] of Judaism and Islam. [The] inclusion of Jews and Muslims inside the category of constitutionally favored religions surely would have shocked [Justice] Story. [The] history of the Establishment Clause's original meaning just as strongly supports a preference for Christianity as it does a preference for monotheism."

In his opinion in *McCreary County,* Justice Scalia replied, "Since most thought the Clause permitted government invocation of monotheism, and some others thought it permitted government invocation of Christianity, [Justice Stevens] proposes that it be construed not to permit any government invocation of religion at all. [Those] narrower views of the Establishment Clause were as clearly rejected as the more expansive ones."

The majority opinion written by Justice Souter in *McCreary County* took the position that Justice Scalia's argument "[failed] to consider the full range of evidence showing what the Framers believed."

> The dissent is certainly correct in putting forward evidence that some of the Framers thought some endorsement of religion was compatible with the establishment ban. [But there] is also evidence supporting the proposition that the Framers intended the Establishment Clause to require government neutrality in matters of religion. [The] fair inference is that there was no common understanding about the limits of the establishment prohibition. [What] the evidence does show is a group of statesmen [who] proposed a guarantee with contours not wholly worked out, leaving the Establishment Clause with edges still to be determined. And none the worse for that.
>
> [Historical] evidence thus supports no solid argument for changing course. [The] divisiveness of religion in current public life is inescapable. This is no time to deny the prudence of understanding the Establishment Clause to require the Government to stay neutral on religious belief, which is reserved for the conscience of the individual.

Professor Jack Balkin asks, "[Why] did Jews and Muslims get thrown in the mix of first class religious citizens? After all, if you exclude them you still have about 91% of the population. So why couldn't the government offer prayers to Jesus Christ, our Lord and Savior?" Blog entry for June 27, 2005, at http:// balkin. blogspot.com/ (used with permission). Is Justice Scalia's response, read in light of the observations of Justices Stevens and Souter, adequate?

Page 1495.   At the end of section 5 of the Note, add the following:

5a. *"Equal Liberty."* Eisgruber and Sager, in Religious Freedom and the Constitution (2007), offer a general theory they call Equal Liberty, which contains two principles: "In the name of equality [no one] ought to be devalued on account of the spiritual foundations of their important commitments and projects." Aside from attention to discrimination and "hostility and neglect," religion should not be treated "as deserving special benefits or as subject to special disabilities." In addition, a broad understanding of general constitutional liberties, such as rights of free speech and association "will allow religious practice to flourish." *Id.* at 52-53. For a collection of commentaries (raising questions about how to identify "hostility and neglect," and about the difference between this approach and others), see Book Review Colloquium, 85 Tex. L. Rev. 1185-1287 (2007).

B.   The Establishment Clause

Page 1522.   At the end of section 3 of the Note, add the following:

For a discussion of the relationship between the "reasonable observer" test and the inquiry into governmental purposes, see Bowman, Seeing Government Purpose Through the Objective Observer's Eyes: The Evolution–Intelligent Design Debates, 29 Harv. L. J. & Pub. Pol'y 419 (2006).

Page 1522.   After section 3 of the Note, add the following:

3a. *Divisiveness as a criterion.* In McCreary County v. ACLU of Kentucky, 545 U.S. 844 (2005), the Court defended the principle of neutrality between religion and irreligion as "respond[ing] to one of the major concerns that prompted adoption of the Religion Clauses. The Framers and the citizens of their time intended [to] guard against the civic divisiveness that follows when the Government weighs in on one side of religious debate." Is the divisiveness occasioned by an enactment, or the potential that a proposed enactment would be divisive, an empirical question? What is the baseline against which divisiveness is to be measured? Consider the possibility that a judicial decision prohibiting a practice as an establishment of religion might be as divisive as, or more divisive than, the legislature's adoption of that practice. If divisiveness or the potential therefor is not an empirical but a conceptual matter, what are the components of the concept?

Consider these observations by Professor Burt Neuborne: "[Why] do we care? I'm sympathetic to the notion that being forced to look at the government's display of someone else's religious symbol can be disconcerting and can send a message of exclusion. [But], tell me that Muslims in this country need a display of the 10 Commandments to let them know they are outsiders. Or, that atheists need government displays of religious symbols to tell them they are on the margin of American public life. To my mind, worrying about the symbols confuses cause and effect. As long as we insist on an equality principle, [I] don't see the value in offending many millions of Americans for whom the displays provide solace and meaning. That's particularly so when the cases enrage millions of persons." Blog entry for June 27, 2005, at http://www.scotusblog.com/discussion/archives/ten_commandments/ index.html (used with permission).

Page 1527. Before the Note, add the following:

What purposes are impermissible ones? McCreary County v. ACLU of Kentucky, 545 U.S. 844 (2005), described the constitutional requirement as one of "neutrality in religion." "[The] government may not favor one religion over another, or religion over irreligion, religious choice being the prerogative of individuals under the Free Exercise Clause." Justice Souter's opinion for the Court treated neutrality as a valuable interpretive principle, providing "a good sense of direction," given the tension in the religion clauses, which express "competing values, each constitutionally respectable, but none open to realization to the logical limit." Chief Justice Rehnquist's plurality opinion in Van Orden v. Perry, 545 U.S. 677 (2005), similarly recognized a tension in the religion clauses. "One face looks toward the strong role played by religion and religious traditions throughout our Nation's history. [The] other face looks toward the principle that governmental intervention in religious matters can itself endanger religious freedom. [Our] institutions presuppose a Supreme Being, yet these institutions must not press religious observances upon their citizens." The plurality opinion concluded that a monument displaying the Ten Commandments on the statehouse grounds in Austin, Texas, "has a dual significance, partaking of both religion and government," and did not violate the establishment clause. Is the acknowledgment that a practice can have a "dual significance" consistent with the principle of neutrality? Does the acknowledgment in *McCreary County* that religion clause principles cannot be "realized" to their logical limits help reconcile the two cases? How great would the religious significance of a practice have to be before it conflicted with the neutrality principle?

Page 1528.   At the end of section 3 of the Note, add the following:

McCreary County v. ACLU of Kentucky, 545 U.S. 844 (2005), revisited the issue of government posting of the Ten Commandments, and applied the "impermissible purpose" test. Noting that "[examination] of purpose is a staple of statutory interpretation [and] governmental purpose is a key element of a good deal of constitutional doctrine," the Court, in an opinion by Justice Souter, adhered to the proposition that "scrutinizing purpose does make practical sense [where] an understanding of official objective emerges from readily discoverable fact, without any judicial psychoanalysis of a drafter's heart of hearts. The eyes that look to purpose belong to an 'objective observer,' one who takes account of the traditional external signs that show up in the 'text, legislative history, and implementation of the [statute.]'" Justice Souter's opinion described prior cases invoking the "purpose" test as holding government action unconstitutional "only because openly available data supported a commonsense conclusion that a religious objective permeated the government's action." Government action does not violate the establishment clause, the Court continued, where it has a secular purpose that is "genuine, not a sham, and not merely secondary to a religious objective."

In *McCreary County,* the Court affirmed a decision by a court of appeals, which itself had affirmed a judgment by the district court, that on the facts presented the county had an impermissible purpose in displaying the Ten Commandments. Initially the county had posted the Ten Commandments in the county courthouse, with no other displays near the posting. Following controversy, and acting on legal advice, the county the expanded the display to include eight other documents in smaller frames, including the passage from the Declaration of Independence asserting that all men were "endowed by their Creator" with inalienable rights, and the national motto "In God We Trust." After litigation began, the county again changed the display, to include nine other documents, in frames of equal size, and called "The Foundations of American Law and Government Display."

On the same day the Court decided *McCreary County,* it upheld the display of the Ten Commandments on the statehouse grounds in Austin, Texas. Van Orden v. Perry, 545 U.S. 677 (2005). For a discussion of the plurality opinion by Chief Justice Rehnquist, see the supplement to page 1527 in this volume. The dispositive vote was cast by Justice Breyer, who wrote, "If the relation between government and religion is one of separation, but not of mutual hostility and suspicion, one will inevitably find difficult borderline cases. And in such cases, I see no test-related substitute for the exercise of legal judgment. That judgment is not a personal judgment. Rather, [it] must take account of context and consequences measured in light of those purposes. [No] exact formula can dictate a resolution to such fact-intensive cases."

Justice Breyer's opinion in *Van Orden* found "determinative" the fact that "40 years passed in which the presence of this monument, legally speaking, went unchallenged. [And] I am not aware of any evidence suggesting that this was due to a climate of intimidation. [Those] 40 years suggest more strongly than can any set of formulaic tests that few individuals [are] likely to have understood the monument as amounting [to] a government effort to favor a particular religious sect, primarily to promote religion over nonreligion, [or] to 'work deterrence' of any 'religious belief.'" In light of *McCreary County* and *Van Orden,* can a government body hereafter, without violating the Establishment Clause, develop a program in which the Ten Commandments are posted with public support?

In *Van Orden,* the court of appeals had affirmed a judgment of the district court, which had found no impermissible purpose. Consider the proposition that *McCreary County* and *Van Orden* substantially commit the decision on impermissible purpose to trial courts, and that in doing so illustrate the tension between constitutional law understood as a system of rules and constitutional law understood as the vehicle by which judgment or common sense is exercised.

Page 1546.   At the end of section 4 of the Note, add the following:

Consider the implications of the argument that voucher and similar programs have a disparate impact on different religious denominations because of their positions on the propriety of accepting government aid even in the form of vouchers. Should the fact that the disparate impact results from religiously motivated choices be sufficient to dispel concerns about sect preference? Consider these observations:

All institutions [have] an intense interest in their own survival. Programs distributing aid under the neutrality principle offer financial inducements for religious groups to participate in certain programs that "government" desires for the nation and that may [conflict] with certain tenets of the nation's faith communities. These programs easily can [tempt] religious groups to go against their basic principles in order to secure government funding and receive the same benefits [as] other faith traditions. [It] will be those programs that center on social issues more "in the gray" respecting a faith community's belief system that will begin the [assimilation] of our nation's religious traditions. [If a group] buckles to [the] government-supplied financial incentive and chooses to participate, after many years [will] the members of the community even remember the original position of their [tradition?] [One] might easily predict the homogenization of America's diverse faith traditions into a form of civil religion that encourages a malleability of doctrine shaped by the designs of government programs.

Davis, A Commentary on the Supreme Court's "Equal Treatment" Doctrine as the New Constitutional Paradigm for Protecting Religious Liberty, 46 J. Church & State 717, 733-734 (2004).

Page 1547.   Delete the last paragraph of section 7 of the Note.

D. Permissible Accommodation

Page 1577.   After section 4c of the Note, add the following:

d. "[The Court's] decisions, taken together, suggest that religious accommodations must satisfy four, linked constitutional norms. First, is the accommodation a reasonable effort to relieve a government-imposed burden on religious practice? Second, do beneficiaries of the accommodation participate voluntarily? Third, is the accommodation available on a denominationally-neutral basis? Fourth, does the accommodation impose significant burdens on third parties?" Lupu & Tuttle, Instruments of Accommodation: The Military Chaplaincy and the Constitution, 110 W. Va. L. Rev. 89, 93-94 (2007).

Page 1577.   After section 4 of the Note, add the following:

5. *The Religious Land Use and Institutionalized Persons Act (RLUIPA).* RLUIPA, enacted in 2000, provides, "No government shall impose a substantial burden on the religious exercise of a person residing in or confined to an

institution," unless the burden furthers "a compelling governmental interest ... [by] the least restrictive means." Cutter v. Wilkinson, 544 U.S. 709 (2005), rejected a facial Establishment Clause challenge to this provision of RLUIPA, finding it to be a permissible accommodation of religion "because it alleviates exceptional government-created burdens on private religious exercise." The provision "covers state-run institutions [in] which the government exerts a degree of control unparalleled in civilian society and severely disabling to private religious exercise." Institutionalized persons "are dependent on the government's permission and accommodation for exercise of their religion." The Court interpreted the statutory standards to conform to prior constitutional decisions indicating that "an accommodation must be measured so that it does not override other significant interests. [We] have no cause to believe that RLUIPA would not be applied in an appropriately balanced way, with particular sensitivity to security concerns." Citing Grutter v. Bollinger, 539 U.S. 306 (2003), which is excerpted on page 594 of the main volume, the Court observed that "[c]ontext matters" in applying the statutory "compelling government interest" standard, and quoted legislative history indicating that "[l]awmakers supporting [the Act] were mindful of the urgency of discipline, order, safety, and security in penal institutions" and "anticipated that courts would apply the Act's standard with 'due deference' " to the judgment of prison administrators. "Should inmate requests for religious accommodations become excessive, impose unjustified burdens on other institutionalized persons, or jeopardize the effective functioning of an institution, the facility would be free to resist the imposition. In that event, adjudication in as-applied challenges would be in order." Compare the standard developed in *Cutter* with that applied in Free Exercise cases prior to *Smith*.

Page 1578.　Before the first full paragraph on the page, add the following:

Consider these comments on *Rosenberger* and related cases:

The student Christian group won the funding of printing for its publication but at the price of having its religious message reduced to the commonality of every other form of human speech. [The] petitioners were willing to give up the special status that religion is otherwise granted. *[Rosenberger]* denies the power of religion by approving state subsidization for preaching of the gospel. By wishing not to deny religion its place in a marketplace of ideas, the Court denied the special place held by religion in our constitutional framework. [If] "preaching the word" [is] only speech, it is outside the restraints of the Establishment Clause. But "preaching the word" is not mere speech; it is religion and must, therefore, suffer the inconvenience of full protection only when disassociated from the power of government. ...

The concept of equal treatment sounds alluringly democratic, pluralistic, and fair. [But] in fact it may signal the triumph of the postmodern relativist mind in which every statement is of equal value to any other. One's religious beliefs would be protected equally and at the same level as one's right to [live] in a certain [neighborhood]. [One's] religious faith will become on par with every other worldview and life belief. [Equality] is a hallmark of American democracy, but it should not rule in every case.

Davis, A Commentary on the Supreme Court's "Equal Treatment" Doctrine as the New Constitutional Paradigm for Protecting Religious Liberty, 46 J. Church & State 717, 720-721, 736-737 (2004).

Page 1581.   After the first full paragraph, add the following:

Shiffrin, The Pluralistic Foundations of the Religion Clauses, 90 Cornell L. Rev. 9, 13-14 (2004), identifies seven values underlying the Free Exercise Clause, and seven underlying the Establishment Clause:

(1) [The Free Exercise Clause] protects liberty and autonomy; (2) it avoids the cruelty of either forcing an individual to do what he or she is conscientiously obliged not to do or penalizing her for responding to an obligation of conscience; (3) it preserves respect for law and minimizes violence triggered by religious conflict; (4) it promotes equality and combats religious discrimination; (5) it protects associational values; (6) it promotes political community; and (7) it protects the personal and social importance of religion. ...

(1) [The Establishment Clause] protects liberty and autonomy, including preventing the government from forcing taxpayers to support religious ideologies to which they are opposed; (2) it stands for equal citizenship without regard to religion; (3) it protects against the destabilizing influence of having the polity divided along religious lines; (4) it promotes political community; (5) it protects the autonomy of the state to protect the public interest; (6) it protects churches from the corrupting influences of the state; and (7) it promotes religion in the private sphere.

Is this a helpful descriptive summary of the doctrines? Does it provide useful guidance in resolving particular controversies?

To similar effect, consider Conkle, The Establishment Clause and Religious Expression in Governmental Settings: Four Variables in Search of a Standard, 110 W. Va. L. Rev. 315, 316 (2007): "Justice Breyer [has] suggested that close cases [require] the exercise of "legal judgment," informed by doctrinal and policy considerations but not controlled by any formal test. Perhaps Justice Breyer is right. Perhaps [the] search for a clear-cut doctrinal test or rule [is] a mistaken or futile venture. [A] different approach [would] attempt to capture the full range of constitutional [values]."

In the context of religious expression in government settings, such as the displays in *Van Orden* and *McCreary County*, Conkle identifies four "variables": "the degree to which the challenged [practice] not only acknowledges or endorses religion but also 'imposes' it in a coercive or otherwise aggressive manner"; "the nature and specificity of the religious expression"; "tradition"; and "the degree to which the religious expression is governmentally [crafted] or sponsored."

9
THE CONSTITUTION, BASELINES, AND THE PROBLEM OF PRIVATE POWER

B. Pure Inaction and the Theory of Governmental Neutrality

Page 1591.   Before *Flagg Brothers*, add the following:

In Town of Castle Rock, Colorado v. Gonzales, 545 U.S. 748 (2005), the Court, in a seven-two decision written by Justice Scalia, rejected a procedural due process challenge to a locality's failure to enforce a restraining order prohibiting an estranged husband from having unauthorized contact with his wife and children. The case is excerpted at the supplement to page 972 in this volume.

Page 1601.   After section 5 of the Note, add the following:

6. Castle Rock. In Town of Castle Rock, Colorado v. Gonzales, 545 U.S. 748 (2005), excerpted at the supplement to page 972 in this volume, the Court seemed to build on *DeShaney*, ruling that a woman did not have a constitutionally protected property interest in protection of herself and her children via a restraining order against her estranged husband (who ultimately took and killed her children). The relevant restraining order appeared to create an entitlement to legal protection. The Court ruled first that the order contained discretion, so that

Gonzales lacked a statutorily protected interest under state law. But it added far more generally:

> Even if we were to think otherwise concerning the creation of an entitlement by Colorado, it is by no means clear that an individual entitlement to enforcement of a restraining order could constitute a "property" interest for purposes of the Due Process Clause. Such a right would not, of course, resemble any traditional conception of "property." Although that alone does not disqualify it from due process protection, as *Roth* and its progeny show, the right to have a restraining order enforced does not "have some ascertainable monetary value." [Perhaps] most radically, the alleged property interest here arises *incidentally,* not out of some new species of government benefit or service, but out of a function that government actors have always performed — to wit, arresting people who they have probable cause to believe have committed a criminal offense.

The Court went on to emphasize "the simple distinction between government action that directly affects a citizen's legal rights [and] action that is directed against a third party and affects the citizen only indirectly or incidentally." Justice Stevens, joined by Justice Ginsburg, dissented.